The Psychiatry of Violence:
A Guide for Lawyers

B Mahendra

JORDANS

Family Law

Published by Family Law
A publishing imprint of Jordan Publishing Limited
21 St Thomas Street
Bristol BS1 6JS

British Library Cataloguing-in-Publication Data

A catalogue record for this book is available from the British Library.

ISBN 978 1 84661 171 1

Typeset by Letterpart Ltd, Reigate, Surrey

Printed in Great Britain by CPI Antony Rowe, Chippenham, Wiltshire

CONTENTS

INTRODUCTION

Even as the world reels from the challenges of a financial crisis of a nature and degree not experienced in several generations and is preoccupied by the adverse effects of changes in climate, overpopulation and threats to the future of the planet, there must be few individuals anywhere on earth whose minds are any distance away from thinking about violence in some form – whether it be inter-personal, intranational, inter-national or international. Violence is a universal experience with numerous facets to it. It is the purpose of this book to consider one aspect of violence, namely the violence associated with mental illness and disorder. There remain many misconceptions in regard to mental disorder and its role in precipitating or contributing to violence and the opportunity will be taken to show that violence due to mental disorder is a small part of violent behaviour overall. Further, it is necessary to consider the background to violence, an exercise to be undertaken in all cases of violent behaviour, before one can conclude that it was the mental disorder *per se* and not some other factor that could have been responsible for an episode of violence. Psychiatry plays an important although limited role in the evaluation of the potential for violence and also in the analysis of violent incidents that have taken place already. The limits of psychiatric risk assessment in respect of violent behaviour must therefore be properly appreciated. Psychiatry deals with illness and disorder. Human behaviour involved in the creation of the risk of violence and the mitigation of those risks comprises a myriad of aspects beyond the psychiatric.

This book is divided into three parts. In the first part of the book the roots of violent behaviour are discussed in outline. The subject is huge and one can hardly hope to do it justice within the compass of a book such as this one. Nevertheless, an attempt must be made to appreciate those factors that could have a bearing on behaviour that turns out to be aggressive and violent. In the second part of the book the general aspects of psychiatric conditions are discussed with special emphasis being placed on the symptoms and behaviour that have a bearing on situations involving aggression and violence. These descriptions are based on the accounts of psychiatric conditions first given in *Adult Psychiatry in Family and Child Law* (Mahendra, 2006) and the opportunity has been taken in the current work to amend, update and clarify the points made in the earlier book. In the third part of the book some special situations involving violence of one kind or another – domestic violence, serial and sexual violence and public and political violence – are taken up in relation to those psychiatric features of relevance that have been discussed in the second part of the book.

The purpose of this book is to promote an understanding of the concepts that are involved to a non-specialist audience. No attempt has been made to offer any comprehensive description of the psychiatric conditions involved – a sufficient number of outstanding works exist already for this purpose. The emphasis is, rather, on understanding and the bias is practical, not academic. There are no footnotes and a few references are given in the form of a select bibliography. The audience for this book is anticipated to come from among lawyers in various fields of specialisation, especially those who are involved in the criminal law and family and child law, but it is hoped that those who work within situations concerning violence – eg social workers and other professionals such as guardians ad litem engaged in family and child practice, probation officers, community workers and counsellors dealing with both offenders and victims, and those involved in making policy – will also find the book of value in their work and especially in those situations where they are called upon to evaluate the risks of violent behaviour. It is to be hoped that this work will prove to be a source of useful information to these professionals.

I must thank Mr Greg Woodgate of Jordan Publishing who commissioned this book, as he did the four predecessors to this work. This series of books has allowed various aspects of psychiatry and psychology to be considered in relation to various fields of legal practice and one hopes a fuller picture of psychiatry and psychology has been drawn thereby for the benefit of interested non-specialists.

B Mahendra

London
Spring 2009

GLOSSARY

Abnormal – Outside of the norm in a statistical sense. Not necessarily pathological.

Aetiology – Cause(s) of a disorder.

Affect – Mood.

Affective disorder – Mood disorder, especially where mood is pathologically elevated or lowered as in mania or depressive illness.

Agoraphobia – A phobic anxiety disorder in which the patient has a pathological fear of venturing into situations where crowds of people may be met.

Alzheimer's disease – A dementing disorder due to degenerative processes taking place in the brain. Believed to be the commonest cause of both senile and pre-senile dementia.

Anorexia nervosa – An eating disorder, suffered predominantly by females, due to a distortion of body image leading to fear of weight gain.

Anxiety state – A disorder in which there is a pathological and disproportionate sense of fear in the presence of trivial or no stimuli. Usually divided as between generalised anxiety disorders and phobic anxiety disorders.

Asperger's syndrome – A disorder placed within the higher end of autistic spectrum disorders due to a pervasive developmental disorder. It is characterised by mild autistic features involving impaired social functioning and stereotypical repetitive behaviour. There is no impairment of intelligence.

Attention-deficit hyperactivity disorder (ADHD) – A disorder of childhood involving overactivity, distractibility and impulsive behaviour.

Autism – A pervasive developmental disorder of childhood within the severe end of the spectrum of autistic disorders. Intellectual impairment is usual.

Benzodiazepines – A group of drugs used as anxiety reducing (anxiolytic) agents. They are depressants of the central nervous system but a paradoxical effect may cause disinhibition and aggression. Highly addictive.

Bipolar affective disorder – A disorder of mood where episodes of mania and/or depressive illness may occur.

Brain scans – Imaging techniques including computerised tomography (CT) and magnetic resonance imaging (MRI) allowing brain structure to be studied.

Bulimia nervosa – An eating disorder in which patients, usually women, display binge eating and preoccupation with weight which is regulated by vomiting, abuse of diuretics and laxatives and excessive dieting.

Cardiovascular – Relating to arterial blood vessels supplying the heart. Impairment of function may lead to ischaemic heart disease and heart attacks.

Catatonia – A collection of behaviours involving disorders of speech, movement, and posture. May be seen in schizophrenia, depressive illness and neurological states.

Cerebrovascular – Relating to arterial blood vessels supplying the brain. Impairment of function may lead to strokes.

Cognitive behaviour therapy – A form of psychological treatment used in dealing with maladaptive behaviours and abnormal mood states by attempting to change negative thought patterns of the patient.

Compulsion – The motor counterpart of obsessional thinking.

Confusion – A symptom resulting from an impairment in consciousness as may be found in acute organic states such as delirium. To be distinguished from disorientation.

Conversion symptoms – A feature of hysterical states. In avoiding inner conflict there is produced psychological energy which is converted into physical symptoms such as paralysis or blindness. There is primary gain for the patient through relief from anxiety.

Creutzfeldt-Jakob disease – The classical illness (and its more recent variant) are rare causes of pre-senile dementia. A viral cause is suspected.

Delirium – An acute organic disorder involving disturbance of consciousness commonly seen in states of alcohol withdrawal (delirium tremens) and infections, especially in the elderly.

Delusion – A false belief unshakeably held despite evidence to the contrary, and out of keeping with the individual's social and cultural background.

Dementia – An acquired global condition which leads to an impairment in functioning of the intellect, memory, personality and social behaviour. The term is entirely descriptive and the causes may be various, for example, degenerative brain disease, endocrine disease, etc.

Depot injection – A drug, usually an anti-psychotic agent, which is given periodically by intramuscular injection. Obviates the need for daily ingestion of medication and thereby improves compliance.

Depression – A pathological lowering of mood.

Depressive illness – A disorder in which the central feature is a pathologically diminished mood.

Dissociative disorders – Formerly hysterical reactions. A disorder in which the integrity in the relationship between memory, identity, sensory perception and motor control appears lost as a result of unconscious mechanisms. Common manifestations include amnesia, fugue (wandering), stupor and motor disorders. An extreme variant is trance or possession states.

Down's syndrome – A disorder with (usually) severe intellectual impairment which is a common cause of mental handicap or learning disabilities. Due to a chromosomal abnormality.

Electroconvulsive treatment (ECT) – A procedure by which seizures are induced by the passage of electricity through the brain. An effective treatment for severe depressive illness.

Epidemiology – The study of the distribution and possible causes of disorders in a population.

Functional disorder – A disorder in which no obvious adverse change in the structure and function of the brain can be discerned in the present state of knowledge.

General paralysis of the insane (GPI) – A condition due to tertiary (ie untreated or incompletely treated) syphilis. In the past a severe untreatable dementia used to be a feature.

Hallucination – An abnormal perception arising in the absence of an external stimulus (cf illusion). May involve any of the senses, for example, auditory, visual, etc. Could be true or pseudo hallucination. Their significance depends on the entirety of the clinical picture.

Huntington's chorea – A cause of pre-senile dementia characterised by abnormal movements and mental disorder including dementia. It is a genetic condition.

Hypomania – A less severe form of mania.

Hysteria – The older term for conversion/dissociative disorders.

Illusion – A misperception due to misinterpretation of stimuli. Usually normal phenomena occurring in such situations as believing a shadow conceals a person.

Incidence – Number of new cases of a disorder occurring within a defined population over a defined period of time, for example, 12 months (cf prevalence).

Insight – The awareness a patient possesses in regard to a condition he suffers from. There are gradations through full, partial and no insight.

Life events – Potentially stressful events such as bereavement, divorce, a house move, loss of employment, etc, which may have a bearing on the onset of psychiatric disorders, in particular depressive illness.

Mania – A form of affective disorder in which the central feature usually is an elevation of mood, for instance, elation. It is associated with increased energy, overactivity, disinhibited behaviour, pressure of speech and grandiose ideas or delusions.

Maternity blues – Transient mood changes involving depression and anxiety occurring in over half of mothers with a newborn baby.

Mental disorder – A compendious term including mental illness, learning disabilities, personality and psychopathic disorders and addiction and other disorders not amounting to formal illness.

Morbid jealousy – A psychotic disorder presenting in its own right or as a symptom of another psychosis such as schizophrenia or alcohol abuse characterised by a false belief in the infidelity of spouse or partner.

Munchausen syndrome – A disorder involving persistent simulation of illness associated with pathological lying, exaggeration of symptoms and the making of importunate demands on hospitals and medical staff. A variant is the controversial, possibly discredited, disorder by proxy in which a carer involves (usually) a child in the simulation or exaggeration of illness. Best understood as a severe personality disorder.

Negative symptoms – (of schizophrenia) Include lack of motivation, apathy, poverty of speech, social withdrawal, emotional unresponsiveness and self neglect. May respond poorly to standard forms of treatment.

Neuroses – Minor psychiatric disorders in which insight and a sense of reality are preserved and there is a discernible contribution of the personality to the disorder. Neurotic conditions include minor depressive illness, anxiety states, obsessive-compulsive disorder and hysterical reactions (dissociative/conversion disorders).

Obsessive-compulsive disorder – A neurotic disorder in which is found ideas and thoughts which are persistent, intrusive, unwelcome and subject to resistance without success on the part of the patient. The motor counterparts are called compulsions.

Organic – Refers to disorders where there is demonstrable structural or functional (ie pathophysiological) disturbance of brain function.

Orientation – An individual's awareness of time, place and person. Disturbed in the dementias.

Parasuicide – Deliberate self-harm in which the element of intention is absent from the behaviour leading to self-harm. Usually associated with reckless behaviour.

Personality disorder – Involves an abnormal personality whose behaviour is at odds with the norms and standards applying in his culture. The disorder is enduring and is separate from any formal illness which may from time to time come to overlie it. The diagnosis is made at presumed maturity but the onset is invariably in childhood as behaviour disturbance. There are problems usually in the personal, social and occupational spheres. Many categories are described (see text).

Phobic anxiety state – An anxiety disorder which is situation-specific such as claustrophobia or social phobia.

Positive symptoms (of schizophrenia) – These include symptoms such as delusions, hallucinations and speech disorder which are features of acute illness and usually respond to standard treatment.

Post-traumatic stress disorder (PTSD) – A delayed and/or protracted response to a stressful event of an exceptionally threatening nature likely to cause distress. Probably overdiagnosed. Clinical utility suspect as features may be subsumed within depressive illness and anxiety states.

Pre-morbid – Antedating illness, especially in the case of personality before onset of illness.

Prevalence – Total number of cases of a disorder in a defined population at any given time (cf incidence).

Pseudohallucination – A hallucination, usually auditory, arising from within an individual's mind and not relating to the world outside. May be seen in states of grief and is less significant than true hallucinations.

Psychopathology – A study of abnormal mental states either in terms of their description (also called phenomenology) or as mode of causation (psychodynamic psychopathology).

Psychosis – A mental disorder which leads to loss of contact with reality and insight along with the presence of symptoms such as delusions and hallucinations.

Psychosurgery – A specialised and controversial form of brain surgery for modifying behaviour and emotions.

Rehabilitation – Procedures aimed at minimising or preventing secondary social disability due to mental disorder by restoring previous levels of functioning.

Schizoaffective disorder – A disorder in which the symptoms of a schizophrenic illness and an affective illness are both present.

Schizophrenia – A psychotic disorder in which pathological changes occur in thinking, behaviour, perception and, occasionally, mood.

Schizophreniform – Schizophrenia-like. A symptomatic form of schizophrenia akin to true illness. May be seen in cases involving drug abuse.

Selective serotonin reuptake inhibitors (SSRIs) – A group of antidepressant drugs including fluoxetine (Prozac) and paroxetine (Seroxat).

Senile dementia – Dementias occurring at the age of 65 or after. Pre-senile dementias occur before that age.

Somatic symptoms – Usually seen in cases of depressive illness. Involve symptoms such as sleep disturbance and changes in appetite, bowel habits, menstrual regularity and libido.

Somatoform disorders – Disorders in which the patient makes persistent complaint of physical symptoms (for which no obvious cause can be found) and refuses to accept the assurances of his doctors.

Suicidal behaviour – Deliberate self-harming behaviour which involves an element of intent.

Tricyclic antidepressants – Older generation of antidepressant drugs including such agents as amitryptiline and dothiepin. Now out of favour on account of adverse side effects and potential for a lethal outcome on overdose.

PART I

GENERAL

CHAPTER 1

AN INTRODUCTION TO VIOLENT BEHAVIOUR AND ITS ROOTS

Violent behaviour is a matter of some complexity, influenced as it is by a variety of factors. As we have noted already in the general introduction, there are two common misconceptions held when it comes to attaining any understanding of violent behaviour. The first of these involves the notion that violence is commonly, if not invariably, related to mental illness and mental disorder. This is plainly wrong on the evidence that is available. Mentally disordered perpetrators of violence exist, in fact, in a minority. The vast majority of the incidents of violence are caused by individuals, or groups of individuals, who have no discernible mental disorder. The second misconception concerns those violent incidents caused by individuals suffering from a mental disorder. It is a common belief that where a situation of violence exists due to mental ill health, the illness or disorder by itself, necessarily and without more, leads to the violent acts that occur. This belief is also wrong, as will be evident to anyone who cares to study these incidents and those perpetrating them in any depth. Mentally disordered individuals are, in fact, subject to the same influences and forces as are the rest of the community. A useful summary approach to take in the approach to understanding violence caused by the mentally disordered is to see how the ordinary or normal factors that could lead to violence are further enhanced or exacerbated by the mental illness or mental disorder present in the perpetrator.

In this chapter we consider the background to violent offending. As the sections that follow indicate, a variety of influences may be present. We learn quickly that violent behaviour may be an intensely personal activity involving elements in the individual who causes the violence. It may also be a communal activity, that is, there could be a background of social, economic and cultural aspects against which violent behaviour is usually set. In the sections that follow we consider some of these factors. The descriptions are brief, summary, selective and simplified, perhaps in some cases even oversimplified. But it is essential to grasp the gist of these matters if one hopes to gain an understanding of violent behaviour in general. In Chapter 2 a general account is given of mental disorder in relation to violent behaviour. In the rest of the chapters that follow in Part II of this book one looks in greater detail at individual groups of mental disorders so as to gain some understanding of how they may cause, or contribute to, violent behaviour.

1.1　ANIMAL BEHAVIOUR

It is to do a disservice to attempts at achieving a human understanding of violence and the behaviours associated with it to disregard the early roots of such behaviour in those animals which preceded humans in the course of evolutionary history. Equally, it would be a serious mistake to think about human aggression and violence only in terms of its earlier animal origins. If one were to be uncritical in the observations one makes of animal violence, it would seem animal behaviour in this respect was dictated by drive and instinct alone. Thus, violence in respect of seizing and keeping territory, finding food and seeking and keeping a mate would all seem responses to the dictates of primitive instincts. A subtler view would be informed by the evolutionary imperative, namely, that animals that were successful in evolutionary terms came to be where they are now by the successful deployment of these forces. If one were to analyse these forces further, one would be drawn to the study of the genetic factors that could have been in operation. We shall further consider these genetic elements in the section below but it suffices here to say that evolutionary progress is underpinned by these genetic mechanisms.

The work of Ellis and Hoffman (1990) is important in this context. They looked at the mechanisms of natural selection operating on genetic evolution to explain aspects of violent behaviour. Their hypothesis is that some forms of violent behaviour involved, say, in assault and rape, are due to genetic forces. Thus, it can be contended that rape attended by violence could have evolved as a result of the male drive to mate with as many females as possible in order to ensure the perpetuation of the gene line. The females resist these violent approaches as their drive or instinct is to exert control over their sexual partners so as to ensure they have the necessary genetic characteristics suitable for propagation. Thus, in numerous non-human species there is evidence of forcible copulation and, also, that the females at highest risk happen to be in the fertile and offspring-bearing age group. The risk of pregnancy from rape also happens to be high. Assaults are also part and parcel of the ritual of finding and retaining a sexual partner, involving as it does fighting off rivals and also ensuring control of partners once they have been found.

There has even been an attempt, based on studies such as these, to formulate a hypothesis for the control mechanisms which could have been the forerunners of the criminal justice system as we know it. It has been suggested that dominant groups, especially in the primate species, may tend to regulate and control behaviour among other groups in their community so as to protect the females and the young. This may appear to be the basis for the protection of the sanctity of both property and of personal security. Needless to say, the aspiration of the these dominant groups to preserve their mating instincts is also served by this form of control and regulation. Therefore, as the victors gain the spoils, the evolutionary process is also served by the *mores* of the dominant group being perpetuated. The strong, indeed, come to prevail in these circumstances.

An extension of this hypothesis seeks to find an explanation for offences against property. It is said that every species aims to ensure the survival of its offspring. To ensure this, the optimal response is for the females to mate with those males who can best provide the resources that are needed for survival. Thus, many offences against property stem from the drive to attract and retain a mate. It is not too far fetched a proposition, if one carried on an argument on these lines, to suggest that males in such communities who lack the resources to provide for the females and their offspring may be drawn into the infractions of the rules and regulations.

This hypothesis is also prayed in aid to attempt to explain the abuse of children. It is well established that abuse is most likely to occur where the offspring are unrelated to the abuser, who may be an adoptive parent or one who has defeated or displaced a weak or ineffectual natural parent. Animal studies have shown that abusive behaviour is most likely to occur where the families are large or where the parents are unable to rear their young or where one or both parents have abandoned their duties and the genetic link between the abuser and the abused is weak or non-existent.

1.2 GENETIC FACTORS

If one looks to the processes of evolution to help understand human violence, the only mechanism that is capable of furnishing any explanatory power is genetics. As almost everyone who has studied the various facets of behaviour – whether it be in the lower animals or man – has known for a long time, genetic factors play an enormously important, if not paramount, significance in all behaviour. In recent years there has been extraordinary progress made in the descriptions of the genetic mechanisms which may be in play. Yet, by a paradox, our understanding of the means by which these genetic factors actually determine behaviour is far from being complete. Indeed, we are as much in the dark now, even with the human genome put together, as we have been before. So close appears to be the superficial genetic resemblance between all living creatures – animals and plants – it is virtually impossible to relate any behaviour to any one genetic element, or gene. There appear to be many *loci* that may be responsible for any given behaviour, and even then there need, it seems, to be many types of interactions between these *loci* before any form of behaviour can be displayed. As has long been suspected in behavioural studies, undertaken from whatever perspective, behaviour is multifactorial in its manifestations. Where violent behaviour is concerned, it appears to be the case that a wide variety of genetic factors, interaction between them and with the environment in general, are necessary before aggressive and violent behaviour are displayed. A particular gene reserved for aggressive behaviour alone appears to be a fanciful notion, for aggression, as is well appreciated, is capable of being channelled into constructive as well as destructive paths. Many creative individuals are notably aggressive and, especially in the fields of commerce, it is this aggression that leads them to the forefront. Sport, too, attracts many aggressive individuals and forcefulness in endeavour is a prerequisite for success. These are constructive forms of aggressive behaviour which lead to social acceptance. The challenge to the biologist engaged in behavioural study is to locate those other elements which may help him separate the roots of socially acceptable aggression from unacceptable violence.

This brings us conveniently to a consideration of the interaction between genetic factors and environmental influences, to cast the aged 'nature versus nurture' argument in slightly more modern garb. It has been evident for a long time that to throw in one's lot with the proponents of the supremacy of genetic factors is to descend into the underworld of determinism, which is no more valid when studying violent behaviour than it is anywhere else in human psychology. Few individuals have their fates decided by their genes alone. Many more are likely to find themselves at the mercy of their experiences, which are derived from the environment. It is far from being an 'all or nothing' phenomenon in either direction. Indeed, the interest is now in the more sophisticated sphere of trying to understand the 'nature of nurture'. That is to say, to try to explain how some individuals find themselves repeatedly in situations which can only lead them to misadventure. This is especially apparent in violent situations to which certain types of individual are attracted even when they are not the perpetrators, indeed those who are resolved to be nothing but innocent bystanders. These individuals may end up being cast as victims repeatedly. It is well known that the statistics on violent offending are to a substantial degree inflated by the presence within them of a relatively small number of young men. When trouble starts in various situations these are the individuals who are also rounded up as the 'usual suspects', leading on occasion to injustice. Morbidity and mortality is high among these groups. As these individuals also, to a disproportionate extent, spring from the more disadvantaged socio-economic groups of the community, there is temptation on the part of some theorists with a tendentious bent to their thought (on the Right and the Left of the political spectrum respectively) to ascribe these violent behaviours to the origins of these young men, either in a spirit of blame or of exculpation. The evidence suggests that such simplistic notions are likely to be wide off the mark. What we inherit by way of genes merely seems to give us a predisposition, or the potential, to behave in particular ways. What determines how we actually behave appears to be due to factors which, in the present state of knowledge, are only dimly apparent to us.

1.3 POSSIBLE GENETIC MECHANISMS

As we have seen already, it is far too simplistic, possibly even plain wrong, to take too deterministic a view of genetic inheritance. It used to be believed that whenever some characteristic, such as a predisposition to violent behaviour, was found among a family or a small close community made up of related individuals, that the cause for such behaviour was genetic. Some of the studies undertaken involved families of well-known criminals. In the nineteenth century one such study involved the Jukes family in New York. The Jukes were the real-life equivalents of the Timson family that kept Mr Horace Rumpole so well supplied with claret and cigars. They were a byword for all manner of feckless conduct. It was postulated that such behaviours indicated that criminality ran in families. Nowadays, such a view would be deemed to be absurd for it does not permit sufficient, or any, attention to be paid to environmental factors. Plain misfortune could run in such a family with little or no scope for the redemptive forces of education, settled occupation or decent habitation. Aggressive behaviours in such unpromising purlieus may become the norm, sometimes the only weapon available against hardship and privation. It could even be the only means of survival. Violent behaviour may even be learned and passed on from generation to generation as being the most effective, or indeed only, means of getting on and getting one's way. It indicates as little by way of genetic influence as one may find when one returns a tame or domesticated animal to the wild when it will, in due course, turn feral.

Every living cell comprises in its nucleus all the chief genetic characteristics of the organism to which the cell belongs. In normal human beings these genetic characteristics are held on 23 pairs of chromosomes of which one pair, the sex chromosomes, will determine if the individual is to be male or female by being represented by, respectively, the XY and the XX chromosomes. These replicate and are united in the act of conception, so that males and female organisms arise. It used to be believed until a generation or two ago that the possession of an XYY chromosome as a result of reproductive aberration would lead to hyper-male type of behaviour, including offending by means of violent behaviour. In fact, it has been found that although XYY males may be overrepresented in samples of offenders, it is because their intellectual endowment is low and, indeed, their offending behaviour, perhaps also for this reason, involves low grade or trivial offending.

More sophisticated approaches to the genetic influence on violent behaviour involve a study of the genes themselves. As DNA analysis shows, virtually every human being is a unique individual apart from the case of identical twins. Identical twins arise from the conception due to a single egg and sperm and are also called monozygotic twins (MZ). Their genetic inheritance is identical, hence the impossibility of separating them on routine tests including DNA analysis. Non-identical twins arise from different eggs and sperm and are, therefore, no different from ordinary siblings. These are also referred to as dizygotic twins (DZ). If genetic influence was wholly or largely determinative of violent behaviour, MZ twins should be similarly violent. If environmental influences are believed to hold sway, DZ twins should show as much similarity in their conduct as ordinary siblings would. In other words, concordance between the individuals making up MZ twins would show the primacy of the genetic factors while concordance between the DZ twins would indicate a much bigger role for the environment. In earlier studies the results appeared to show a tendency to the first among these hypotheses. However, there were serious methodological problems afflicting the early work on twin studies. Later studies, carried out primarily in Denmark and Norway, tended to show some genetic influence, but by no means to any overwhelming effect. It had by then been suggested that any similarity in behaviour between MZ twins could also be explained in terms of closeness in their upbringing, ie similar environmental influences could have been in play even among genetically identical pairs of twins. There may also be interaction between siblings who tend to influence one another's behaviour. Thus, there were these limitations to be considered when twins, whether MZ or DZ, were studied within their own families.

The next logical step was therefore to consider MZ twins who had been separated at or close to birth and, thus, notwithstanding the same genetic inheritance, who were brought up in different families.

This is what adoption studies attempt to do. If the determinism of genetic influence is to prevail, by separating MZ twins at or close to birth, to be adopted within different environments, it must be shown that the childhood influences were of little value, the genetic inheritance proving conclusive. If, on the other hand, the two individuals from an MZ pair behaved differently upon separation, then, notwithstanding their common genetic endowment, it had to be concluded that it was the environment that mostly mattered.

The early studies in adopted MZ twins, mostly undertaken in the Nordic countries, seemed to suggest that genetic influences tended to be supreme. In other words, a twin with criminal and violent propensities who was adopted still showed a similar predilection when placed in another setting. But methodological objections were still raised, as there is a tendency among adoptions to place like with like, that is to say, to choose consciously or not an adoptive family similar in characteristics to the biological family. As larger cohorts were studied and the methodology was improved, it seemed in general that the genetic influences became less and less in evidence. This accords with common sense and general observation and experience that law abiding and peaceable individuals can be drawn from even the most violent of families while, in the converse sense, that recidivist thugs can arise from families which have provided them with every advantage. It is perhaps fair to say that where studies are well designed, the evidence supporting the link between genetics and violent criminality appears more tenuous than in earlier, less well designed studies. The conclusion that may be permitted overall is that genetic and environmental factors both have a role to play in determining the propensity to violent behaviour, depending on the particular circumstances that any individual may find himself in.

1.4 OTHER BIOLOGICAL CONSIDERATIONS

Whatever genetic influences may be in play, and however they may interact with environmental factors, the ultimate agent of all behaviour, including aggressive and violent conduct, must be the brain. The effect of other influences is to make an impact on the brain, directly or indirectly through the medium of neurochemicals. In the next chapter we shall take an overview of how mental disorders may be related to violent behaviour. These mental disorders also have their origins in the brain. In the chapters succeeding that we shall consider how individual forms of mental disorders may be involved in violent behaviour. In this section we shall now consider how some of the commoner chemicals found in or introduced to the brain may affect that organ in relation to violent behaviour.

Virtually every lay person is aware, however vaguely, of the effects of the male sex hormone, testosterone. It is well associated with aggressive or assertive tendencies and a particularly spirited effort in any situation may be described as having been 'testosterone-induced' or, more crudely, of the protagonist concerned as having possessed 'balls'. As such, the properties of testosterone have become part of lore. Studies in non-human primates have shown that a tendency to aggression and assertiveness can also be related to the levels of testosterone found in these creatures and such matters as social status in hierarchies and success in finding and keeping female partners were related to the levels of testosterone flowing through male monkeys. Moreover, masculine behaviours such as increased aggression and a more predatory approach to sex could be induced in female monkeys by injecting them with testosterone.

In humans, such a relationship between testosterone levels and aggressive behaviour, does, in general, exist but is far less marked than in non-human primates and other animals. It appears from studies on human subjects – who have included violent convicted criminals – that testosterone levels are but one variable among many that may determine the levels of aggression and violence that are seen. The personality of the subject is one of those other variables, there being different approaches taken to violent and potentially violent situations by subjects differing in the make up of their personalities. The situation itself is important to consider, there being a difference between situations where the subject is the aggressor and where the subject defends himself against aggression, and also on how much provocation has been given to the subject. Alcohol and illicit substances may also add another layer of chemical complication.

One of the more intriguing findings in studies on criminal behaviour is that violent offences, including those involving sexual violence, are committed mostly in adolescence and the early adult life of male offenders. This also happens to be the period when the testosterone coursing through the body is found at its peak levels. It is also a universal truth for in virtually all cultures violent crime is preponderantly perpetrated by adolescents and young adult males. It is attractive to postulate some direct link between this chemical and violent conduct, but more detailed consideration has failed to show an invariable relationship between testosterone levels and violent crime, there being aggressive individuals with relatively low levels of testosterone. It appears truer to say that it is the fact of being adolescent or in early adult life, rather than giving harbour to one chemical, albeit one implicated in aggressive behaviour to an important extent, that is responsible for the aggressive and violent behaviour in these age groups.

Nevertheless, the drive to employ corrective measures on these individuals has been informed by the belief that there exists a simple relationship between testosterone and violent behaviour, especially where sexual violence has been involved. This has been the basis for employing castration – surgical at first, by way of anti-androgen drugs more recently – in an attempt to curb excessive and perverted desires in some of these offenders. As might be expected, given so many variables in play in violent situations, whether or not sexual violence is also involved, the results are far from being unequivocal. In fact, castration is of limited application for the vast majority of these offenders – to the disappointment and frustration of the editors of the tabloid newspapers – the preferred management approaches now involve rather more subtle therapeutic strategies whose aim is to correct any cerebral lesion through indirect means rather than by recourse to knife or drug. Ellis and Coontz (1990) have attempted to explain the role testosterone may have in violent behaviour. They postulate that the brain may show a differential response to arousing stimuli depending on the rate at which stimuli reach it, and this may demonstrate a gender difference which itself is determined, at least in part, by the exposure of the male foetal brain in the course of its early development to male sex hormones. The testosterone levels may also affect the development and integrity of the limbic system which mediates emotional responses (see Chapter Two). These authors have also suggested that dominance of one cerebral hemisphere at the expense of the other may determine violent criminality. This domination is particularly marked in males.

Where excitement and aggression are concerned, testosterone is matched in popular lore by adrenaline. In the case of the latter, the paradox appears to be that violent antisocial activity is associated with low levels of adrenaline in the perpetrators, at least when they are at rest. The level of this hormone is linked to the level of cerebral cortical activity, which has been found to be notably low in criminal offenders. They are slow to arousal and also slow to recover from arousal, which has implications for learned behaviour which has been linked to rapid recovery from heightened states of arousal. Low levels of cortical arousal are also related to easy boredom and a craving for excitement which may, of course, be satisfied by legitimate means such as, for example, by participation in 'extreme' sport. So there are obvious personal, social and cultural factors also in play.

Some other hormones may have an indirect effect on the causation and exacerbation of violent behaviour. One of these is insulin, which influences the levels of blood sugar. Insulin itself has no effects on aggressive behaviour, but in the increased presence of insulin – either in absolute terms by an excess of the hormone given by injection or in relative terms by the blood sugar levels not being kept up by adequate nutrition – there arises the condition of hypoglycaemia in which violent behaviour may be associated with confusion, emotional instability, marked anxiety, convulsions and, in time, coma and death. There is also a link between excessive alcohol use and hypoglycaemia, a possible contributor to the levels of aggression associated with this substance. There has also been postulated a condition called reactive hypoglycaemia where subjects given doses of glucose react by showing low blood sugar levels, presumably through stimulating excess insulin production. Low levels of blood sugar have been found in some series of habitually violent and antisocial offenders.

While violent behaviour is usually a predominantly male activity, there are a couple of instances where the female sex hormones may cause, or contribute to, aggressive and violent behaviour. One of these situations involves the hormonal changes associated with the menstrual cycle which, especially in the pre-menstrual period, may lead to irritability and which may provoke violence. It is a factor that is occasionally taken into account by a sentencing court as a mitigating element in an individual who has been convicted of a violent assault. The other situation involves the surge of hormones that occurs during and after pregnancy, especially in the course of lactation. This has led to the availability to a mother of the partial defence of infanticide in cases where she has killed her own child in the 12 months following her giving birth to it, which gives recognition to the fact that her mind could have been disturbed by the event of the birth or the period of lactation. While it may seem simplistic to attribute all of a mother's vulnerability at these times to her hormones, and one must pause to consider the social and personal factors that could also be making an impact during this period, some recent research has indicated that the period of lactation may be associated with a rise in levels of some neurochemicals which have previously been implicated in the onset of psychotic illness.

A few words need to be said about some chemicals that may be commonly found in nature and that are distributed in common foodstuffs and drinks. Some extravagant claims have been made for the effects of these chemicals – especially in the form of 'additives' – on behaviour that may lead to aggression and violence, and claims have even been made that improving or modifying the diet of recidivist criminals may make them see the light even where punishment has failed to do so. No worthwhile scientific case has hitherto been made in respect of common chemicals preferentially leading to aggressive and violent behaviour. However, the increasing environmental impact of one chemical, in the form of the metal element lead, and its possible incorporation into the brain of young children, has been studied with some interest recently. The lead, having reached the atmosphere as a pollutant, is said to have toxic effects on the brains of children, leading to slowed learning, impaired intelligence, loss of concentration, impulsiveness, hyperactivity and aggression. Further studies on lead pollution and other environmental toxins are being carried out in the spirit of increasing awareness of the effects of pollution and the damage it does both to individuals and the environment they live in.

1.5   SOME PSYCHOLOGICAL FACTORS

Psychology, in very general terms, deals in behaviour. Naturally it concerns itself with aggressive and violent behaviour. The subject matter of psychology is vast and the literature is extensive and variable in its scientific merit and usefulness. Yet, it is an important subject for it deals, by and large, with normal behaviours which are beyond the scope of psychiatry, dealing as the latter does with abnormal, indeed pathological, behaviour involving mental illness and mental disorder. A historically important part of psychology is psychoanalysis. This deals in the main with unconscious forces. In very broad terms the psychoanalytic understanding of aggression and violence involves the study of unconscious dynamic forces which result in a conflict between the demands of reason and conscience and those of instinct. If the forces of instinct overcome the forces of reason and conscience, the result could be antisocial behaviour. Out of deference to history, and also in attempt to keep this section within a manageable compass, we may start with and concentrate on the thoughts of Sigmund Freud, a seminal figure in psychoanalysis and one, though not the only begetter, whose ideas about the unconscious were arguably the most persuasive of the modern propagandists of these notions.

Freud considered the personality as existing in three parts – the id, the ego and the super-ego – and antisocial behaviour may be understood in terms of the relationship between these three parts. The id reflects the primitive, unconscious areas of the mind and is the source of the most basic and primeval of the instincts, which includes the instinct to be aggressive and to seek self-gratification. If unchecked the id will lead to the most monstrous displays of behaviour which will be quite at odds with the needs of a civilized society. The task of taming and controlling the id falls on the ego and the super-ego. The ego is developed through social learning. Its business is to control the id and any success in this endeavour owes most to successful learning of social rules and standards. Standing over the ego as it accomplishes this task is the super-ego which exists in the unconscious and is the important part of the conscience. Any human who is fully socialised and accepts the *mores* of the community that he lives in will have a satisfactorily developed super-ego.

In psychoanalytical theory, therefore, the satisfactory development of the super-ego is the key to developing a conscience and thereby avoiding antisocial attitudes, including the resort to violence. The child learns the rules, standards and limits of the society it will exist in through the examples and precepts of its parents who are believed to uphold the values of society. Thus, the ego finds itself pushed and pulled in two directions, trying to meet the demands of both the id and the super-ego. There will inevitably be conflict and the well-balanced mind is one that is able to master this conflict for, if there is a lack of balance, there could be antisocial behaviour in one direction and excessive anxiety leading to neurosis in the other. It could be surmised that a lack of attachment to the parents, absent parents or neglectful parents may lead to a failure in developing the super-ego. This explains the widespread belief that a parent (or a suitable parental substitute) is essential for proper development of the super-ego. If the child, removed from unsatisfactory parents, is placed in an environment which provides appropriate parenting, the damage could be undone. Conversely, if the substitute atmosphere is also unsatisfactory, the damage will continue. Hence, the reason to believe that poor quality institutions and unsatisfactory fostering arrangements may be as capable of doing as much damage as inadequate biological parents.

In psychoanalytical theory the issue for successful social integration is a balancing of these conflicting demands. A proper balance does not mean the full resolution of conflicts. It is possible to sublimate or displace the forces that remain unresolved. Thus, the aggressive and destructive instinct could be channelled into sporting activity, in sports like boxing and into fields such as 'extreme' sports. These socially acceptable activities have the merit of satisfying the demands of both the ego and the super-ego. Those who have failed to become socialised in these ways may be drawn into antisocial behaviour including criminal violence. Unresolved conflicts may also lead to persistent criminal conduct. A repressed individual with many feelings of guilt arising out of an unsatisfied ego and super-ego may be drawn to crime and the suffering of punishment. The punishment may lead to the anxiety and the guilt being assuaged for the time being at least. Any recrudescence of these feelings may lead to renewed offending, with scope for more punishment, a model for habitual criminality.

The difficulty with all psychoanalytical theories is that, dealing as they do, with unconscious forces, they are not readily susceptible to hypotheses being formulated and tested. Hence, they must be deemed to remain as unscientific speculation, and their chief merit lies in them offering scope for another approach to understanding mental phenomena, not for any explanatory power they possess. Their role in managing violent offenders and preventing repeat offending is of limited value.

Some followers of Freud, such as Carl Jung, later a bitter rival, developed the notion of introversion and extraversion as tools for the understanding of the nature of criminal behaviour. Introverts were believed capable of learning from their errors and therefore better able to incorporate the rules and standards of society, while extroverts were more likely to be subject to violent emotions which rendered them incapable of learning new behaviour. This simplistic theory was soon discredited. Later efforts by behavioural psychologists such as Eysenck to improve these ideas by introducing a three dimensional scale to incorporate also 'neuroticism' and 'psychoticism' (roughly equivalent to psychopathic traits) appeared at first to hold greater promise but have also fallen by the wayside for there was little evidential support for any of these notions. What appears to be the case is that a detailed study of an offender's personality, from as many directions as possible, is one that usually repays the investment in time and effort.

Other psychological approaches have also been taken using apparently objective tools such as personality measurements. Claims made for the detection of certain personality types being predisposed to criminal behaviour have not been sustained. There have been numerous problems of methodology and definition, including the size of the samples used and the employment of definitions of offence which are artificial, as Parliament hardly uses psychological methods of definition when framing legislation. Farrington (1994) has noted that the truly significant differences lay not between personality traits and offending behaviour, but between impulsivity and offending behaviour. This view was based on the Cambridge study in which a cohort of young boys was followed up into adult life. Impulsivity carries the ordinary meaning found in the English language in which actions are taken heedless of consequences and the subject is at the mercy of rogue impulses arising in his brain which he finds difficult, if not impossible, to master. As noted in a previous section, impulsivity may be linked to low levels of cerebral arousal which are believed to lead to overconfidence, the seeking of new sensations and uninformed risk taking, all behaviours related to offending. A low heart rate, which is one measure of low arousal, is also associated with violent offending. Being shy, nervous or withdrawn, on the other hand, suggests high arousal and the Cambridge study further suggests that possessing these characteristics, which are widely deemed to be socially negative, may actually protect a boy coming from a high risk environment from turning into a criminal offender himself.

1.6   SOME SOCIOLOGICAL FACTORS

Much sociological speculation has had its focus on criminal behaviour, including violent offending. Several leading figures, including the French sociologist Emile Durkheim and his American counterpart Robert Merton, may be deemed to be seminal thinkers in this field. In essence, workers in this area attempt to link criminal behaviour to the organisation of the societies in which offenders exist. Life was simple in early society, but as this evolved complex rules had to be formulated to ensure the security of those who dwelt in these communities and their property. It has been postulated that for crime to occur there must be some degree of disaffection between the offender and society. The incomplete degree of integration into society gives rise to the phenomenon of 'anomie', a term first used by Durkheim, whose primary interest lay in the study of suicide. Financial crises and industrial conflict could give rise to this alienation from society. Another situation could involve rigid class divisions, affording little scope for social mobility, leading to the oppressed starting to rebel and to lash out. A third situation could involve the exploitation of labour where dispossessed workers could feel a sense of alienation and a lack of interest in the enterprises for which they laboured. The 'anomie' that results in these situations could be mirrored in the lawlessness and 'normlessness' which is seen especially vividly at times of social upheaval. The result is not only social breakdown, but a feeling of psychological isolation in the face of undermined confidence in the social structures.

The expectations of individuals and the ability of society to satisfy these is also part of the tension that tests the bonds of society. Individuals in an aspirant society are under pressure to succeed, but the scope for advancement by legitimate means may be limited, hence the recourse to illegitimate, ie criminal, means of advancement. This idea was taken up to explain the discrepancies in the criminal rates among the various social classes in society. It was said in the American context that every citizen there believed there was equality of opportunity. Yet, the reality was that numerous constraints also existed to blunt attempts at advancement. The feelings of disappointment and unfairness that resulted could lead to criminality. Thus, those inhabiting the lower reaches of society, who are most likely to be disadvantaged by lack of educational opportunity or by racial discrimination, were the least likely to succeed in fulfilling the 'American Dream' through legitimate means. It was this that led to criminality and violence, the result of the 'strain' between individuals from the lower social classes and the limitations imposed on them by society.

It could be inferred from these ideas that the important consideration is not deprivation or poverty, but the inequality in wealth and the unfairness in its distribution that could give rise to the breaking of rules and, hence, lead to offending behaviour. The theory of relative deprivation addresses this issue. It deals with individuals and groups in society who feel hard done by because they perceive they have little or no chance of satisfying their desires in any legitimate way. Their criminal behaviour is then influenced by these feelings.

The early thinking concentrated on economic deprivation, but later thinkers have also turned to considering the 'strain' or 'tension' that could apply in other areas of human endeavour and lead in certain circumstances to violent offending. One of these situations is trauma resulting from bereavement through death, divorce, migration (and loss of existing social support) and loss of friendship. This is a situation in which positively valued stimuli have been removed, resulting in trauma being experienced. Other situations may involve the strain resulting from negative stimuli which may occur when an individual faces domestic or child abuse, family breakdown, pain and disability and involvement in criminal proceedings. The resulting behaviour could involve further offending or the seeking of revenge. Workers believe that the strongest emotion experienced in these situations is anger. How well the individual will deal with this situation will depend on his coping mechanisms and his success in using them.

1.7   JUVENILE DELINQUENCY

The early work on juvenile criminality concentrated on the subcultures which these youthful offenders inhabited. These subcultures arose in rebellion against what were perceived to be 'middle class' values, namely the values of individual responsibility, personal achievement, the control of aggression, restraint and respect for the integrity of the person and property. The rebels' values tended more to toughness, the pursuit of excitement and gratification without delay.

How youths become socialised is the basis of the control theories, a mix of psychology and sociology, that have attempted to explain juvenile deviance. Control may be broadly subdivided into 'personal control' and 'social control'. Where 'personal control' is concerned, the onus is on the individual youth and it is a measure of the development of his conscience and the degree of his socialisation that he comes to accept socially approved methods of reaching his goals. 'Social control' is the ability of social groups or institutions to make the norms and rules of society effective. In other words, it requires submission and conformity of the individuals to the rules and norms of society.

Extensive work has been done in regard to the control theories, and although the results vary, with the emphasis on individual factors differing, some conclusions are capable of being drawn for present purposes. One of the most important of deterrent factors appears to be shame, which is related to the conscience. That is to say, that if an individual felt shame at the prospect of doing some act, this factor would induce him to resume his fidelity to conformity. This is taken to support the value of the processes of socialisation which have long been valued as being essential to the processes of maturation and on which so much emphasis is laid. Legal punishments, if they were certain to be applied, also tended to be fairly effective in inhibiting non-conformist delinquency. The disapproval of 'significant others' does not appear to be as effective, perhaps because of the chances of being excused or in the belief that 'significant others' would not learn about the infractions of the rules. Some individuals appear to be beyond the reach of control theories. These include those whose calculation of risk against reward tempts them into offending, even when high gain has to be set against high risk. This situation applies to illicit drug dealing where the prospects for violent offending and gang warfare are high. The mentally disordered offender may also be beyond the constraints of these forces of control.

One of the criticisms made of conventional control theory is that it does not give sufficient weight to the issue of motivation. An individual may be highly enough motivated to offend whatever the claims of conformity are; another who is poorly motivated will not offend even where there are no or only few social controls. The former situation is again exemplified by the illicit trafficking in drugs, while the latter illustrates the point that apathy is perhaps the best deterrent against criminal offending, and that turning the other cheek the best safeguard against escalating a potentially violent conflict.

PART II

THE PSYCHIATRIC DISORDERS

CHAPTER 2

INTRODUCTION – VIOLENCE IN RELATION TO MENTAL DISORDER

As we have seen in Chapter 1, the roots of violence are manifold. Many factors appear to be responsible, causative or contributory to the manifestations of aggressive and violent behaviour. In this chapter we shall focus on one of those factors, namely, mental disorder, which is naturally appropriate to a work aiming to explore the psychiatric roots of aggressive and violent behaviour. Fairly detailed descriptions of the mental disorders are given in Mahendra (2006, 2008a, 2008b). We shall also consider these disorders in some detail in the chapters that follow. In this chapter we shall attend to general considerations of the psychiatric aspects of aggressive and violent behaviour. We must begin, however, by discussing the nature and scope of psychiatric disorders.

The term mental disorder occasionally leads to confusion among the lay public. One may say that it is a collective term used to include formal mental illness and also what amounts not to illness but involves behaviour of such a kind that makes it appropriate for inclusion among the subject matter that is studied within psychiatry, the medical speciality that deals with such disorders. The test of what is a mental disorder is just that, namely, whether or not it is a condition that is deemed fit for study by a psychiatrist. A more detailed study of the background to the mental disorders has been undertaken in the general part of *Adult Psychiatry in Family and Child Law* (Mahendra, 2006). In this chapter a brief summary of the issues involved is given in relation to mental disorders with regard to aggressive and violent behaviour.

2.1 THE PROVENANCE OF PSYCHIATRIC DISORDERS

A little thought will convince us that all mental illness, mental disorder and violent behaviour must have their ultimate origins in the brain. There is nowhere else, as far as we know, for these behaviours and symptoms to originate from. But, in the present state of knowledge, while we are aware that all mental disorders must originate in the brain, we do not have sufficient information concerning the precise locations in the brain and the mechanisms of function involved therein to establish the study of mental disorders as a branch of the applied neurosciences. That is a task for the future. In the present all we can do is to describe and classify the symptoms and behaviours we can observe. But we must note the lively controversies which are still stirred by arguments over whether a disorder has its origins in the 'brain' or 'mind'. As we see at regular intervals, this unedifying argument taints the discussion of the origins of such conditions as the chronic fatigue syndrome or the Gulf War syndrome. Many of those suffering from, or those caring for those suffering from, these disorders appear to feel insulted by being told there is no convincing evidence for an 'organic' origin for these conditions. All this means is that techniques available at present cannot locate the cerebral lesion, if one indeed does exist. That does not mean that these symptoms do not have a basis in the brain. No doubt, in the fullness of time, we shall be able to see what exactly is wrong and be better placed to give explanations for these symptoms.

2.2   ILLNESS AND DISORDER

Formal mental illness includes such conditions as schizophrenia, depressive illness and bipolar affective disorder. The mental disorders have included among them conditions such as the personality disorders and the behaviours due to the misuse of alcohol and illicit drugs, among others. The broad test to be applied is whether there are observable symptoms attaching to any condition. If there are, and a systematic study can be made of these symptoms, the condition involved comes to be called a mental illness. If it is behaviour rather than symptoms that is available for study, the condition may be, subject to the qualification discussed below, called a mental disorder

2.3   ABNORMALITY AND PATHOLOGY

One could ask if there is any matter of reason or logic that determines some behaviours to be part of a mental disorder and others not to be. While reason and logic cannot, in the present state of knowledge, play any overwhelmingly important part in psychiatric classification, for now the test for inclusion within the ranks of the mental disorders is whether pathology is involved in the behaviour concerned. A delusion, which is classified, broadly speaking, as a false belief held with unshakeable conviction in the face of compelling evidence to the contrary against a background of the social and cultural beliefs of the individual concerned, is clearly pathological. But there are other beliefs that are not so clearly demarcated but which may still be odd, eccentric and bizarre. Auditory hallucinations may or may not amount to pathology; the bereaved, the learning disabled and the lonely may be subject to these phenomena. One must, therefore, be able to distinguish between what is normal, abnormal and pathological. The distinction between normal and abnormal may be made by means of statistical measurement. If some measure is common to 95 per cent of the population, all those within it may be deemed normal. Where excessive height is concerned, for example, the very tall and the very short may be deemed to be abnormal but only a few rare disease conditions will cause excessive tallness or shortness. Where intelligence is concerned, an IQ measure of 70 is conventionally taken to be the point below which learning disabilities or mental handicap exists. An IQ of 140 or greater is generally taken to indicate genius. The learning disabilities are deemed to be pathological states and constitute one of the mental disorders. There is no pathological cause of genius. The inclusion of a condition such as pathological gambling – said to afflict 300,000 individuals in Britain – among the mental disorders (F 63.0 ICD-10 Classification of Mental Disorders) may appear to be problematical, except for the fact that its subject matter is a form of addictive behaviour which already finds representation among the mental disorders in the form of behaviours due to misuse of alcohol and illicit drugs.

2.4   ORIGINS OF MENTAL DISORDERS

As we may note, in general terms progress has been made in respect of the greater understanding of the genetic basis of illness and disorder. While these developments have been steady, knowledge has been accrued and there is much promise, for the present we can only make very general statements about the genetic basis to most psychiatric disorders. Such a basis definitely exists, as can be seen with conditions such as schizophrenia and the bipolar affective disorders, where the closer the relationship is between a sufferer and his descendant, the greater is the probability of the condition arising in the latter. However, except in rare situations like that obtaining with Huntington's disorder or some metabolic disorders leading to the learning disabilities, one cannot generally make any confident prediction of the onset of any disorder in any individual who could be at genetic risk for any given condition. The overwhelming impression that is created at present is that while genetic vulnerability may exist, it requires interaction with one or more environmental factors before illness or disorder is manifested. This means that environmental factors are given a role to play in the onset of most mental disorders. This is a matter of considerable importance for, in the present state of knowledge, while the chances of intervention to correct a genetic deficiency or aberration are next to negligible, there usually exists significant scope for environmental manipulation. One is invariably asked about the genetic prospects for a child about to be placed for adoption, where one or both of its parents have suffered a mental disorder such as schizophrenia, when the answer usually given is that a stable and nurturing environment provided for the child could go a long way in mitigating any genetic risk he or she could have inherited. The influence of the personality of the individual could also be crucial, for many psychiatric disorders could be studied in terms of the interaction between personality and the impact upon it of adverse life experiences, including trauma. The important role played by both personality and the environment in the causation and maintenance of disorder and recovery from it will become apparent throughout the course of this part of the book.

2.5   DIAGNOSIS

As will be apparent from the previous description, the study of mental disorders involves descriptions of symptoms or behaviours. These have been placed into clusters which have been given names called diagnoses. The diagnosis of psychiatric disorders has often been a controversial matter. An outline of how diagnostic classifications arose and evolved and the questions that have been asked of, and remain about, these systems has been given in *Adult Psychiatry in Family and Child Law* (2006). As far as this present book is concerned, one will do well to appreciate the limitations of the diagnosis arrived at in any given case. A diagnosis is a short hand method of conveying medical information, as between doctors. It has its value in surveys on the epidemiology of disorders. It is obviously useful when research is undertaken, including that which involves the testing of new drugs, as agreed criteria must be satisfied in the selection of subjects for study. But in individual cases, where a particular aspect of a patient's functioning is what is in issue, there are shortcomings in any attempt to extrapolate from diagnosis to behaviour, an issue that must be understood. To say that a patient has suffered from schizophrenia does not, on the basis of the diagnosis alone, answer the question as to whether or not he is fit to undertake parenting or employment, or what kind of insurance risk he might be. In order to attempt to answer these questions the patient needs to be studied in the entirety of his functioning and any medical condition he may have suffered from is only one of the factors to be taken into account. Another way of putting this sentiment is to say that behaviour is more important than diagnosis when some particular function is to be addressed (Mahendra, 2008c).

2.6   TREATMENT

Broadly speaking, treatment of the psychiatric disorders involves both drug treatment and psychological treatment. Drug treatment is predicated on the belief that the underlying brain dysfunction gives rise, by some mechanisms that are far from fully understood, to disturbances in the chemicals mediating functions in the brain which may be corrected by means of similar or related chemicals that are given to the patient. As the mechanisms of their actions remain largely unknown in the present day, much drug treatment is little better than a shot in the dark, based as it is on empirical rather than fundamental evidence. The results, however, from drug treatment are generally satisfactory where the patient and his condition have been carefully chosen. The acute mental illnesses respond best to drug treatment, while behaviours are mostly beyond correction by this means. Treatment largely produces symptomatic improvement and the ameliorated clinical state is probably best described as a state of remission rather than a cure. Treatment may need to be continued for several months, occasionally for the rest of the patient's life, and maintenance treatment may also play a prophylactic function. Psychological treatment is primarily aimed at behaviour whose modification may lead to an improvement in the symptoms also. Generally speaking, a combination of drug and psychological treatment furnishes better results than one of these alone. Learning disabilities are a life-long affliction and beyond conventional treatment and the same could be said for the personality disorders, although there are those who claim they are able to bring about fundamental changes in the personality. Other forms of treatment that may be used as ancillary measures may not be as specific as drug treatment or the psychological treatments are but play an important role in 'getting a patient better' as opposed to attempting to cure him. In this respect supportive treatment plays a very important part. Support is required, for example, in keeping patients suffering from learning disabilities functioning effectively in the community. Supportive therapy is also the cornerstone in the treatment of cases of misuse of alcohol and illicit drugs, there being little by way of specific measures for these conditions. Allied to supportive therapy are all the measures taken for the rehabilitation of the patient. It is not at all uncommon for the symptoms to be dispersed in a patient without him being able to resume the functioning he had before he fell ill. As will be seen when individual disorders are discussed in detail, inadequate rehabilitation may lead to secondary disability supervening and prolonging the malfunctioning of the patient. In fact, there is increasingly good evidence that what prevents patients suffering from even serious mental illness from resuming the functioning they are capable of, including a return to employment, is a lack of rehabilitation, especially specialised vocational rehabilitation. The processes of litigation – which reward prolonged incapacity – may also play a part in perpetuating disability.

2.7 MENTAL ILLNESS AND BEHAVIOUR

It is a popular misconception to believe that the behaviour involving those suffering especially from mental illness is wholly or chiefly due to the condition or the symptoms themselves. Observation will reveal that this is not the case. Even when florid symptoms of illness are present, the behaviour of any patient will be determined, in addition to these symptoms, by a variety of other factors, which include his personality and also his personal and social circumstances. Culture is always a heavy influence on behaviour, as much on that of the mentally disordered as on others. Patterns of violence, whether involving suicide or violence directed against others, vary as between different communities even when the symptoms of illness are similar, even identical. Prejudice can be created by the belief that patients with mental illness, as a result of that illness alone, are prone to maladaptive behaviours, including violence. That is far from being the case. Only a small minority of patients with mental illness are involved in conduct that may breach the rules and norms of a community. There are some exceptions. The condition of morbid jealousy, for example, may lead to a situation of risk involving a spouse or partner through the fact of the diagnosis itself. But this is a rare instance. Situations of risk involving mentally disordered patients concern primarily the behaviours of individuals. We have already referred to the influence on violent behaviour of factors other than the disorder itself. In family and child practice, the functioning of spouse, partner or parent must be evaluated *qua* spouse, partner or parent and not merely *qua* patient. Parenting, in particular, involves many elements beyond the pathological. As can be seen in situations involving employment and the post-traumatic states, recovery from the symptoms of illness does not necessarily equate with a resumption of full functioning, any disability capable of being perpetuated by a variety of personal, social and cultural factors. Even whether an individual ought to be deemed unduly suggestible as a suspect undergoing interrogation following arrest may depend on the circumstances at the time of his interview. Mental disorder is an uncommon presence in cases of nuisance behaviour but even when it is present it tends to be heavily affected by other factors that apply in situations involving nuisance behaviours. It cannot be stressed too often that the proper assessment of risk in any situation involves elements that go well beyond the merely psychiatric.

2.8   FORMS OF AGGRESSIVE AND VIOLENT BEHAVIOUR

We shall now consider aggressive and violent conduct as it is directed against the self (suicidal behaviour and deliberate self harm) as well as against other persons and property. The special case of sexual violence will also be taken up. These behaviours form the basis for the risk assessment exercise concerning violence which involves all psychiatric practice.

2.9   SUICIDAL BEHAVIOUR

About a million people die by suicide world wide each year. In England and Wales there are between 4500-5000 suicides per year. A distinction is to be made between suicidal behaviour (including attempts) and behaviour leading to deliberate self harm. Suicidal behaviour is distinguished by the presence of intent as a mental state required for the act or omission involved. What 'intent' is may be explored by means of the proposals put forward by the Law Commission (*A New Homicide Act for England and Wales?* Consultation Paper No 177 of 2005) which is a proposed attempt to statutorily define what is at present a common law concept. By this proposed definition a person acts intentionally with respect to a result when he or she acts either: (1) in order to bring it about, or (2) knowing that it is will be virtually certain to occur, or (3) knowing that it would be virtually certain to occur if he or she were to succeed in his or her purpose of causing some other result, with the proviso that a person is not to be deemed to have intended any result which it was his or her specific purpose to avoid. In practice, whether there is suicidal intent is to be determined by the stated views of the individual if these are available (usually conveyed orally or by the writing of a 'suicide note') and the surrounding behaviour of the individual which may perhaps be best illustrated by way of a couple of examples.

A 40-year-old single mother could no longer cope with the increasingly disturbed behaviour of her 14 year-old son who was later diagnosed to be suffering from one of the autistic spectrum disorders. She planned to kill herself. She left notes, also made elaborate plans for the future care of her 10-year-old daughter, settled her affairs and asked in a note for her possessions including her jewellery to be passed onto the daughter. Suicidal intent was therefore clear in this case but it may not be so clearly observed in many other cases, a fact explaining the reluctance of some coroners to bring in a verdict of suicide in the absence of incontrovertible evidence of intent being present.

The unusual facts of a second case also illustrate the concept of intent in these circumstances. A 39-year-old man, separated from his wife, had contact with his three-year-old son who resided with his mother. The man suffered from severe and enduring physical illness which necessitated treatment with methotrexate (an anti-cancer drug which may occasionally be used to treat some intractable physical illnesses) and also a steroid drug. Both these agents may precipitate or exacerbate mood disorders and the man had in any event for many years suffered from depressive illness as a result, it was believed, of his chronic physical illness. Soon after the man separated from his wife he suffered a further bout of severe depressive illness. In a state of deep despair and depression he proposed to drive to an isolated spot and there gas himself and his child by means of the exhaust fumes emitted by his car. The car, a fairly up-to-date model, was equipped with a catalytic converter which is believed to prevent the normal kind of exhaust fumes, laden as they are with the lethal carbon monoxide gas, from emerging. This fact was not, however, known to the man at the time and he insisted at a later examination that his intention had all along been to die with his son. In the event, no injury due to the actions of the father resulted to either father or son. It is, however, the point that the impossibility of bringing about an intended outcome does not preclude there having been made a genuine attempt with intent as the underlying mental state. This was, in fact, a genuine suicidal (and homicidal) attempt.

Pure chance might also have determined the end result in another case. A 40-year-old chartered accountant, beset by many problems and facing possible indictment on a charge of mortgage fraud, decided to end his life also through gassing himself by means of his car's exhaust fumes. The turmoil in his mind was such that he had failed to ensure the car had sufficient fuel in its tank for this purpose. The engine accordingly cut out in due course in the isolated woodland spot he had chosen for his deed and he was rescued by some sightseers. He was left with severe, uncorrectable brain damage which virtually completely destroyed his memory. Suicidal intent was nonetheless clearly present.

Contrary to popular notion, the fact of death or near death through dangerous behaviour does not necessarily distinguish between intentional behaviour and merely reckless action. It is perfectly possible to die following an impulsive act if the means employed are dangerous enough, eg swallowing a sufficient dosage of paracetamol tablets if they are to hand. Some tragic consequences have resulted even in situations where the victim probably did not intend to die but the circumstances were against her (females more commonly engage in reckless rather than intentional acts of self harm). Even an apparently trivial consideration such as the day of the week when the act takes place may make a difference as to whether an individual lives or dies. If, say, towards the end of the week, when the supply of paracetamol tablets in the household drug cupboard is running low, an impulsive act takes place, it may well lead to the individual surviving. If the act had taken place, on the contrary, at the weekend, say, when the supply has been replenished after the week's shopping has been done, enough tablets may be available to make death the outcome, as sufficient poison would then have been ingested. Recent legislation restricts the amount of paracetamol available for sale in packages; therefore stockpiling may be evidence of intent, for the reckless self-harmer usually merely swallows what is to hand.

Risk factors for suicidal behaviour include male sex, unemployment, a single state, psychiatric disorder (especially depressive illness, schizophrenia, anorexia nervosa or abuse of alcohol and/or illicit drugs or the personality disorders), chronic physical disability, recent bereavement and personality malfunction not amounting to disorder. Some 50 per cent of successful suicides have previously made an attempt to end their life. Swinson et al (2007) have shown that 25 per cent of suicides have been in recent contact with the mental health services. 160-200 psychiatric in-patients die by suicide annually, most commonly by hanging. The period of highest risk after discharge from hospital in-patient care appears to be in the first 14 days. Over one-fifth of individuals dying by suicide have not been adhering to their medication regime in the preceding month and nearly one-third appear to have disengaged themselves from the services.

Hunt et al (2006) have shown the differences between younger and older suicides. Deaths of younger patients were characterised by jumping from a height or in front of a vehicle, and these patients suffered from schizophrenia, personality disorder, unemployment and substance misuse.

In older patients, drowning, depression, living alone, physical illness, recent bereavement and suicide pacts were more common. Individuals with schizophrenia were often in-patients and died by violent means. About a third of individuals with depressive disorder died within a year of illness onset. Those with substance dependence or personality disorder had high rates of disengagement from services. Prevention measures likely to benefit young people including targeting patients who had schizophrenia or a dual diagnosis and had lost contact with the services; those measures aimed at depression, isolation and physical ill health were likely to have more effect on elderly individuals. Suicide prevention in those under 25 may require comprehensive care packages for patients with schizophrenia, co-morbid substance misuse and poor engagement with the services, whereas improving the recognition and treatment of depression, the care provided at times of bereavement and the mental health care of those with physical illness could reduce suicide among older patients (Hunt, *op cit*).

In the assessment of suicidal risk the examination of the mental state appears to be the most important element. The presence of any psychiatric disorder (and not merely the conditions mentioned above) increases risk. A depressed mood – which may be found as a symptom in any psychiatric disorder – associated with feelings of pessimism, despair and worthlessness, will elevate risk. The psychotic disorders are generally believed to carry a lower risk although, as already noted, an appreciable number of schizophrenic patients proceed to kill themselves. Auditory hallucinations may impel a patient to take his life by ordering him to do so. Suicidal ideation is an important sign to elicit in the mental state examination. There is a gradation in those thoughts and we shall consider them in an ascending order of risk. The most innocuous are fleeting thoughts that life may not be worth living. This is followed by momentary notions where actual suicide is contemplated. Next comes recurrent and persistent thoughts of putting an end to one's life. At the extreme end is found actual planning of the kind we have described. It has been shown that suicide attempts among patients with major depressive disorders are strongly associated with the presence and severity of depressive symptoms and predicted by lack of a partner, previous suicidal attempts and the time spent in being depressed. Suicidal thoughts must be actively sought and it is a false sense of propriety and delicacy that decides not to intrude into private matters or even causes one to be fearful of putting such thoughts into an innocent mind. The purpose of the enquiry is to be able to arm oneself with the information which may dictate the necessary responses to be made including, where the conditions merit it, compulsory hospital admission under the Mental Health Act 2007. The actual treatment to be given is, of course, dictated by the underlying disorder when it is treatable. Social measures are very useful in the long-term, even those involved in giving such simple information as the availability of the Samaritans organisation. As noted above, treatment, even in a hospital setting, does not always provide the necessary security for it is well known that the recovery phase in a depressive illness is a particularly dangerous period for further suicidal attempts The explanation usually given in respect of depressive illness is that the marked psychomotor retardation found in the acute stages of the illness is selectively eased with treatment, with improved physical activity coming before psychological uplift so that the patient previously physically incapable of carrying out a suicidal act now has the means as well as a still persisting intention, a case of the flesh becoming stronger while the spirit remains weak.

2.10   DELIBERATE SELF HARM (DSH) OR PARASUICIDAL BEHAVIOUR

This is to be distinguished from attempted suicide which, as with any attempt, is marked by the possession of intent. In fact, the behaviour seen in DSH is usually characterised as reckless, for the individual knows that some harm may befall him if he proceeds with the actions he is about to take but he continues with it nonetheless. It should be remembered that mental states, in both the medical and legal sense, can change and vary, and recklessness may give way in time to intentional behaviour. In fact, it is known that in the 12 months following an act of DSH there is an increased incidence of both further acts of DSH (some 20 per cent of cases) as well as acts of completed suicide (1-2 per cent of cases). While death may follow an unintentional act in ways described before, there is some evidence that the perpetrator of DSH might also have had some time before the intention to take his life.

Deliberate self harm is a fairly recent phenomenon which, at one stage in the 1960s and 1970s, threatened to attain epidemic proportions. Even now there are about 150,000 cases of DSH admitted to the casualty units each year. It is difficult to find many examples in the historical literature of deliberate self harm unrelated to hysterical states (except, of course, as acts of mutilatory malingering to avoid going to war) while attempted suicide was, of course, not uncommon. Why this should be so is unclear although the identity of the perpetrators of self harm – mostly adolescent and young women of lower social origins than is associated with suicidal behaviour – may furnish a clue. Perhaps it results from social emancipation from previously fairly tightly regulated lives. Whatever the cause may be, the methods used in DSH now involve prescribed and off prescription drugs (which account for some 90 per cent of cases of DSH) and some form of self-mutilation which involves (usually) superficial cutting of parts of the body, chiefly the limbs.

The causes of this behaviour are not uniform. While a significant number of these individuals exhibit features of personality disorder (or behaviour disorder if younger than the age of deemed maturity), quite a few have no discernible psychiatric abnormality at all. The commonest factor in the act is a precipitating event preceding the act which has caused distress or is perceived as threatening. As many of these acts are impulsive – done in 'moments of madness', as it is commonly described – it is difficult sometimes to identify any persisting personal or social difficulty, but there is not uncommonly a pervasive or smouldering feeling of unhappiness or dissatisfaction – neither of which is, of course, a psychiatric symptom – which is waiting for some stimulus or spark to set it off by way of an act of self harm. Alcohol is commonly involved as a disinhibiting agent.

The assessment of DSH is as for suicidal behaviour, for no conclusions can be arrived at as to whether intent is or was present or the act followed recklessness without proper assessment. It is now routine for psychiatric assessments to take place in Accident and Emergency departments of hospitals to which the patient is taken in the first instance following an overdose. Transfer to a psychiatric unit takes place when there is an underlying disorder detectable or when there is uncertainty about the clinical picture and the patient is believed to be at risk of repeating such behaviour. Treatment is, as with suicidal behaviour, for any underlying psychiatric condition if one exists. Some social and personal problems are amenable to advice and practical help such as rehousing or debt management, which is often more appropriate than formal psychiatric treatment. The risk of further DSH and suicidal behaviour is always present and the most useful duty of the attending psychiatrist is to detect the presence of some treatable condition in the individual who has engaged in DSH. It has been shown that those patients who display an escalating severity of self-poisoning episodes are at high risk of completed suicide. In a review by Crawford et al (2007) it was shown that there was little evidence that additional psychosocial interventions following self harm had a marked effect on the likelihood of subsequent suicide. Individual trials of psychosocial treatments might have demonstrated statistically significant reductions in the likelihood of repetitions of non-fatal self harm, but such findings do not necessarily mean that these treatments would reduce the likelihood of subsequent suicide. These authors suggest that a range of public health measures should be pursued in an attempt to reduce rates of suicide.

2.11 AGGRESSION TURNED OUTWARDS

Violent behaviour directed outwards is a complex subject and its roots go beyond the psychiatric, yet it is the professional in this field who is often asked to evaluate violent behaviour as part of a risk assessment and management.

2.12   VIOLENCE ASSOCIATED WITH MENTAL DISORDER

When formal mental illness can be identified, an understanding of the psychiatric origin of cases of violent behaviour may be achieved without too much difficulty. Psychotic violence is not uncommon and conditions such as schizophrenia and mania may feature highly in such violence although overall, despite popular prejudice, violence associated with mental disorders is comparatively rare. Perhaps reassuringly – for it confirms what has long been suspected by informed persons – a recent study from New Zealand has reported that homicides by the mentally ill have not increased as a rate and also that people in close relationship with the perpetrator, rather than strangers, are most at risk of being the victim. In schizophrenia the violence may be associated with underlying symptoms such as delusions (persecutory delusions may cause a patient to protect himself against his imagined tormentors) or hallucinations (voices may urge the patient to act violently) though violence may also remain an unexplained feature, indeed leading to the first presentation of the condition. In the days when it used to be commonly seen, catatonic excitement (when the patient had roused himself or was roused from stupor) used to be a particularly frightening phenomenon and hard to control. Among states of psychotic violence one may also class the condition of delirium or acute confusional states in which lashing out on the part of the patient is not uncommonly seen. Confusional states may or may not be associated with dementia, another condition in which violence is occasionally seen when it may be associated with agitation and wandering behaviour and appears related also to the previous personality of the patient, a matter previously discussed. Both the carer and the cared for in cases of dementia not uncommonly experience violence at each other's hands. As has also been noted, and will be discussed in the chapters that follow, the risk to the spouse or partner of a patient suffering from morbid jealousy is a very real one, a risk that should be taken seriously in all cases for it brings together various strands involved in violent behaviour such as the victim being closely related to the assailant and therefore at the highest risk of violence from a psychotic patient and also the known statistical risk of violence to spouses or partners (a couple of whom are killed every week). It must be acted on urgently.

The affective disorders may also lead to violence. Depressive illness, contrary to popular belief, is not all about slowed down physical and mental functions. There is an appreciable risk of violence in this condition, most often directed against the self as in suicidal behaviour, but other aggressive, even homicidal, features are not unknown. One particular form of violence associated with depressive illness is murder followed by suicide, cases occasionally featured in the media when a depressed individual kills one or more persons, usually those who have had an intimate relationship with him, before turning on himself, perhaps by using the same murderous weapon. Some months ago one read about the successful middle-aged man, estranged from his wife and waiting to be divorced, who had had a long history of depressive illness. He discharged himself from being a voluntary patient at a psychiatric hospital in the south of England, drove to the matrimonial home where he bludgeoned his wife to death before proceeding to kill himself by driving his car into a tree. These tragedies are also not uncommon especially where the father has been in dispute with the mother over their children who are then killed by the father before he kills himself. It is, of course, by no means the case that depression – in the form of illness – has been suffered in all these instances and there are, in addition, numerous other contributory factors usually involved, but the features of an affective illness are not uncommonly reported in such individuals before the act. Affective disorders in the post-partum state, including the most common, namely post-partum depressive illness, are a source of risk to the newborn child and one must ensure the relatively common nature of the condition does not lead to the minimising of the need for risk assessment of the potential for violence.

Systemic disorder is a possible cause of violent behaviour. Head injury, in particular where it involves personality change, as in the case of *Miah* that will be discussed in the chapter on the personality disorders, could be a potent cause of such aggression. Brain tumours may present themselves with aggressive conduct. Epilepsy – especially in the post-fit state – is another cause and what used to be called 'post epileptic furore' used to match catatonic excitement in its scope for and degree of violence. A well known physical state involved with violent and other uncharacteristic bouts of behaviour involves the hypoglycaemic state which follows over corrected diabetes mellitus, usually after the patient has taken his insulin or oral medication but has then failed to keep up his blood sugar levels by eating sufficiently or at regular intervals. One must also bear in mind the use of steroids – by renegade professional sportsmen or by body builders – which is a class of drug which can not uncommonly lead to aggressive behaviour.

By far the commonest psychiatric condition associated with violent behaviour is personality disorder, including its most severe form called psychopathy. Aggression in these individuals is commonly attributed to poor impulse control and lack of restraint though it has to be said their lack of remorse or feelings of guilt may also contribute by means of the absence of personal or social 'brakes' which are so vital for harmonious life in any community. Personality disorder is also commonly associated with the abuse of alcohol and illicit substances, a matter which will be discussed in some detail below, though an underlying psychiatric disorder is not required for these substances to act as instruments of violence. Alcohol is widely known to precipitate violence though sophisticated analysts of the phenomenon accept that there are crucial personal, social and cultural factors also influencing the behaviour when alcohol fuels violence. The disinhibiting effects of alcohol often require some other factor such as the comforting presence of a like-minded mob before appreciable violence is precipitated. The rampaging behaviour of football hooligans is due to both drink and the mob influence. A clear distinction has to be drawn in such cases between public violence and private violence involving individuals who might have been caught up in acts involving the former. Many public exponents of such violence may be peaceable individuals in private. A 35-year-old father, a notorious football hooligan with many convictions and 'away match' bans, wished to have contact with his young child. The public violence he had indulged in had been undertaken under the influence of alcohol and at other times he had also abused cannabis among other illicit substances. Yet, there was no evidence of any violence on his part in private, especially against the child or any other children or, indeed, other individuals. Other cultural factors may also be found operating. In some ethnic minority populations there is perceived to be a greater degree of violence in association with mental disorder. Black patients in high-security psychiatric hospitals are overrepresented by eight times. Unmet needs are more common among black than white patients in these hospitals. Higher prevalence rates of mental illness, particularly schizophrenia, have been found for black Caribbean patients than for white patients. Higher rates of compulsory admission have also been reported and also higher rates of contact with the police and forensic services and with intensive care facilities.

Along with alcohol – a lawful and freely available substance – one must consider the possible role of prescribed drugs in the precipitation of violence. We have already referred to the possibility that the newer antidepressant drugs, the SSRI agents such as fluoxetine (Prozac), could precipitate violence in some predisposed individuals. Diazepam (Valium) is widely known to be, and is taken as, a sedative and anxiolytic drug. Yet, it could paradoxically release aggression and violence as happened on the facts of *R v Hardie* (1984) 3 All ER 848. The appellant's relationship with his girlfriend had broken down. He became upset and consumed several tablets of Valium which, in fact, had been prescribed for his girlfriend for use as a sedative. Under the influence of this drug he started a fire. On a charge of arson he submitted he had had no *mens rea*. The trial judge refused him on the ground of voluntary self-administration of the drug. The Court of Appeal allowed his appeal on the grounds of misdirection to the jury, noting that Valium is a drug 'wholly different in kind from drugs which are liable to cause unpredictability or aggressiveness'. This paradoxical disinhibiting effect is, of course, a cause of violence due to alcohol or any other normally sedative or anxiety-relieving agent. In these cases a close study needs to be made of the individual propensities of the patient concerned and the manner in which he has behaved on previous occasions when he has been under the influence of these drugs.

Similar considerations apply to cannabis, usually also taken for its sedative or calming properties but which, in some individuals and in large quantities, is capable of precipitating violence or aggravating aggressive conduct. That cannabis is not entirely innocuous as previously believed – and the focus of campaigners demanding its decriminalisation – is now accepted for there appears to be a significant minority of individuals with a predisposition who may be turned towards violence – and also into suffering psychotic conditions – by the consumption of this drug. The position with the amphetamines, cocaine and many other illicit substances is much clearer, for violence is to be expected in certain cases following their use. These stimulant drugs cause an apparent increase in energy along with surging self confidence and self esteem which could spill over very easily into aggression, especially in the atmosphere and circumstances in which these drugs are usually taken. In the course of illicit use the purity of these substances can also by no means be guaranteed and in those circumstances there is a wholly new dimension to be considered – for the contaminants themselves may be capable of causing aggressive behaviour. Paradoxically, on occasions when there are no contaminants and the drug is taken in pure form, there could also be aggressive behaviour on account of the unwonted effects of the pure substance. It is easy now to see how the analysis of violence attributable to these drugs and their impact on different individuals is a subject fraught with complexity and uncertainty. While the general principles are clear enough it cannot usually be said with any great conviction, as far as any individual is concerned, that any drug or group of drugs, by their actions alone, will cause particular effects or could have been responsible for specific past behaviours.

2.13   VIOLENCE UNASSOCIATED WITH MENTAL DISORDER

When mental disorder is not part of the picture, the analysis of violent behaviour becomes even more difficult. One searches for any available rules that can be applied in these circumstances. Of all the available rules there is one of especial value which has survived the test of time when it comes to predicting the risk of future violent conduct; and that rule involves a history of previous violent conduct which is a strong predictor of future violence. This behaviour has been tested in relation to previous history of offending. One study showed that 14 per cent of those with a previous conviction for violence, 40 per cent of those with two previous convictions, 44 per cent of those with three previous convictions and 55 per cent of those with four previous convictions were likely to have a further conviction for violence. Overall, violence is also still more common in men than in women, although it is said that teenage and adolescent girls are catching up with their male peers in that age group. A man who has behaved violently on one occasion is more likely to behave in such a way on a future occasion than one who has no history of violent behaviour. That is a general truth which is subject to qualification. As we have seen with the football hooligan whose case was mentioned previously, violent behaviour can be situation-specific. The hooligan can be predicted to behave violently at football matches in the future, especially when he is under the influence of alcohol and illicit substances and when he is surrounded by like-minded supporters. But it is by no means certain that he could be expected to behave violently in other circumstances. In fact, there was little evidence that this particular individual behaved aggressively elsewhere, a point made in childcare proceedings in his favour where he had applied to have supervised contact with his young daughter. This illustrates a key point – the precise circumstances of previous episodes of violence need to be studied as well as the situation for which risk is being assessed. The facts required for this analysis include, among other details, the identity of previous victims, their gender, the particular circumstances (eg whether the individual and victim were previously acquainted and, if so, at what level of intimacy), the role played by alcohol and/or illicit and prescribed drugs and the outcome of the violence including any convictions and the penalties that came to be applied. These are the objective facts. A subjective account should also be obtained from the individual who is being assessed. This is both fair to him and may also help to correct any disputed facts but it may also indicate the attitude he has towards violent behaviour in general and the previous victims in particular. A lack of remorse or regret is taken to be a reliable indicator of future violence and any attitude that is specific (eg hostility to a spouse or partner) or more general (eg against women) is often a dangerous sign.

The role of alcohol and illicit substances has already been touched upon. A rule can be given at a fairly low level of generality that future indulgence in these substances will probably lead to a repetition of acts of violent behaviour, but the facts must still need to be analysed with care for even substance-induced violence can be situation-specific, eg domestic violence.

Violent behaviour, if one is to believe what psychologists and anthropologists say, should be commonplace but it is, in fact, an uncommon phenomenon in most civilized societies, though the levels may not be any less worrying for that. Man is supposed to be an inherently aggressive animal. He would not have succeeded in evolutionary terms if he had not been assertive and ruthless in his dealings with the environment. In fact, social and cultural rules that have been developed and are inculcated in children from a young age may be seen to be attempts designed to curtail this aggression so as to enable life to go on in tolerable tranquility among members of a social community. This restraint is meant to apply to all members who are expected to curb their aggressive thoughts and impulses. These are surprisingly common to experience, and are found in the most unlikely of individuals, but are relatively uncommonly acted upon. It follows that anything that interferes with normal impulse control in respect of aggression will be conducive to violence. Poor impulse control is a feature of personality disorder and psychopathy, and it is the usual finding in clinical psychiatric practice that a crucial element in future risk assessment is an evaluation of the individual's personality. Impulse control is also associated with the expression of anger and reactions to stressful and provoking stimuli. Anger is well recognised to be a source of violence and anger management is the approach usually suggested to deal with excessive and inappropriate anger. Anger management deals with the problem at the behavioural level and a close analysis is still required of factors such as personality and the misuse of alcohol and illicit substances.

Another factor often suggested to function as a protective influence against habitual violent behaviour is the degree of socialisation achieved by individuals. This phenomenon is related to the successful incorporation of social rules. The thinking here is that a person who has been properly integrated into the requirements of society, and in whom the rules of society have been embedded into those centres of the brain which govern socially appropriate behaviour by suppressing impulses and emotions, achieves proper social integration. Such individuals are less likely to resort to violence either because they can successfully master their impulses or they have otherwise learned to take the co-operative and lawful route to achieving their needs and desires and do not have to resort to the 'coerced transactions' (as the economic philosophers characterise robbery) when individuals have failed to use negotiation and persuasion in the market place for transactions but have turned instead to force to achieve their ends. The lesson to be learned for purposes of risk assessment is that a poorly socialised individual may pose a higher risk of future violence than one who is normally socialised and in whom a solitary act of aggression may be attributed to aberrant behaviour on one occasion. Social isolation with poor social networks, a lonely existence and solitary interests are believed to indicate a lack of proper socialisation.

Violence, of course, occurs against the person or property. The interaction between the assailant and his victim has attracted enormous interest in recent years. At one level, it could be said there is always some interaction, however minimal in degree, between attacker and victim even when a victim might only have found himself, as is said, in the 'wrong place at the wrong time'. We are here, however, concerned with more substantial levels of contact and in the relationship that has existed between attacker and victim. The features present in the victim must also be studied, wherever possible, with care. The age of the victim is of importance for while most assailants and their victims are young men, the selective and purposeful targeting of victims of a certain age, e g at the extremes of age, the elderly and the very young, may give a clue as to the prospects for future violent conduct. The gender of the victim is an obvious consideration. The personality of the victim, whether it also underlies some mental disorder, may be as important to take account of as that of the assailant. One must seek to find out, especially in situations where recurrent violence has taken place, whether the victim himself is aggressive, unduly anxious or overly dependent on a potential assailant for these features are often associated with individuals who tend to become victims, especially in the domestic context. We shall consider some of the more specific features of this condition when we later take up domestic violence but the attitude of the victim is always important to evaluate. If recurrent violence has taken place, involving one set of assailant and victim, has the victim complained and supported previous proceedings? If not, why not? It is an obvious inference that if an assailant knows he can get away with violence he will be more prone to violence or aggressive conduct for even the most impulsive of persons usually has some idea of self-preservation and normally has little wish to entangle himself unnecessarily with the criminal law. The role of mental disorder and the misuse of alcohol and illicit substances in the victim may also be material considerations. It follows that in the ideal situation the assailant and any identifiable future victim should both be assessed, although the absence of resources (and possibly consent) do not usually permit this endeavour.

2.14   MENTAL DISORDER AND OFFENDING

Studies in forensic psychiatric practice have been usefully summarised (Power *et al*, 1996) in terms of risk factors influencing offending and reoffending:

1. The mental disorder itself and its lack of recognition by professionals. In a study at the Rampton Hospital of those mentally ill patients who had committed homicide it was found that all these patients had been mentally disordered at the time of committing the offence but only some 25 per cent of them were receiving treatment. Premature discharge from hospital adds to the risk. Repetition of violent acts may be determined by the situation in which a mentally disordered offender finds himself in and the emotional demands that are made on him. It is vital before discharge from hospital to ensure that the offender's psychological resources are sufficient to cope with the vagaries of life in the community. More recently, Swinson *et al* (*op cit*) have found that around 50 homicides per year are committed by those in recent contact with mental health services, a figure that represents 9 per cent of all homicides. About 5 per cent of the perpetrators of homicide have a diagnosis of schizophrenia. Perpetrators with mental illness are less likely to kill strangers and the rate of 'stranger homicide' by those with mental illness has not increased with national trends.

2. The tendency to engage in impulsive anti-social acts on little or no provocation is another pointer towards increased risk. If aggressive anti-social tendencies co-exist with mental illness or other disorders the risk may increase.

3.   The nature of the index offence may give clues as to future risk, especially if the victim had been specifically targeted e g as being a member of a particular age group (the elderly or children) or of a particular gender. This may indicate a habitual pattern of serious anti-social behaviour. Random killings by individuals suffering from schizophrenia or other psychotic disorders involving strangers may indicate continuing risk to the public. Incidents prior to the index offence, which if they had not involved prosecution might not have revealed the full facts, could be important. In the notorious *Zito* case, Mr Jonathan Zito had been stabbed to death at a London Underground station by Christopher Clunis who had a history of paranoid schizophrenia and of violence. It transpired at the official inquiry into this case that Clunis had stabbed a fellow resident in a hostel some five months before his attack on Mr Zito but had not been prosecuted, a matter which came to be criticised.

4.   The uncertainty of the clinical prognosis, especially where there are multiple diagnoses, e g mental illness with learning disabilities or mental illness associated with a personality disorder, may increase the risk or, at any rate, make it even less predictable.

5.   Persisting lack of remorse or continuing denial in the face of overwhelming evidence may be a sign of high risk. This will be enhanced if the clinical condition associated with previous violence – persecutory symptoms, morbid jealousy – persist. A declared intention of future violence in the midst of an unsettled mental state is obviously of considerable concern.

6.   The continuing presence of sadistic fantasies even after incarceration and attempts at treatment may be indicative of a high risk of reoffending.

7.   A history of misuse of alcohol and/or illicit substances, even if the behaviour is in abeyance on incarceration, may be a sign of risk if it is believed the patient may resume his patterns of substance abuse, especially on release from custody. Swinson *et al* (*op cit*) have also found that alcohol and drug misuse contribute to homicide in 61 per cent of cases, a figure which has major public health implications.

8.   A paradoxical situation involves the offender, often a psychopath, who learns to work the system, appears to be most amenable and succeeds in fooling the professionals evaluating his progress. He may pose a serious risk if only because it is never wholly possible to properly assess future risks to be posed in the community by an individual who is being evaluated in an artificial situation of containment. Good behaviour in an institution does not necessarily mean it will be translated to conditions in the world outside.

In recent years there have been attempts to standardise assessment of the risk of violence and the management of that risk. This has included the introduction of structured approaches to risk assessment. The rationale for this is that there is believed to be both clinical and actuarial approaches that can be taken in regard to risk assessment and aspects of both these approaches could be included in a structured approach. Studies have shown there not to be any significant relationship between specific diagnosis and future violence in the community. There is also support for the view that after care arrangements can offer a degree of protection against future violence on the part of patients. Psychopathy, when diagnosed, was, however, predictive of future violence. While the assessment of future risk of violence remains essentially a clinical procedure at present, a rating scale has been put forward in the form of HCR-20 Violence Risk Assessment Scheme (see Appendix 1) and may come to find more widespread acceptance in the future (Webster *et al*, 2002). It provides an outline of the factors clinicians could use in assessing risk and provides a structured basis for doing so. This instrument contains 20 items organised around three scales: historical data (ten items), clinical evidence (five items) and risk (five items). The ten historical items include history of violence, age at first violence, relationship history, employment history, history of substance misuse, previous mental illness, psychopathy, early maladjustment, personality disorder and previous conditional release failure. The five clinical evidence items include lack of insight, negative attitudes, symptomatology, lack of behavioural stability and lack of treatability. The five risk items are concerned with forecasting the patient's future social, living and treatment circumstances, as well as anticipating the patient's reactions to those conditions. This includes lack of plan feasibility, access to destabilisers, lack of support, future non-compliance and stress. Reviews have suggested that the HCR-20 was the most robust predictor of subsequent violence in the community and that the clinical and risk management items (referred to as the 'dynamic' element) add significantly to the validity of risk assessment as compared with the more 'static' factors such as the items listed under the historical scale of the HCR-20. The historical data appear to be of limited predictive value in clinical risk assessment. It appears that strategies for risk management could be successful if they are feasible, treat active symptoms of mental illness, address issues of attitude, impulse control and emotional regulation in patients, reduce the likelihood of non-compliance and improve insight. In summary, it appears that while 'static' measures of risk relating to past history and personality may make some limited contribution to the assessment of risk violence, consideration of current 'dynamic' factors relating to illness and risk management significantly improves predictive accuracy.

2.15   SEXUAL VIOLENCE

This subject, too, may be studied as a sub-species of general violence, though, of course, some special factors also apply. We have already learned that a process of socialisation undertaken in childhood leads, by learning to control primitive instincts, to the development of responsible adult behaviour. Persistent violent behaviour, whether it involves sexual misconduct or not, often shows a failure of this process of socialisation and many of the risk factors involved with aggressive behaviour in general are also applicable here. The social elements involved, including those affecting the victim, are also important to consider.

Formal mental illness is uncommon to find among sex offenders, although a manic illness may involve aggressive sexual conduct and morbid jealousy is a special case further taken up in the next chapter. Brain degenerative processes and the consequences of head injury, as in the *Miah* case, are occasionally present in sex offenders, as is dementia in the early stages of that degenerative condition. Where mental disorder is present in an offender, as with violence generally, the condition most often met with is personality disorder. This is commonly associated with misuse of alcohol and illicit drugs, substances which lead to disinhibition in terms of sexual behaviour, as well as of violent conduct generally.

Given the diverse circumstances involved with sexual offending, general rules are hard to lay down. It seems the following points could be reasonably made.

1.   The vast majority of sex offenders do not appear to be suffering from a recognisable psychiatric disorder. In other words, they are not ill in a way that a doctor or lay person would recognise. They may have a psychological disturbance which may, at least in a statistical sense, indicate abnormality.

2.   As far as we can tell, most sexual offences, and those involving rape in particular, occur between parties who are acquainted with one another, often intimately so. In other words, most sexual offences involve the issue of 'consent', not 'identity'.

3.   Where mental disorder is found, personality disorder is the most common of the conditions involved.

4.   Substance misuse is commonly involved. This may involve a situation where the rapist has gone 'too far' in presuming consent when under the influence of a substance (that is, he might have abused consent which might have been given), those situations involving 'date rape' resulting from administered drugs (likely to be far less common in incidence than is portrayed by the popular

media) and the rare 'sprees' which follow the ingestion of substances, most commonly the stimulant drugs such as cocaine and the amphetamines.

5.   Where there has been significant victim complicity, substance misuse is usually an important factor.

6.   Many of the studies purporting to study the characteristics of rapists involve 'serial rapists' and their conclusions are as limited in application to the most common type of 'one-off' sexual offender as a study of serial murderers is to the study of the average murderer.

7.   The absence of mental illness and mental disorder in the usual run of cases limits the effectiveness of psychiatric treatment. Medical and surgical treatment involving drugs and/or surgery are also very limited in scope, beneficial perhaps to an occasional offender but not generally.

8.   The risk assessment of sexual offending is probably best approached in the terms employed for the study of violent behaviour generally. Where the best predictor of future conduct is being deemed past behaviour, those factors that applied at the time of the index offence need to be analysed. It is salutary to remind oneself of the low reliability of most predictive indices. To give but one example, it used to be believed that a lone individual who was poorly socialised was most prone to sexual violence. The number of married and otherwise apparently socially adept men being thrown up by DNA analysis several years after the commission by them of sexual offences, which long lay unsolved, reveals that generalities are just that – with little application to the individual case. There is no alternative, it seems, to a detailed study being made of all the available facts of the case, paying attention to all the surrounding circumstances as well as the behaviour of the victim.

Part III of this book has chapters devoted respectively to domestic violence, serial and sexual violence and also to public and political violence in their psychiatric aspects.

CHAPTER 3

ORGANIC MENTAL DISORDERS

Whenever psychiatric disorders come up for discussion, convention dictates that we describe the subject matter of this chapter as the organic mental disorders as opposed to the functional mental disorders that will be taken up in the chapters following. This distinction is somewhat illogical. As far as we know, all psychiatric conditions are ultimately traceable to origins in the brain. There is no evidence that there is some parallel medium mediating animal behaviour. All roads therefore lead to the brain, as far as mental phenomena are concerned. Psychiatric disorders should therefore, strictly speaking, be considered brain disorders. The fact that the external environment may influence behaviour should be irrelevant – the brain still needs to intervene before behaviour can be demonstrated. Seeing an object or hearing a sound are cerebral phenomena. However, unassailable logic has got to confront, in the present state of knowledge, the inconvenient fact that we do not possess sufficiently precise knowledge of brain function and dysfunction to delineate the origins of most psychiatric conditions in terms of the brain. Thus was born the distinction between organic mental disorders where a cerebral origin can be fairly clearly established, even when the precise details of pathology may be lacking, and the functional mental disorders where brain dysfunction has still, by and large, got to be presumed.

It is customary to classify organic mental disorders as between acute disorders such as confusional states or delirium and chronic conditions such as the dementias. Further, consideration in this category is also given to the psychiatric consequences of head injury and to the psychiatric effects of systemic illness such as endocrine disorders. Even this inclusion carries with it an anomaly. Learning disorders or the cerebral manifestations of alcohol and illicit drug use, the subject matter in the chapters following, are examples of conditions which involve lesions in the brain but, once again by convention, we study these conditions separately as we do in this book. Further, one must also bear in mind that external or environmental factors, which are given greater prominence in the consideration of functional mental disorders for want of known cerebral pathology for study, are of importance also in the study of mental disorders due to brain dysfunction, for the brain is also affected by external stimuli as one can see when the nature and frequency of epileptic fits, for example, are influenced by common environmental stimuli.

3.1   THE DEMENTIAS

Dementia refers to a condition in which there is an acquired global impairment of brain functions which usually leads to a progressive loss of intellectual and memory powers and a deterioration of the personality and in social behaviour. These are conditions that have come upon the public consciousness fairly rapidly in recent years on account of an ageing population, for many of the dementias have an incidence in the population which is related to age. At the age of 65 some five per cent of the population is believed to be affected, the figure rising to 20 per cent when the population reaches the age of 80. There are believed to be some 750,000 individuals suffering from the dementias in the United Kingdom, though the precise figure cannot be reliably established. There may be underdiagnosis in some parts of the country for want of adequate diagnostic services, while in others there may be an overestimate by including cases with age-related memory loss which is a normal process and which by itself does not amount to dementia. Despite the growing prominence given to this condition, there still tends to be a degree of confusion concerning these conditions. The first element causing confusion is the term 'confusion' itself. It is common to hear even health care professionals referring to a demented patient being 'confused'. This is an inaccurate use of the term. Confusion, as we shall see in the next section of this chapter, is a result of a disturbance in consciousness. A demented patient is not confused, his consciousness is normally clear and unimpaired. What he usually displays is disorientation, that is to say he does not know where he is, what day or place it is, what the date or year are or who his intimates might be. A demented patient may, like anyone else, become confused as well, say, as a result of an infection but the primary underlying feature in dementia is a brain disorder which has global effects on the intellect, memory and personality which, at some stage in the course of the disorder, also comes to include disorientation.

As the definition of dementia given above suggests, it is also an acquired condition. Congenital or childhood brain dysfunctions which lead to impairment in intelligence, memory and character (as personality can be called before maturity has been reached, at least in chronological terms) is more properly referred to as mental handicap or learning disabilities which we shall take up in Chapter 9. A patient with learning disabilities may, of course, like anyone else, become demented in later life. As the definition also suggests, the impairment in dementia is global, that is, it refers to a considerable range of the brain's functions being affected, a state of affairs to be distinguished from focal deficits where one part of the brain eg the parietal or frontal lobe is the specific area of the brain to be affected. Finally, dementia refers to a clinical description of the phenomena observed. It does not suggest the cause of the brain dysfunction leading to the features of dementia which requires further investigation and analysis for its elucidation where this is possible.

The term senile dementia is to be found in popular usage. In its strict sense the term is doubly descriptive as it refers to a dementia found in the senium. The senium is conventionally defined as being the period after the age of 65 has been reached. The origins of this figure – which, of course, now has enormous social, financial and political significance the world over – are usually attributed to the age at which in 1884 Otto Von Bismarck, then Chancellor of Germany, decreed that citizens became entitled to their state old age pensions. There is no discernible medical significance in this age. Therefore any dementia arising after the age of 65 is a senile dementia, if before that age it is called a pre-senile dementia.

3.2 DEMENTIA – CLINICAL FEATURES

The symptoms of dementia are attributable to the global nature of the brain dysfunction involved. Their course is usually insidious and it is usual for the short-term memory to be first affected, invariably unnoticed at first when it may be put down to the forgetfulness long associated with ageing. The growing impairment of intellectual functioning may also be similarly dismissed at first. Changes in personality may, however, cause early concern. There may be what is called a 'coarsening' of personality. Any individual is usually made up of many elements forming an amalgam of his personality, there being good, bad or indifferent parts to any personality. The whole is usually held together with the glue usually attributable to good manners and the appreciation of the need to conform and behave according to the expectations of a civilized society and adjust to its norms. Dementia has a tendency to cause this glue to dissolve or, perhaps as it may be more aptly described, this coat of civilising varnish to be removed, making more apparent the elements within and the rougher edges to an individual's personality. The result could be the emergence of an exaggerated or parodic picture of the characteristics in the individual's habitual personality. Thus, a person known to be careful with money now begins to acquire a reputation as a miser and a hoarder of objects, mostly valueless except in his eyes. An assertive person who managed nevertheless to keep his need to dominate others within acceptable bounds now turns into an aggressive, even violent, bully. This has implications for the manifestation of aggressive and violent tendencies. Dementia may also give rise to disinhibited behaviour. Individuals who had been able to keep rogue impulses in check while their personalities were intact and reasonably well adjusted may now cease to conform to the needs and expectations of social and legal norms. Violent behaviour, along with antisocial conduct, sometimes involving sexual matters, including those in relation to young children, are occasionally the result of such aberrant behaviour. The criminal law and family and child law may both express an interest in these circumstances. Mood changes, whether due to the brain dysfunction itself or as a reaction to the realisation of waning powers, are not uncommon. Neurological features such as deficits in speech may also be revealed. Insight is progressively lost as the commoner dementias advance at varying speed. The terminal phase of the illness is characterised by a return to a state of infantilisim with loss of speech among other powers, and incontinence supervening.

3.3   DEMENTIA – THE CAUSES

It is believed there are scores of dementing conditions. The commonest cause is believed by far to be a degenerative brain disorder called Alzheimer's disease, suspected to account for 80 per cent or more of all dementias. The diagnosis of this condition is entirely by means of neuropathological analysis, usually undertaken post mortem. There are no valid laboratory or other tests as yet to aid in the diagnosis and a clinical diagnosis of the condition is usually little better than an informed guess. Parts of the brain in this disturbance show abnormal structures which are believed to be the result of the pathogenic process rather than being the cause. A clear genetic basis has not as yet been established, but it appears that the presence of a first degree relation with the condition leads to a doubling of the risk for a subject developing the condition. A clear genetic risk may also be observable in cases with pre-senile dementia where the illness runs a notably aggressive course. Various other causative environmental factors have been proposed from time to time but it does not appear that any one of these is the causative factor in the generality of cases. There is also a neurochemical disturbance which is at present believed to be secondary to the structural changes in the brain and which involves acetylcholine metabolism, but other chemicals have also been implicated. Among the other dementias are the group called the vascular dementias which are associated with small strokes and disturbances in the arteries supplying blood to the brain. There are rarer degenerative conditions of the brain such as Huntington's disease, Pick's disease, Creutzfeldt-Jakob disease (in its classical form as well as the more recently emerged variant CJD), the latter acquired from the meat of cattle infected with bovine spongiform encephalopathy (BSE) and the dementias associated with Parkinson's disease. Huntington's disease involves clear genetic transmission. Other causes of dementia include endocrine disorder (eg thyroid deficiency), head injury, poisoning (eg by heavy metals), excessive alcohol consumption, brain tumours and a variety of infections affecting the brain. Drugs used in the treatment of various conditions may sometimes lead to the clinical presentation of a dementing illness. Their importance lies in the fact that dementias due to some of these conditions or factors may be reversible if prompt steps are taken.

3.4   DEMENTIA – THE MANAGEMENT

This is almost entirely palliative in the present state of knowledge. There was much clamour – due to the carers as well as the drug companies – about drug treatment, especially in the earlier stages of dementia due to Alzheimer's disease. It is probably fair to say on the available information that there is no consistent evidence for sustained improvement in the condition in any group of patients whatever the stage of illness they are in. This is not surprising as the causes of the dementias appear to be manifold and also because the chemical basis to the condition is in all probability much more complex than is commonly understood. If several chemicals are associated with degenerative dementia, drugs involving just one type of chemical are likely to be limited in their efficacy. It may be that an effective cocktail of drugs is what is needed. Nevertheless, a primary purpose of prompt investigation of a dementia is to establish the presence of a treatable cause such as an underfunctioning thyroid gland, a condition which is treatable by means of a replacement hormone. Prompt treatment of this kind by treating some deficiency appears to lead to the symptoms of dementia being corrected in a minority of cases.

3.5 DEMENTIA – THE RISKS OF AGGRESSION AND VIOLENCE

The risks associated with the dementias, in particular those involving violence, need to be appreciated. We have already noted the possible interest the criminal law and family and child law could have in this respect of the evaluation of risk posed by these patients. It appears true to say that disinhibition of brain functions is the most likely cause of aggressive and violent conduct involving dementing patients. There appears to be a loss of control over impulses which might have been kept in check when cerebral functions were intact. As already pointed out, there may also be aggressive and violent tendencies on display as a result of the exaggeration of personality traits which surface as cerebral functions are impaired. Dementing patients notoriously wander and get lost, especially in situations which are unfamiliar to them, and can turn truculent when a carer intervenes. Disinhibition may also lead to sexual misconduct which may lead to concern being expressed in a wide variety of situations involving both adults and children.

3.6 THE CONFUSIONAL STATES

As we have already noted, confusional states are characterised by a clouding or an impairment of consciousness. The patient may exhibit drowsiness, a diminished awareness of his surroundings, distractibility and also disorientation. Unlike dementia, where the onset is slow and insidious, confusional states are usually acute in presentation. Their course fluctuates, with a diurnal variation with a worsening at dusk. There may also be associated visual hallucinations (characteristically small animals are perceived although larger creatures including the fabled pink elephants may be seen in *delirium tremens*, the acute confusional state that may follow withdrawal from alcohol). There may also be present persecutory ideas, typically fleeting and in keeping with the distractibility of confused patients. These patients may also show increased motor activity, ranging from anxiety and agitation to aggression and violence. This behaviour may alternate with periods of drowsiness and somnolence.

3.7   THE CONFUSIONAL STATES – CAUSATION

The commonest cause of confusional states is probably infections. As with dementia there is an element of age-related risk with the confusional states and therefore the elderly have a greater tendency to become confused. Thus, the demented patient – who, as we saw, is not normally confused – could become so as a result of some incidental infection. Prescribed drugs also have a well-known tendency to induce confusional states, especially in the elderly. The confusional states due to alcohol withdrawal have been noted and a variety of illicit drugs may also lead to this condition following their consumption.

3.8   THE CONFUSIONAL STATES – MANAGEMENT

The rule in treating confusional states is to seek a cause which is invariably present, though by no means always found. In its absence some practitioners may even resort to 'blind' treatment with antibiotics. Review of all medication given, and a check being made on other drugs ingested by the patient, especially when young, is a crucial part of the investigation. The results with treatment are usually good except when the patient has some terminal underlying condition.

3.9   THE CONFUSIONAL STATES – RISKS OF
AGGRESSION AND VIOLENCE

Some of the risks of developing confusional states have already been noted. An elderly demented patient who is being prescribed medication is clearly at risk of developing a confusional state. Previous episodes of the state, especially in an elderly individual who already also has some sensory impairment eg blindness or deafness, may be important as these individuals appear to be preferentially at risk. Risks that follow confusional states may involve, as already noted, aggression and violence that these patients may occasionally display. Aggression and violence are by no means uncommon in the confusional states and some expressions of violence may be frightening to the onlookers. The usual rule is that the violence tends to settle as the confusional state is dispersed either by means of treatment of the underlying cause or with the passage of time.

3.10   HEAD INJURY

This is a vast subject primarily of neurological and neurosurgical interest. Unlike the dementing illnesses, however, which preferentially afflict an older age group, the psychiatric complications of head injury may affect all age groups. Younger individuals, in particular, on account of their diverse activities, may come to the attention of clinicians as a result of the various consequences of head injury. Head injury being a common phenomenon, its victims not uncommonly interest the psychiatrist on account of the behavioural changes that may follow any insult given to the brain. These behaviours may involve aggression and violence. Head injury may cause obvious brain damage although much psychiatric time is usually taken up with cases of head injury where there appears to be no obvious brain damage and the blow to the head might seem to have been minor or trivial. This results in the post-concussional state, which we shall consider later. It may generally be stated that the result of a head injury in psychiatric terms is determined partly by the extent and location of the brain damage (whether provable or not) and partly by the pre-existing personality and the psychiatric state of the patient.

Head injury which actually affects the gross structure of the brain may leave behind specific defects. One such state is the frontal lobe syndrome following injury to that part of the brain. There is often dramatic change in personality and behaviour of patients so affected. These patients may become euphoric or apathetic. Their character can turn gross and they may come to have little regard for social norms and conventions or for the concern of others. They can be irresponsible and cruel and prone to excesses involving all their appetites. Their amoral aggression and violence may lead to involvement with the criminal law and family and child law. They tend to lack foresight, are impulsive and are also heedless of the consequences that may follow their actions. Lesser degrees of damage to the brain may be associated with mood changes, in particular depression or anxiety. Some cases involving damage to the frontal lobes may go on to develop bipolar affective disorder which, as we shall see later, may also involve aggression and violence.

3.11   HEAD INJURY – POST-CONCUSSIONAL STATE

An intriguing form of a post-head injury psychiatric condition involves the post-concussional state. This may follow a minor or even trivial head injury. As a rule, no neurological lesion is demonstrated despite extensive investigation involving a panoply of tests and scans. In this state are to be found numerous symptoms, some vague, some described with greater precision, which include headache, giddiness, irritability, fatigue, depression, sleep disturbance, frustration, restlessness, excessive sensitivity to noise, blurred vision, double vision, excessive sensitivity to light, nausea, tinnitus, poor attention and concentration with impaired short-term memory and an intolerance of alcohol. Mild organic dysfunction is not uncommon in the early days following minor head injury and the subsequent few months. Post-traumatic epilepsy may also be found although that is commoner with penetrating wounds of the head where up to 50 per cent of patients may develop this condition. During this time psychological features can develop and/or pre-existing psychological vulnerabilities may be activated. When post-concussion syndrome persists, psychological factors may entirely account for the symptoms in some individuals, and organic or quasi-organic features will entirely account for the symptoms in others. Most patients will be found in between these extreme situations. A complicating feature in symptoms persisting over six months may be the expectations from a claim for compensation. Treatment of the post-traumatic state is often difficult partly because the patient is convinced that there is organic pathology underlying his symptoms, partly as the symptoms are often so vague and also in part because the personality of the patient may be the most important factor behind the symptoms and, accordingly, so much harder to deal with.

King (2003) has reviewed the post-concussion syndrome which appears to have intrigued clinicians for 130 years. 75 per cent of all head injuries are mild. Half of these experience some post-concussion symptoms. Most recover completely within three months of injury but around a third have some persisting symptoms beyond this time. Around eight per cent have significant symptoms at one year and in some cases the symptoms are possibly permanent. There is also good evidence from the literature that early intervention, within the first few weeks of mild head injury, does significantly reduce post-concussion symptoms and limits the emergence of persisting problems. There is an association between the severity of post-concussion symptoms or time taken off work after mild head injury and the seeking of compensation. It should be noted, however, that although twice as many patients seeking compensation have post-concussion symptoms compared to those who are not, few show significant improvement following settlement of their case, even a few years afterwards.

Personality change following concussion or more serious injury to the brain is occasionally to be found. Sometimes the change in personality can take a dramatic turn as a previously peaceable and respectable citizen commences a career of psychopathic excess. A couple of examples of this phenomenon are given in Chapter 8 when we take up the personality disorders. Those are personality changes of a fairly gross kind but many patients following head injury leaving little or nothing by way of obvious physical *sequelae* complain they are not 'the same person' following an episode of trauma involving their heads.

3.12   HEAD INJURY – RISKS OF AGGRESSION AND VIOLENCE

Symptoms such as irritability, apathy, poor tolerance of frustration and the hypersensitivity to light and, in particular, to sounds, are features which bring these cases to the attention of those also in the fields of family and child law and, occasionally, the criminal law. The irritability may give rise to aggression both in the home as well as in public situations where some minor frustration, such as met with in the course of negotiating road traffic, may lead to disproportionate levels of violence being shown by the subject. The frontal lobe syndrome, associated with a lesion in that part of the brain, may also lead to a kind of violence being shown that is indistinguishable from psychopathic violence. A common sequel of many forms of head injury is epilepsy, which is itself associated with explosive violence often in the face of little or no provocation.

3.13 SUMMARY

1. Dementia is associated with disinhibited and occasionally aggressive behaviour which could become a matter of concern for those caring for these patients. These behaviours may have implications for the practice of the criminal law as well as family and child law. Dementing patients are also susceptible to infections which may cause a confusional state, thereby worsening the mental state and leading to further potential for aggressive and violent behaviour.

2. Confusional states are mostly due to infections and other physical causes. These states also are related to age and also to sensory impairment. It leads to very changeable mental states in which agitation, aggression and grossly impaired cognitive states may be seen, but there is recovery when the cause of the confusional state is corrected. Many drugs, both prescribed and unprescribed, can induce a confusional state and details of their consumption must always be sought. Drug-related confusional states may also lead to aggressive and violent conduct.

3. Minor head injuries can lead to the post-concussional state in which vague and indefinite symptoms may be seen. The pre-existing personality appears to play a significant part in this condition which is, therefore, similar in this respect to the neurotic conditions. These symptoms may be resistant to conventional treatment and may become chronic. The irritability often found in this condition may lead to violent behaviour in the face of trivial or no provocation. Head injury with more obvious brain damage may also be associated with aggressive and violent behaviour and the frontal lobe, when damaged, may lead to serious displays of violence. Head injury commonly leads to epilepsy being suffered and there is an association between epilepsy and aggressive and violent behaviour.

CHAPTER 4

THE PSYCHOTIC DISORDERS

These psychotic disorders – and those that follow in the next chapter – are the major psychiatric disorders and involve the patient losing touch with reality, with also loss of insight, and displaying symptoms such as delusions, hallucinations, and disorders of thinking and of speech. As such, these features demonstrate a quite fundamental disruption of the higher functions of an individual and it is easy to see how many branches of the law, including the criminal law and family and child law practice, may become involved with an individual who suffers from such a condition. In this chapter we shall concern ourselves with schizophrenia and related conditions but not with those affective disorders of a psychotic kind which we shall leave for consideration until the next chapter.

4.1 SCHIZOPHRENIA

Schizophrenia refers to a group of disorders which are a major worldwide cause of psychiatric disability. It is also the condition which is probably the commonest to be associated in the public imagination with aggression and violence. It is best considered as a form of brain dysfunction whose neurological lineaments are still far from well understood, thereby reducing us to a study of the illness (or, more accurately, the group of illnesses) at a descriptive rather than at any deep pathological level. One matter we shall summarily dispose of at the outset. Lay persons – encouraged by the more thoughtless elements in the media – appear to hold onto a notion that schizophrenia involves some entity called a 'split personality'. It is nothing of the kind. The 'split' in schizophrenia refers to the dissociation between the various functions of the mind such as thinking, feeling, behaviour and perception so that contact with reality comes to be lost. This is a serious medical condition, far removed from any form of personality disorder.

4.2 SCHIZOPHRENIA – CLINICAL FEATURES

The mode of onset of the illness may be variable. Some patients may harbour the illness for months or years and come only casually to medical attention. Others may suffer an explosive presentation which is drawn to the attention first of the police force or the criminal justice system as a result of the patient's aggressive or violent conduct. The symptoms associated with this condition used to be described as being positive, (such as hallucinations) or negative (such as apathy and social withdrawal) and extensive classificatory systems used to be drawn up with many sub-categories. These are of little practical help nowadays. The symptoms may nevertheless still be varied in presentation. Self neglect or a bizarre appearance and behaviour may be in evidence. Speech disorders indicating disordered thought used to be believed to be virtually pathognomonic of schizophrenia. Concrete thinking, neologistic constructions, irrelevant sentence structures and illogical speech patterns may be seen. Disorders of thinking may be further manifested by the possession of delusions, usually persecutory in kind. A delusion may be defined as a false unshakeable belief held despite the evidence to the contrary and out of keeping with the social norms and the cultural practices of the individual in question. Discussion of the features of a delusion arising in terms of such a definition has kept phenomenologists and philosophers happily occupied for years. It is plain that no false belief by itself necessarily amounts to a delusion. A belief in God may not appear rational by the usual standards but, quite apart from there being lack of definite proof to the contrary, it is also a belief sanctioned by social norms and cultural practices. Patients from parts of Asia and Africa may hold varying beliefs in 'evil spirits' or witchcraft but these may also be appropriate according to the norms obtaining in their cultures. More problematical diagnostic considerations may arise when an individual complains, say, of being hounded by the security services which, on investigation, turns out to be true. He may still be mentally ill if the means by which he arrived at his belief are shown to be pathological. This matter does not feature in the definition of a delusion given above but one needs also to enquire in practice as to how the belief was come by. Thus, the story is told of the man who, having paused at a red traffic light, came to the overwhelming conclusion that his wife was being unfaithful to him on account of the colours changing from red to amber. That state of affairs was true, as it happened, but the way the belief arose suggested it as being pathological. So, one may say that just because they are really after you does not necessarily rule you out as also being paranoid. The usual form of delusion seen in schizophrenia is a persecutory delusion, although grandiose delusions may also be come across.

The other dramatic symptom is auditory hallucination. A hallucination is a perception experienced as real in the absence of a sensory stimulus. Thus, any of the senses may be involved in the manifestation of a hallucination. The commonest of these in schizophrenia is an auditory hallucination, ie one involving the hearing of voices. In this disorder it may take the distinctive form with voices talking about the individual in the third person, even offering a running commentary, the tone often being derogatory, and there may also be voices commenting on the individual's actions and thoughts.

Mood changes may not be remarkable in this condition, but depression not uncommonly co-exists with other phenomena. Whether the behaviour is related or not to this mood change, there is an increased risk of suicide in schizophrenia, especially in the early phase of the illness when the changes in the mental processes may be bewilderingly incomprehensible and therefore distressing to the still insightful patient. There has been considerable recent interest in suicidal behaviour among schizophrenic patients. Previously, a depressive component in schizophrenia was believed responsible for this behaviour. Then it became known that the disorder, without any obvious depressive element, could also give rise to this phenomenon. The incidence of suicide in schizophrenia was put at about 10 per cent. Recent studies have shown this figure to have been exaggerated and, at any rate in the pre-community care age, it does not seem to have exceeded one per cent. What the post-community care era will bring forth remains to be seen, for it is believed that the single most important factor determining suicide rates in patients with schizophrenia is deinstitutionalisation – that is, the protective asylum function of institutions having now been lost – although drug treatment seems also to make a contribution to increasing risk. It seems a patient in the community has also to assume the cares of the community.

Schizophrenia may also be associated with cognitive changes, in particular with impairment of memory. The precise cause of this change, or its significance, is not understood with any precision but it may, of course, illustrate the ultimate cerebral provenance of the disorder and usually also indicates a poorer prognosis.

Insight, by which one means in this situation an appreciation by the patient that he is ill, that the illness is caused by a mental disorder that is the cause of his problems, and that he should seek and receive treatment, may be lost when the illness progresses but it is often preserved in the early stages, a feature which, as we said, compounds the distress experienced. Cultural factors, as we have already noted, may inform the issue of insight. In many cultures, especially of Asia and Africa, there is a notable lack of enthusiasm for acknowledging mental disorder, whether on the part of the patient or his/her family and the wider community. It is customary among these persons to try to understand the phenomena of disease in physical terms. In such cases it would be wrong to suggest that insight has been lost when all the patient is trying to do is to understand and explain his/her symptoms in terms of the acceptable cultural norms he/she subscribes to.

4.3 SCHIZOPHRENIA – CAUSATION – GENETICS

The schizophrenic disorders are found the world over in virtually all communities and in fairly uniform distribution, apart from a few pockets of increased incidence. They affect young men and women in late adolescence or early adult life. Men have the more severe illness and the worse prognosis. It is a not uncommon condition with about five in every thousand of the public affected. Although nowadays there is not believed to be a social class difference in the affliction, the tendency of patients with these conditions to drift socially downwards may suggest a preferential poorer class distribution in surveys. There is sufficient evidence now of a genetic predisposition, although the precise mechanisms still elude us. The closer the relationship to a schizophrenic patient a person has, the higher the risk that individual runs of developing the illness. The risk appears to increase with the closeness of the familial relationship. Twin studies and adoption studies have confirmed this point. There appear to be multiple genetic *foci* involved rather than a single gene. However, the genetic risk is not 100 per cent, which allows scope for environmental influences, both good and bad, to affect both onset and outcome. In fact, it appears it is a predisposition or vulnerability that is inherited, rather than the illness itself. It has long intrigued observers that some of those who could have inherited this predisposition often tend to be gifted and highly creative individuals who, moreover, do not go onto develop the illness. There is a suggestion therefore of evolutionary advantage to be had in possessing some of this genetic material which is thereby propagated and kept in circulation. Schizophrenic patients themselves traditionally have had low fertility. There appears to be interaction between genetic vulnerability and environmental influences. It is these environmental influences – such as stresses of a diverse kind, illicit drug consumption, trauma, physical injury or illness – that may help to steer a vulnerable individual over the threshold. There may be an overlap between true schizophrenia, the paranoid disorders to be discussed later in this chapter and the stress-induced schizophrenic illnesses which are sometimes referred to as the schizophreniform disorders. With the recent fashion for the use of the term, we could say there may even be a schizophrenic spectrum of disorders.

4.4 SCHIZOPHRENIA – CAUSATION – THE ENVIRONMENT

The environmental influences remain unclear. However, that the environment does play some part in the causation of schizophrenia has long been suspected. A viral theory has been mooted, viruses having been in the frame, so to speak, for a long time. Over the past generation or two the condition appears to have become milder in presentation, at least in some cultures, and less chronic in outcome. The kind of inhabitant seen in the old lunatic asylums – still to be recalled by an older generation of psychiatrists – is now rare and the change is exemplified also by the 'care in the community' approach, much traduced on account of its shortcomings, but an infinitely better and more humane way of dealing with the appropriate patient than incarcerating him, perhaps for ever, in primitive institutions offering little by way of comfort or treatment. The diminished severity of the condition has suggested to some observers there could be a possible infective aetiology for viruses which, in common with other micro organisms, have a well recognised tendency to mutate rapidly to greater or lesser virulence. That apart, there have been some neurological changes noted on brain studies of patients with schizophrenia although these findings, as yet, do not provide any reliable basis for diagnostic purposes. The role of environmental pollutants also remains unclear. There have also been a reduced incidence of some symptoms of schizophrenia which were common in earlier years. One of these is catatonia which in the past was considered to be a characteristic symptom of the condition and, indeed, attracted a sub category to itself in classificatory systems. The symptom is now rarely found in the developed world and, even then, appears to be preferentially distributed among patients from migrant communities. There is also the phenomenon that antibodies to various viruses such as the herpes simplex virus are found in the blood of patients with schizophrenia, although the precise significance of this has not yet been explained. Closer to home, pathological and dysfunctional family relationships have been suggested both as being aetiological as well as relapse-inducing elements. Finally, some presentations of schizophrenia-like conditions are virtually indistinguishable from the traditional presentations of the illness and may arise in the presence of systemic illness or following some illicit drug taking.

The strong association between self-reported cannabis use and the earlier onset of psychosis provides further evidence that schizophrenia may be precipitated by cannabis use and/or that early onset of symptoms is a risk factor for cannabis use. One study showed that half of all patients treated for cannabis-induced psychosis will develop a schizophrenia-like disorder and that almost a third will be diagnosed with paranoid schizophrenia. The first episode of schizophrenia occurs several years earlier in these patients compared with those with no history of cannabis-induced psychosis. Another study has suggested that compliance with antipsychotic medication by someone with schizophrenia may not prevent a relapse or worsening of psychotic symptoms if stimulant drugs (such as the amphetamines and cocaine) are used. Another study has reported that cannabis use in adolescence leads to a 2–3 fold increase in relative risk for schizophrenia or schizophreniform disorder in adulthood. The earlier the onset of cannabis use, the greater appears to be the risk for psychotic outcomes. Cannabis does not appear to represent a sufficient or necessary cause for the development of psychosis but seems to form a part of a causal constellation. A minority of individuals therefore experience a harmful outcome consequent on their use of cannabis. However, this minority is significant from a clinical point of view as well as at a population level. It is estimated that about eight per cent of cases of schizophrenia could be prevented by elimination of cannabis users in the population. Given all this evidence, it is tempting to believe that the picture of schizophrenia one sees in a clinical setting is but the result of some 'final common pathway' of brain dysfunction which may be instigated by diverse means.

4.5   SCHIZOPHRENIA – TREATMENT

The cornerstone of modern treatment of schizophrenia is drug treatment. In broad terms, the drugs used may be classified as the 'old' type and the 'new' type of drugs. The older drugs – the stalwarts among them were chlorpromazine, haloperidol and trifluoperazine – tended to be effective but were also sedative and in addition caused movement difficulties, some of which became permanent, causing a considerable degree of secondary disability. Versions of injectable depot preparations of these types of drugs, by which a patient may be given periodic injections thereby reducing the risk of non-compliance (a notoriously intractable problem in all medical practice), were also available.

The newer type of anti-psychotic drugs include agents such as amisulpride, clozapine, olanzapine, quetiapine, risperidone, sertindole and zotepine. These drugs, it is claimed, have fewer of the adverse effects, especially the atypical movement disorders, associated with the older drugs. By and large the efficacy of both sets of drugs is comparable. Special mention may be made of clozapine which is said to have properties against the 'negative' symptoms of schizophrenia – apathy, lack of motivation etc – which appear to be largely beyond the reach of the other agents more commonly used. However, clozapine is a notably toxic drug capable of producing lethal adverse effects by causing bone marrow suppression of white cell formation. It is therefore never to be considered as a first-line treatment in the average case of schizophrenia, its utility being rather in its availability when the conventional drugs have failed to produce improvement, especially with the negative symptoms which may also be present. It has to be used under strict medical supervision with periodic blood testing being a mandatory requirement. It goes without saying its use is limited to those who are specialists in this field who are able to weigh up the balance of benefits and risks. The patients being considered for this treatment must show motivation – however apathetic they may be – to take the drug as well as being able to submit themselves to regular blood testing.

If a firm diagnosis is made of schizophrenia, drug treatment, following a first episode of illness, is normally required for a period of at least two years. If there have been recurrent episodes of illness, this period of treatment may have to be extended. If stresses are present – whether personal or social – longer periods of treatment may need to be advised to avail of the protective functions of drug treatment. Therapeutic drugs have been shown to have a prophylactic function in the face of most stressful situations but not, it appears, against persistent illicit drug use. Recourse should be had, wherever possible, to depot anti-psychotic injections which will also ensure a reliable record being kept of compliance with medication. Contact with doctors, community nurses and other members of the mental health team is advantageous, as is the prompt reinstatement of vigorous treatment early in the course of any relapse. Modern drugs, including clozapine, offer alternative choices which were not available in the past.

The drugs commonly used today are usually successful in controlling the acute symptoms of the illness and, unlike in the past, in-patient treatment is not always necessary. This shift of treatment to the community has also the supplementary benefit that rehabilitation can be started straightaway. This is essential for one can be successful in treating the disease and yet end up with a patient that becomes a chronic invalid who tends to make the most of his illness for conscious and unconscious motives. The rule should always be to aim for as rapid a return as is safely possible to the patient's pre-morbid state of physical, psychological and social functioning and minimise, as far as possible, the dangers of secondary disability and chronic invalidism.

4.6 SCHIZOPHRENIA – PROGNOSIS

The prognosis of schizophrenia has notably improved in the past generation or two. The starkly disabled patients shuffling, muttering, disengaged, seen in such vast numbers inhabiting the Victorian lunatic asylums – and their more recent successors – is a thing now of the increasingly distant past, although if the theory of viral infection as a possible cause of schizophrenia holds any water it is not wholly inconceivable that the condition could once again in the future regain its previous severity. Viruses, after all, are known to mutate in all directions. The improvement in prognosis cannot be attributed, to any significant degree, to the drugs used or the diagnostic or treatment approaches employed, although the importance of early rehabilitation is better appreciated now than in the past. It used to be believed that a schizophrenic illness of early onset and of insidious progression associated with prominent negative symptoms heralded a poorer prognosis than an illness which came on at a later stage of life announcing itself with an acute onset and the spectacular presence of positive symptoms such as delusions and hallucinations. A clearly identifiable stress factor acting as a precipitant, good compliance with medication, satisfactory social support and a sympathetic family environment are all known to improve prognosis. Good recovery from a few episodes of illness presages a reasonably sound prognosis while recurrent bouts of illness may be associated with a poorer prognosis. Abuse of alcohol or illicit drugs – along with non-compliance with prescribed drugs – remains a potent cause of future relapse and consequently of a poorer prognosis. However, most patients with this condition, with treatment and support, could reasonably expect to reclaim the life they used to lead before the illness struck. It used also to be believed that few sufferers from a schizophrenic illness could successfully resume a professional, academic or social life. This is no longer necessarily true – a function of the reduced severity of the illness and the generally good prognosis it carries now.

4.7   SCHIZOPHRENIA – THE RISKS OF AGGRESSION AND VIOLENCE

Such is the universal nature of schizophrenic illness that it will come as no surprise that practitioners in several branches of the law may find themselves involved with patients suffering from such an illness. Their unpredictable and occasionally aggressive behaviour interests the criminal law as it does family and child practice. Which aspects of this condition cause or contribute to the displays of aggression and violence are by no means clear. The symptoms of the illness themselves may be causative in any untoward behaviour. It is easy enough to understand that a patient suffering from a persecutory delusion may be impelled to act against his imagined tormentors by visiting violence on them. Similarly, auditory hallucinations may command the patient to take some violent action. However, it is too simplistic to believe the symptoms themselves are the sole or even main cause of any violence associated with these patients. Their personalities may be involved as with any individual whether suffering from an illness or not. Social and cultural factors may influence schizophrenic patients as they do everyone else. The misuse of alcohol and illicit drugs may lead to displays of violence involving these patients. One cannot even discount the possibility that some drugs used in the treatment of this condition or for some intercurrent disorder contribute to aggressive behaviour. This is a reminder to any observer that all the facts associated with a patient must be taken into account in trying to understand any patient in regard to his potential for violence and to make rational predictions on the probability of that violence occurring.

4.8   OTHER PARANOID DISORDERS

There are paranoid disorders – usually involving persecutory delusions with little or nothing else by way of other psychotic symptoms – which for a long time have been observed not to fit into the diagnostic categories reserved for the schizophrenic illnesses. The primacy of delusions was always evident in these cases. When the onset of these paranoid disorders is acute there is present an acute delusional disorder in which may be seen persecutory delusions with a mood of suspicion. The cause of these states may be illicit or prescribed drugs, and adverse life stresses are not uncommonly implicated as precipitants. The more chronic or more persistent forms of delusional disorders involve systematised delusions – meaning these exist as a near complete system within the patient's mind and usually involve a belief in conspiracies against him – and there is little other impairment, intelligence and the personality in other respects being well preserved. These delusional beliefs and systems may also exist in isolation – they are then referred to as being encapsulated – and there is usually little other impairment in functioning or of the personality in other respects. A famous case – and a patient of Freud's – involved a German judge who apparently carried out his judicial tasks satisfactorily even while harbouring such a delusional system in his mind. The term paranoia used to be given to this class of paranoid disorders. Another kind of paranoid disorder afflicts the elderly in whom it showed virtually all the features of a paranoid schizophrenic illness, apart from the obviously late onset, and this condition usually carries a good prognosis. This condition was referred to as paraphrenia or, where appropriate, as senile paraphrenia. All these conditions have now been brought under the heading of persistent delusional disorders which are to be diagnosed in the absence of brain damage or schizophrenia. There are a handful of other paranoid disorders such as morbid jealousy which, as will be discussed later in Chapter 10, is especially important as being a cause of violence between, in particular, individuals who are in an intimate relationship. The treatment of these paranoid disorders is essentially on the lines taken in cases of schizophrenia. This involves the use of anti-psychotic drugs. The acute forms of the illness respond reasonably well to treatment and the patient should be able to make an uneventful recovery. Good results are usually also to be expected in those cases previously called paraphrenia but there is usually little impact on well established cases of chronic or persistent delusional disorders, or paranoia, as they used to be called, and these patients carry on with their life with their delusions well encapsulated in their minds.

4.9 OTHER PARANOID DISORDERS – THE RISKS OF AGGRESSION AND VIOLENCE

The risks are as for schizophrenia with the difference that apathy and poor motivation are not usually associated with the paranoid disorders. The criminal law and family and child law may become involved in litigation with these patients on account of their unreasonable and occasionally aggressive and violent behaviour. The violence due to patients with paranoid disorders is to be subject to the same analysis as is employed with patients suffering from schizophrenia.

4.10 SUMMARY

1. Schizophrenia is essentially an illness which afflicts young adults. There is known genetic risk, susceptibility to the illness rising according to how closely related one is to an affected family member. Schizophrenia-like conditions may be produced by some physical causes, including the use of illicit drugs. There has been recent interest in how cannabis may cause or contribute to the development of the condition. The prognosis of schizophrenia appears to have improved in recent years. Its symptoms are amenable to drug

treatment and active rehabilitation should prevent secondary disability arising. There is a known relationship between schizophrenia and aggressive behaviour but the relationship is complex and needs to be subjected to detailed analysis. The personality of the patient and the concurrent misuse of substances may play a part in the violence associated with these patients. Apathy and lack of motivation are occasional features of the illness, made worse for want of active rehabilitation. There is evidence that with adequate rehabilitation patients will become less disabled and more capable of employment. The better the social functioning of these patients, the lower the risk of inappropriate behaviour concerning them.

2.   The risks associated with the paranoid disorder are similar to those involved with schizophrenic illness. Interpersonal relationships may be affected with problems arising in respect of employment and housing. Aggression may also be involved with these patients. The acute state is susceptible to drug treatment and good results may be anticipated. The underlying personality may be a significant factor in the long-term prognosis.

CHAPTER 5

DISORDERS OF MOOD

As far as the psychoses are concerned, the modern understanding of mood disorders is that it involves mania, depression or a combination of the two conditions which are called bipolar affective disorders or manic-depressive illness. These conditions are all characterised by pathological mood changes, usually in the form of depression or elation. In fact, it is a useful rule of thumb to remind oneself that the symptoms found in mood disorders should generally be capable of being explained by the central change in mood, whether downward or upward.

5.1 DEPRESSIVE ILLNESS – CLINICAL FEATURES

The term depression, used without qualification, is not wholly satisfactory for it is capable of bearing many meanings. It could refer to a mood state, a personality type or the constellation of symptoms that makes up a depressive disorder. These symptoms can involve bodily or physiological changes such as those concerning sleep, appetite, sexual desire, gastro-intestinal function or the menstrual rhythm. Symptoms may also involve psychomotor function.

The mood change in depressive illness must involve a pathological diminution of mood. This refers to a significant and sustained reduction of mood which transcends the regular variations of mood that all human beings (indeed, probably all animals) are subject to. Where normal variation ends and pathological change begins remains a problematical area of definition for there are no objective measures available to discern this shift unlike, say, with the measurement of body temperature or blood pressure. There is no alternative to a detailed enquiry being undertaken into the individual's perceptions of changes in mood, for different persons may also differ in their habitual setting of mood. Any change must be sustained and persistent, normally lasting for at least four weeks. The mood change may lead to a variety of ancillary subjective changes such as the inability to enjoy the things the individual habitually previously used to. There may also be present a pervasive feeling of gloom, pessimism and dark foreboding which is not in keeping with the previous character of the individual concerned. The sufferer may echo Shakespeare by saying, 'How weary, stale, flat and unprofitable/Seem to me all the uses of this world.'

These feelings may intensify to accommodate ideas of guilt and worthlessness which may extend even, in severe cases, to expressing delusions of guilt and worthlessness such as being convinced that one is responsible for all the ills, sins and wickedness found in the world. A related delusion is one involving a sense of nihilism in which the patient believes he does not exist, that his mind and body do not exist and that the world itself does not exist. As these delusions are to be derived from a pathological lowering of the mood, these ideas far transcend any philosophical notion one can hold that the world and the individuals within it are but an illusion. As might be imagined, these pathological ideas may co-exist with a sense of bleak hopelessness which leads on, with perverted logic, to suicide, an ever present risk in any patient with a depressed mood.

The changes in physiology or bodily function are common in depressive illness and have long indicated to some observers the ultimate biological provenance of any significant depressive disorder. The sleep rhythm may be early upset in the course of the illness. Although the classical feature is noted to be early wakening, that is waking two or more hours before the usual time of awakening for the patient, in practice sleep may be disturbed in diverse ways. There could be difficulty in getting to sleep, repeated wakening during the course of sleep, waking early or a combination of all these disruptions over several nights. Sleep may also be disturbed by intrusive dreaming. The upshot is disrupted sleep of poor quality which leaves the patient unrefreshed even after he has apparently been sleeping for several hours. This ensures the next day is started off on a shaky footing and, thereby, a vicious circle is also set in train, making the consequences of a depressed mood worse through a lack of any 'balm of sleep'. Many patients complain it is their poor sleep, above all other symptoms, that contributes most to their feelings of black despair and demoralisation. However, a small minority of patients tend to oversleep, giving the impression to observers that they could be attempting to escape their torments in a periodic loss of consciousness. These patients do not, however, appear to enjoy much refreshment as a result of their prolonged somnolence.

Parallel biological change may be seen in respect of appetite. Loss of appetite is common and may be severe with consequent weight loss which, in graver cases, could come to cause a medical emergency through loss of nutrition and hydration. Changes in bowel function may reflect poor appetite with ensuing constipation the common feature, although diarrhoea may also be present when it is usual to attribute it to features of anxiety which are commonly found in depressed states. There could in some cases be a paradoxical feature of over eating when with the over consumption of what is called 'comfort food' there could be excessive, even gross, weight gain. Reduction in sexual interests – as with other appetites and sources of pleasure – is a common feature in depressive illness, as are changes in menstrual rhythm.

Psychomotor retardation refers to slowness of both mental and physical activity. It is a common observation that patients with depressive illness often appear to be functioning like an under-powered engine, being laboured in thought, word and movement. In extreme cases – rarely seen these days – stupor can overcome patients when, mute and immobile, they enter into a catatonic state. On the other hand, minds can, in equally severe depressive illness, become seemingly overactive when agitation may be an accompanying feature. In severe psychotic forms of depressive illness, delusions of a kind already mentioned could be seen along with auditory hallucinations – the voices characteristically saying things in keeping with the patient's mood, abusing him, invoking feelings of guilt and, sometimes urging him to commit suicide to put an end to a worthless existence. In these cases the differential diagnosis must also consider other psychotic conditions such as schizophrenia. The implications for violent behaviour in these circumstances are obvious.

An invariable feature in a depressive illness of any significant severity is loss of attention and concentration. Patients may report having difficulty keeping track of events when following popular pastimes such as watching the television. Serious intellectual activity may become impossible. A common complaint is also made of a poor short-term memory, of being forgetful and mislaying objects. A picture of dementia may be presented to the world. However, there is usually no evidence of anything unduly serious underlying these memory difficulties which are attributable to poor attention and concentration, and full recovery can be confidently predicted with successful treatment of the depressive illness.

5.2 MANIA – CLINICAL FEATURES

Mania is popularly regarded as being the mirror image of depressive illness. It appears to sit on the other pole of bipolar illness, although this stark distinction between 'polar opposites' is not by any means entirely accurate either in description or in terms of an analysis of underlying pathology. As with depressive illness it should be possible, at a superficial level at any rate, to derive all the features of a manic illness from the central pathological elevation of mood. In mania this elevation of mood is elation, a sustained elevation of mood. It must be stated, however, that in many cases what strikes (occasionally possibly in more senses than one) the observer is not elation or pathological happiness but a mood of aggression mixed with irritability and hostility. Nevertheless, many of these patients do appear unduly cheerful, for a time at least, with a limitless supply of energy which – in stark contrast to the more severe cases of depression – causes them to act like an overpowered engine, fuelled by rocket fuel, being in constant overdrive, humming with activity and exhausting those around them. These patients may talk without end, make endless and increasingly ambitious plans and are pathologically optimistic. The future is scanned by them with lofty regard, money may be scattered on all and sundry, extravagant purchases (including the fabled elephant ordered through Harrods, other exotic creatures, jewellery) made, largesse bestowed. Relations usually have to pick up the pieces at the end of the episode of illness.

Their excessive talk is characterised by what is referred to as a pressure of speech and the overpowered mind may give rise to a 'flight of ideas' which means a form of speech disorder is present.

So active are some of these patients that they have little time for food, drink or sleep and very occasionally they may collapse into utter exhaustion. Elation of mood is also mirrored in the patient having a grandiose or even fantastic conception of himself, occasionally believing he is of noble or royal birth, possessing special talents or powers and given also to possessing limitless wealth. There is also disinhibition in sexual matters and unwanted pregnancies in women patients is not uncommon. With the lack of any insight being present, all these excesses may appear to give the impression of behaviour by a celebrity albeit one who actually possesses little or no talent, which may, of course, be not unusual these days.

5.3 BIPOLAR DISORDER

Depressive and manic illness may be, and indeed are commonly, found as separate and discrete illnesses. However, when serially combined, for instance, when depression and mania alternate or appear in irregular series in the same patient, the appellation bipolar affective disorder, replacing the formerly used manic-depressive disorder, is given.

5.4 BIPOLAR DISORDER – CAUSATION

As with schizophrenia, all the evidence suggests that pathological disturbances of mood originate in brain dysfunction, although the precise mechanisms are far from clear in the present state of knowledge. The structure of the brain, especially in the parts below the cerebral cortex, appears to be implicated, the lesion detectable by scanning of the brain. It is believed that where obvious lesions exist, the prognosis is poorer. At the neurochemical level changes have long been known to exist, although the precise mechanisms involved continue to elude us. The finding of chemical disturbance of some kind being present offers the rationale for drug treatment. There is a discernible genetic influence (greater in bipolar than in unipolar disorders) and close family relations may show an increased tendency to these disorders. Relations of patients with a bipolar disorder have a higher risk of both bipolar and unipolar depressive disorder. The risk of depressive disorder in women is higher, although the risk of bipolar disorder is comparable in men and women. But the environmental effect, as might be imagined, is also strong and in any given case of these disorders it is not uncommon to find an interaction between genetic susceptibility and environmental effects (eg an individual with genetic susceptibility falling ill having experienced some adverse life event) bearing responsibility for the illness. The role of life events may be particularly decisive. It appears to be the case that it is not so much the effect of the adverse life events themselves – which, after all, everyone is heir to – but the impact they could have on a person who might have been rendered vulnerable as a result of genetic and prior psychological influences. An intriguing question is to what extent genetics and the environment, in combination or separately, determine not merely how an individual faces up to stressful life events but how he has got into the situation of having to experience them, the so-called 'nature of nurture' argument. Among the psychological factors deemed significant in making an individual vulnerable to disorders of mood, especially depressive illness, are unemployment, having several young children living at home and having no confiding or intimate relationship to sustain the individual. Other psychological factors include parental loss, emotional deprivation or abuse and abnormal personality. Those with disordered personalities may appear to be drawn into situations which lead to mood disorders, in particular depressive illness, as a result of their reactions to these situations. Alcohol misuse may lead to a depressive mood and both depressed and manic patients may drink heavily as well as consuming illicit drugs. Many of these patients have low self-esteem and may be hypersensitive to criticism and not a few have a tendency to think negatively about themselves and the world, the focus of cognitive behavioural therapy.

Neither depressive illness nor mania need to be of primarily psychiatric origin. These disorders can follow a host of medical or surgical conditions or the treatment given for those. The primary cause in such cases could be systemic illness of infective, metabolic, endocrine, haematological or neoplastic origins. Some of the conditions involved include cerebrovascular disease, brain tumours, hypothyroidism, steroid drugs, amphetamine and other stimulant abuse and multiple sclerosis. Treatment of the underlying condition may be sufficient in some cases to improve the mood disorder although not uncommonly both the secondary depressive illness or mania requires treatment in its own right whatever other condition might have been primarily causative of the mood disturbance.

5.5 BIPOLAR DISORDER – TREATMENT

The treatment of depressive illness usually involves some combination of drug and psychological therapy. The mainstay of drug treatment for many decades used to be the tricyclic group of antidepressant drugs. This group includes such drugs as amitryptiline and dothiepin. Their efficacy was, on the whole, acceptable but their adverse effects occasionally proved tiresome. They could be unduly sedating and thus be inconvenient for use in situations requiring alertness and, more crucially, they could be dangerous, even lethally so, in overdose, a situation that is potentially capable of arising in every case of a depressive illness. These drawbacks led to a search for drugs with different modes of action and in time was born the group of drugs called the selective serotonin reuptake inhibiting agents (SSRIs). As the name suggests, their biochemical action is to block the reuptake of an important brain chemical called serotonin, thereby, in effect, flooding the nerve endings where this chemical is believed to modulate mood function. Some other drugs are known to have analogous effects in respect of noradrenaline metabolism. These drugs do not have the same sedating properties as the older tricyclic agents and, more pertinently, are believed to be far less dangerous in overdose. Among their number are fluoxetine, citalopram, paroxetine and sertraline. In time other atypical drugs such as mirtazepine, nefazodone, reboxetine and venlafaxine also made their way to the market place. There is no doubt that we now possess a considerably improved armoury of drugs for use in depressive illness but in all drug treatment there is a cautionary tale to be told and remembered when it comes to the use of any pharmaceutical agent.

These newer atypical drugs were taken up with an almost messianic zeal, the drug fluoxetine (Prozac) in particular achieving notoriety by being promiscuously exhibited in subjects for whom it was never intended – very young children, domestic pets, not to mention individuals who were disaffected with life rather than suffering from a depressive illness – and the term Prozac nearly came to signify a synonym for panacea. Over a period of time adverse reports gathered and there is some evidence now that these newer agents may not be as risk-free, never mind of universal benefit, as they were once believed to be. In particular this group of drugs has been implicated as a possible cause in some cases of suicide and homicide where it is believed they might have enhanced aggressive tendencies already present in some depressed patients – might even have precipitated these tendencies in other patients – causing them to turn on themselves or towards others with violence. Litigation was mooted. The caution that was enjoined following these reports was wholly beneficial for in all medicine a balance has to be struck in every patient between the reward and risks possible with any treatment that is being contemplated. The result now is that a more balanced view appears to be once again taken of all antidepressant drug treatment. Treatment is usually required for at least six months, after which the drug dose may be gradually reduced and the drug treatment may be stopped altogether. Gradual reduction in medication reduces the risk of relapse and also prevents withdrawal effects, seen with some drugs, emerging. It has been shown that maintenance drug treatment reduces relapse rates by 50 per cent in cases of recurrent depressive illness.

Drug treatment works most effectively when allied to some form of psychological treatment. The role of conventional counselling and therapy is probably overestimated. Psychological treatment is labour – and, therefore, time and cost – intensive and resources are scarce. The motivation of the patient is the paramount requirement and relatively few patients appear to have the patience and the commitment necessary to achieve good results. As up to 50 per cent of patients are non-compliant even with medication, simple enough to consume, a great deal of motivation is demanded of any patient being offered psychotherapy. Where litigation is involved, there are two additional factors also to be taken into account. Firstly, the motivation always required of the patient becomes mixed if he engages in treatment so as to impress a court. Secondly, litigation usually envisages a short time scale for treatment which may be insufficient for success. Most forms of psychotherapy are therefore to be ruled out for parties involved in the usual forms of litigation. Nevertheless, in carefully selected patients, considerable benefit may be reaped through the deployment of psychological methods of treatment used as an adjunct to drug treatment. The role of cognitive behavioural treatment (CBT) in particular has been studied with interest and there is no doubt that in suitable groups of patients better results may be obtained by the use of this technique with medication than by drug treatment alone. The purpose of CBT is, to put it at its simplest, to attempt to refocus a patient's approach to thinking. A patient's problem may not be due to some objective and inherent property in the problem itself but the way his thoughts or cognitions come habitually to interpret the situation. The patient and therapist work out methods of challenging unhelpful and negative thoughts in relation to situations and to focus instead on thinking in positive and helpful ways. There may be role play, homework (the keeping of diaries involving cognitions) and practice involving situations that the patient could encounter, then and also in the future. An associated form of treatment is what may be called social therapy. There is often little doubt that in a significant number of depressed patients, underlying the disorder are adverse social factors such as uncongenial or non-existent employment, unmanageable debt, poor marital relationships, adverse housing and a host of similar influences. If anything can be done to ameliorate these adverse influences there is greater scope for successful treatment and rehabilitation involving these patients.

Brief mention must be made of electroconvulsive treatment (ECT) given the notoriety the procedure has attracted over many years. It is a procedure that is not without its risks but there is no gainsaying its potent efficacy in the most severe forms of depressive illness involving a seemingly intractable disorder that could be leading the patient into a serious state of ill health. It can be a life saving intervention. Its use lies in specialist hands and with carefully selected cases.

The treatment of mania involves the use of the kind of antipsychotic agents that were discussed in the management of the schizophrenic disorders. The essence of treatment is to bring symptomatic relief and curb the various excesses involving the case of a manic patient. But in the case of depressive illness or mania or both (bipolar states) there is also scope for prophylactic treatment, that is attempting to prevent the recurrence of these conditions. The primary agent available for the use for such purposes is the salts of the metal lithium which has now been employed for this purpose for four decades. The benefit from lithium use can be considerable but, once again, it is not without risk, especially in terms of kidney and thyroid functions. There are also other adverse effects associated with this drug. Further, it is safely and satisfactorily used only with regular blood level monitoring available to the patient and accepted by him/her. The demands on the patient may be considerable and some selection as to who might be suitable is necessary. Risk of relapse, when the drug is used, may be reduced by up to 30 per cent, results being better with the prevention of manic relapse than the prevention of depressive relapse. Other drugs pressed into service in this regard are carbamazepine, valproic acid and lamotrigine. There is some evidence that the course of the natural history of bipolar affective disorder can be advantageously altered by the use of lithium. Hence, the tendency now to embark on prophylactic treatment after even one episode of illness rather than wait for recurrence, which was the approach previously taken.

5.6   BIPOLAR DISORDER – PROGNOSIS

The prognosis for individual episodes of illness, whether of depression or mania, is generally good these days. Fairly rapid response to modern drug treatment may be expected. If recovery from a depressive illness appears to be slow, apart from non-response to medication (which may necessitate a change of drug), other factors may need to be considered or reviewed, in particular the personality and the social elements in the patient's life. Alcohol and illicit drug misuse are important factors interfering with successful treatment. Recurrence of illness is always possible. It is usual to advise that drug treatment be continued for six months following full recovery from symptoms so as to minimise the risks of relapse. The role of lithium in prophylaxis has been mentioned above. Recurrence following specific risk factors eg the post-partum state is always possible (see later).

5.7   BIPOLAR DISORDER – RISKS OF AGGRESSION AND VIOLENCE

Both depressive and manic illness have implications for the law. Both conditions are associated with the risk of violence, which explains the interest of the criminal law and family and child law in these conditions. The potential for violence in cases of depressive illness is not uncommonly underestimated. While the risk of suicidal behaviour is well understood, depressive patients can also turn violence on others, sometimes turning on themselves after attacking someone else. Cases of murder followed by suicide are occasionally reported. Mania is more easily understood in terms of the scope for aggression and violence that it presents as the demeanour of manic patients with their overactivity, aggression and hostility lends itself to aggressive conduct. It should also be borne in mind that both depressive and manic illness may lead patients to misusing alcohol and illicit drugs which, in turn, may increase the potential for violent behaviour. Finally, the points made about the use of some antidepressant drugs and their potential for causing or exacerbating violent behaviour must be borne in mind.

5.8 SUMMARY

1. The risk of developing an affective disorder such as depressive illness or mania is affected by genetic factors, there being a greater risk of developing bipolar disorder when the genetic loading is elevated. Environmental factors also play a significant part in causing or contributing to the onset of these conditions. These disorders are also associated with physical and systemic illness. There is also a well known relationship between the affective disorders and the misuse of alcohol and illicit substances. Modern treatment is generally successful in containing symptoms and also in the prevention of further episodes of these disorders.

2. While the risk of violence associated with mania is well appreciated, it appears not to be with depressive illness with a result that the prospects for violence with depressive illness have come to be underestimated. Suicide is an ever present risk with any depressive illness or where depressed mood is present in another condition. But there may also be an appreciable risk of violence directed outwards, also associated with depressive illness. Murder followed by suicide is well established in cases of depressive illness. The risks may be heightened by the concurrent misuse of alcohol and illicit substances and some antidepressant agents have also been implicated in the violence that may be seen with depressive illness.

CHAPTER 6

THE NEUROSES

The neuroses refer to those conditions which make up the minor psychiatric disorders. The qualifying term 'minor' refers to the presentation of symptoms as seen from the perspective of a detached professional observer who finds the symptoms associated with these conditions to be less severe than the features of a psychotic disorder. To a patient with a neurotic condition it may be anything but minor as he carries around pressing symptoms of greater or lesser chronicity which respond poorly to conventional treatment and cause him to become the despair of doctors. The old joke with an American flavour – that 'the neurotic builds castles in the air, the psychotic lives in them and the psychiatrist collects the rent' – conveys much truth as jokes often do. A neurotic patient, whatever his symptoms may be and however inexplicable they are, usually has some grasp on reality and, generally, some measure of insight; the psychotic patient may invariably fall down on both scores. A cardinal rule with most neurotic disorders is that there is also a strong contribution made to neurotic conditions by the personality of the patient whereas psychotic conditions are usually studied as 'true' disease conditions with distinct biological origins and with the disease condition usually overwhelming any observable feature in the habitual personality and forming a distinguishable break from it. The neuroses may also be approached from the point of view of conditions that arise from the interaction between a patient's personality and the impact upon it of some external stressful event. This analysis may help to understand the acts of aggression and violence that these patients may be engaged in.

6.1 MINOR DEPRESSIVE ILLNESS

The first of the conditions to be considered under this heading are the minor depressive illnesses. We have already considered depressive illnesses under the psychotic conditions and, at one level, the differences between the conditions appearing under the two rubrics is merely quantitative – depressive neurosis may appear to be a less severe illness and is not usually associated with a bipolar affective disorder. If the term is to be taken literally, depressive neurosis also will be expected to lack psychotic features such as delusions and hallucinations which may be a feature in some very severe depressive illnesses. These patients also keep a good hold on reality and their insight could be considerable and, in fact, contribute to their perception of their disorder. However, it is usual also to observe other differences between the two forms of depressive disorder. One of these, as already suggested, is the contribution made by the patient's personality to his disorder, which may be of greater significance than with cases of 'psychotic' depressive illness where the illness element is usually the more prominent observable feature. That apart, the symptoms may appear to be similar, with, as stated, the obvious absence of any psychotic features. Onset of illness may be less marked and there is a 'grumbling' (in all senses) feel to the condition as reported by the patient. In other words, the distinction between the patient's habitual mood state and the way he usually feels and the state of disorder seen at an objective examination may be far from clearly drawn. It is a feature of the neuroses that there is considerable interaction between personality and response to stress or life events in the causation of the conditions and this is usually seen in cases of the depressive neuroses. The management of the condition is on similar lines to any other depressive illness with the difference that more obvious attention should be paid to psychological approaches to deal with elements in the personality once the symptoms have been dispersed, or at any rate controlled, with the help of medication. Cognitive behavioural therapy is probably the approach of choice and holds far greater promise than any assault directed at the core personality where attempts at amelioration usually result in, at best, equivocal results. The prognosis for this condition is invariably guarded. Where personality is so intimately involved in symptom formation and even influences the patient's attitude to life and the situations that he finds himself in, little else can be said with any confidence. As with all personality disorders, and defects in the personality not amounting to the disorder, the suspicion remains that the patient's clinical improvement or deterioration will depend largely on the prevailing circumstances of his life. Aggression and violence appear to owe more to the impact of the personality of the patient and the stresses he faces rather than to the condition itself.

6.2   ANXIETY STATES

One of the commoner neurotic states involves the presence in the patient of pathological levels of anxiety. Anxiety in this context refers to unnatural and inappropriate feelings of fear. It is normal – and an important part of survival, both personal and collective, in the evolutionary sense – to feel fear. Most animals keep an eye watchfully open for predators. The human animal is naturally concerned for its personal security when living in its modern habitation and is understandably concerned for the future. Even a measure of anxiety – short of pathological levels – appears necessary for success in life for it fuels motivation. In anxiety states this natural and appropriate fearfulness appears translated into an overwhelming sense of fear in regard to ordinary and seemingly normal situations. A patient may feel a sense of impending disaster when seated indoors, behind locked doors and in the absence of any obvious threatening stimulus. Another patient may become fearful about walking outdoors among people going about their routine and unremarkable business. A third may become exceedingly fearful in ordinary situations or in the presence of mundane objects or common and generally harmless creatures such as domestic pets where, in no obvious way, is such feeling serving any protective purpose. Anxiety states may be classified as being generalised anxiety states, panic states or as phobic disorders.

6.3   GENERALISED ANXIETY STATES

In generalised anxiety states the patient is subject to 'free floating' anxiety which may arise without any provocation or warning and in the absence of obvious stimuli. There is a feeling of great unease and of foreboding, a sense of some disaster waiting to strike imminently. The feeling of persistent anxiety differs from the episodic or paroxysmal feelings of anxiety which occur in panic disorders and are unrelated to specific situations, as happens with the phobic disorders. This feeling is accompanied by physical symptoms such as palpitations, a dry mouth, a tightening in the chest, excessive sweating, a tremor of the extremities, sleep disturbance (characteristically an inability to get off to sleep), diarrhoea and increased feelings of urgency and frequency of the urge to urinate and evacuate the bowels. There are also symptoms of physical tension such as a particular type of headache (usually described as feeling like a band around the head) and stiffness in the region of the back and neck. There is loss also of attention and concentration which, in turn, may lead to poor short-term memory. Insight is normally preserved, meaning the patient can recognise all these effects (and will, indeed, complain about them and ask for help), attribute them to a nervous or mental phenomenon and confirm that something has definitely gone wrong with the mechanisms.

6.4   PANIC STATES

Panic attacks were previously considered to be part of any state of generalised anxiety, but are now believed to occupy a discrete sub-category among the anxiety states. The symptoms of a panic state are well known and combine the physical symptoms seen in generalised anxiety states with an overpowering mental reaction – as a result of severe, periodic and paroxysmal attacks of anxiety – which may give rise also to feelings in which the patient's life may seem unreal or the world itself may appear unreal (depersonalisation and derealisation). Attacks tend to recur and are unpredictable, a state of affairs leading to much distress and also tending to feed the anxiety.

6.5   PHOBIC DISORDERS

In phobic disorders the anxiety is experienced in relation to a situation and is usually restricted to the experience of or anticipation of the stimuli associated with that situation. Phobic anxiety states refer to pathological and irrational fearfulness experienced in these specific situations. There are both quantitative and qualitative elements distinguishing these phobic states from normal responses. Children may fear the dark as a normal response and anxious adults become apprehensive in unlit locations. That these fears do not usually handicap them in their daily existence, is a response shared by several persons and may, in fact, both be seen to be normal and sensible responses to reality. Phobic anxiety states are of a different order for the fear may be out of proportion to any threat inherent in the situation, it cannot be reasoned away, is beyond the control of the individual and leads to the avoidance of these situations. These fears are not shared by any large number of other citizens and, on occasion, may be socially disabling. Common phobias involve outside locations (agoraphobia), confined spaces (claustrophobia), social settings (social phobia) and such situations as heights, flying, spiders, domestic animals, needles and of contracting illnesses.

One of the commonest of the phobias is agoraphobia (whose name is derived from the Greek for fear of the market place) which involves intense fear of open spaces or large spaces which are built up and difficult to escape from such as supermarkets and shopping centres. It appears, at any rate in some cases, it is not so much the market but the situation of social contact that provokes the anxiety experienced, indicating an overlap with social phobia. The phobia may also involve the fear of physical symptoms of anxiety and panic attacks, in which case there is also overlap with the panic disorders. Young women appear to be preferentially involved and in extreme cases the patient may be reduced to being housebound. Social phobia extends well beyond normal shyness and bears all the hallmarks of an anxiety disorder. There could be difficulties in the personalities of these patients, with a lack of confidence and self esteem, and there is commonly a history of involvement in some incident or situation in the course of which the patient had not appeared to his best advantage. (One recalls the story about the eminent Cambridge economist whose arguments had been comprehensively demolished in a coruscating attack in a learned journal. He had not returned to Cambridge for some time afterward, pleading plaintively, 'I dare not return. Even the porters at the station will be laughing at me.' Happily he recovered without further incident.)

6.6   ANXIETY STATES – CAUSATION

Anxiety states are common and their prevalence comfortably outstrips the distribution of the psychotic conditions. The symptoms of anxiety are strongly suggestive of the involvement of a part of a brain called the limbic system. There is a significant genetic component and features of anxiety may be seen to run in families where sometimes psychological contagion may also be implicated as a cause, unnaturally fearful parents infecting children under their influence. The environment undeniably plays a part. Anecdotal observation suggests that the modern overprotective parent can induce unnatural fearfulness in children so much so that a child today appears to be more apprehensive of situations, especially concerning outdoor activities, than its predecessor of a few generations ago (similar explanations are given for the apparent increase in allergies to all manner of stimuli among children and young adults believed to have been reared in excessively sanitary conditions). The other psychological explanation of note regarding causation involves faults in attachment in childhood, where early feelings of insecurity may be reactivated later in the form of anxiety in relation to the world and the objects within it. Whatever the suggested explanations, it seems certain that that the primary *foci* responsible for these disorders will be found in some part of the brain.

6.7 ANXIETY STATES – TREATMENT

Treatment of the anxiety states involves both pharmacological and psychological approaches. The best known drugs for use in anxiety states are the benzodiazepine group including such agents as diazepam (Valium) and lorazepam. There is no doubt these drugs are effective in treatment in virtually all forms of anxiety but for some considerable time now their primary adverse effect has become all too well known – that they are also remarkably addictive. In fact, the anxiety in the patient having been successfully dealt with, the problem then arises that the patient needs to be weaned off these drugs, a process which sometimes causes far greater trauma to the patient than the symptoms of anxiety did in the first place. There is still a place for these drugs in the treatment of anxiety but that lies in the hands of specialist practitioners who may use it under strictly observed conditions – for short periods of time and as an adjunct to other treatments. These drugs may also have a place in the treatment of some phobic anxiety states where the anxiety-provoking situation is only met with occasionally, eg when the prospect of air travel looms to a patient suffering from anxiety in such a situation or a visit to a dental surgeon beckons for another who becomes anxious in those situations.

Other drugs have useful anxiety-relieving properties as side effects of their primary therapeutic use. The tricyclic antidepressant drugs discussed in the previous chapter have such effects which can be usefully mobilised in the treatment of anxiety. However, the more serious adverse effects of these drugs such as a fatal result in overdose constrain their widespread use. The modern SSRI group of drugs such as paroxetine and citalopram also have well recognised effects in reducing anxiety, although the paradoxical effect of making anxiety worse in some susceptible cases must be borne in mind. For all these reasons drug treatment of anxiety should be approached with care and left in specialist hands. Another group of drugs with useful anxiety-reducing features are the beta-blocking group of drugs such as propranolol. Their effects are on the physical manifestations of anxiety such as palpitations, which they may be successful in reducing. The mind-body relationship may well be in evidence in these situations for it is believed a reduction in physical symptoms may lead in turn to an amelioration of the psychological effects and a virtuous circle is thereby caused to come into being.

Psychological treatment is well established in the management of anxiety states. At its simplest the procedures involve techniques of relaxation and anxiety-management being taught to the patient. Phobic anxiety states, in particular, submit well to psychological approaches. Perhaps the best known of the techniques employed with cases of phobic anxiety is called graded exposure, by which the patient very gradually becomes attuned to approaching the object or situation that has caused dread previously and either comes to deal with the situation with greater equanimity or has his previous feelings replaced by not too disabling nervousness. Panic attacks and phobic anxiety states may also respond well to cognitive behavioural treatment which involves shifting – by means of reframing – the existing cognitive bias of the patient in a more positive direction. Social approaches must not be neglected as the patient's personal and social circumstances could, at least in part, be responsible for his anxiety state, causing it or maintaining it. It is necessary to deal with the mundane stresses the patient may be experiencing for his personality is, by and large, beyond correction.

6.8   ANXIETY STATES – PROGNOSIS

The prognosis of anxiety states is variable but is generally satisfactory. If an anxiety state is of acute onset and has followed discrete trauma such as, say, a road traffic accident leading to a phobic state about driving or travelling in a motor car, and the patient has a reasonably stable personality, the results are generally good if treatment is undertaken swiftly. As a general rule, the longer the symptom persists the less good is the outcome as any treatment for symptoms can become entrenched. Chronic anxiety states are much harder to deal with and delays in offering treatment may worsen the prognosis. An important point to bear in mind – as with all psychiatric disorders – is the danger of secondary disability supervening and exacerbating the primary difficulty. For unconscious and conscious reasons of gain – relief from some inner anxiety or some more obvious profit – the patient's symptoms could worsen, become entrenched and become unresponsive to treatment. The rule therefore is always to treat with vigour and to rehabilitate the patient promptly. With generalised anxiety states the previous personality of the patient may intrude upon treatment and may be a bar to successful recovery. Such patients may continue to be predisposed to relapse even while temporary short-term improvement can be produced. As might be imagined, the exigencies of the modern world inform the anxieties of many patients. Relationship insecurities, financial difficulties, employment uncertainties, poor housing or a run of misfortune, eg being a victim of street crime when one is recovering from a previous assault (something not unknown to happen in certain neighbourhoods) may defeat the best efforts of the most skilful of therapists.

6.9   ANXIETY STATES – RISKS OF AGGRESSION AND VIOLENCE

As will be appreciated, anxiety states are so pervasive in the community that many branches of the law may become involved with patients suffering from anxiety states. Chronic disabling anxiety may impair employment duties and family and child law practitioners may come across a spouse, partner or parent whose duties have become compromised through the symptoms of anxiety. These situations of stress may cause or exacerbate the feelings of anxiety. Anxiety states are also well known to lead to substance misuse, especially alcohol and cannabis misuse, which may bring about complications including aggression and violent behaviour that attract the attention of the criminal law. Indeed, there is often suspicion that it is an individual's state of anxiety that has led him into some situation which, when it threatens to overwhelm that individual, leads to his lashing out in an attempt to protect himself from perceived assailants. Very anxious individuals may also react by attacking property or by harming themselves, actions which often lead to a dissipation, albeit temporary, of the anxiety experienced.

6.10   OBSESSIVE-COMPULSIVE DISORDER

A relatively uncommon neurosis but one which has become better appreciated in recent years is obsessive-compulsive disorder. This condition is characterised by obsessional thinking and/or compulsive actions. The former involves persistent and intrusive thoughts which are unwelcome to the patient, who attempts to resist them and yet fails. This is not to be confused with being preoccupied with some thought, a common enough and perfectly normal experience. Compulsions or rituals are their motor equivalents leading to repetitive, usually non-productive or inefficient, behaviour. The patient may spend many hours engaged in rituals of diverse kinds which are meaningless to the observer. The commonest feature among these patients involves repeated handwashing. Thoughts and actions of this kind involving a patient can cause immense distress to the patient and eventually lead to destruction of family, social and occupational life.

An obsessive-compulsive disorder may exist in its own right or it could be part of the symptomatology of a depressive illness. Also, as some forms of brain damage can cause the features of obsessions and compulsions to emerge, it is believed the locus for pathology in this condition exists somewhere in the brain (very severe forms of the disorder are one of the rare indications for modern psychosurgery which may achieve good results where all other treatment has failed). However, as with all neuroses, the personality of the patient cannot be ignored when evaluating this disorder, for a substantial majority of patients do have a pre-morbid obsessional personality which is characterised by a tendency to unusual orderliness and conscientious attention to detail, admirable characteristics in those in clerical or administrative occupation but not always tolerable when it forms the basis for pathology of this kind. It is common to see some stressful life event precipitating the neurosis in a susceptible individual who previously might only have displayed the features of an obsessional personality. Treatment involves both drugs and psychological approaches. Antidepressants, both of the SSRI group as well as the tricyclic agent clomipramine, have been shown to be useful. Behaviour therapy is also effective and a combination of drug and psychological treatment may well be the most effective approaches to the management of the condition. Untreated, there is risk of the condition becoming chronic. Treatment undertaken reasonably promptly after onset can achieve reasonably good results in the average case, although recurrence is not uncommon.

6.11   STRESS REACTIONS

While all neurotic conditions may generally be understood as being the reactions of vulnerable personalities to stress of some kind as perceived by them, stress reactions involve situations where the stress has been overwhelming or threatening in some way to the patient. It can be an acute reaction, arising immediately after the stressful event, or it could be delayed.

Acute stress reactions are emotional reactions that follow in close temporal proximity to some stressful event. The patient may become dazed or distressed with little recollection of the precipitating event and he could react by withdrawing himself or, conversely, by becoming excessively active. Many of the features of an acute anxiety state may be present. Treatment is by means of removing or alleviating the effects of the stressors, reassurance and a short course of medication which, in this instance, could be a member of the benzodiazepine group of drugs such as diazepam.

A more prolonged reaction to stress may lead to an adjustment disorder. The symptoms, similar to those found with the acute stress reactions, may last up to six months. There is a clearer presentation with symptoms such as anxiety and depression being present. Treatment approaches are similar, although the use of standard antidepressant drugs may be more appropriate than employment of the benzodiazepine group of drugs. Counselling may be offered in addition to reassurance.

A more serious form of stress reaction is what is commonly referred to as post-traumatic stress disorder (PTSD). The probably much overused diagnosis remains controversial. It is moot whether a severe acute anxiety state associated with depressive symptoms is truly distinguishable from what is called PTSD, and whether the latter term adds anything to an understanding of the severe emotional reactions which have been long been known to follow exceptionally traumatic events, eg 'shell shock'. PTSD follows serious trauma eg major disasters, violent personal assaults, grave road traffic accidents and its association with war continue with its modern description being born out of the Vietnam war. This condition may be defined as 'a delayed and/or protracted response to a stressful event or situation of an exceptionally threatening or catastrophic nature.' One of the commoner features of the condition is the tendency of patients to re-live the experiences of the traumatic event either in nightmares or as 'flashback' phenomena during their waking hours. There may be present the more usual symptoms of anxiety and depression along with a detachment displayed by the patient from ordinary concerns. There may also be avoidance of situations related to the precipitating trauma and the anxiety may provoke hypersensitivity to light and sound and cause also a startle response. There is a common association with misuse of alcohol and illicit drugs. If it is to be diagnosed at all, strict diagnostic guidelines should be followed.

Treatment of the condition, as previously mentioned, has raised surprising controversy given its widespread diagnosis in recent years. There is a place for drug treatment in the form of antidepressant agents such as paroxetine and sertraline. Cognitive behavioural therapy is known to be effective, especially in combination with drugs. The technique of eye movement, desensitisation and reprocessing (EMDR) in which the patient is encouraged to think of an image of the trauma while his eyes move from side to side has been claimed to be effective, but it is still not clear what form psychological intervention should take. The extensive 'debriefing' that was routinely practised soon after the victim had emerged in the immediate aftermath of the tragedy has been questioned in some quarters, with some holding this activity may tend to make things worse or even retard recovery. Some others have even gone as far as saying these victims should be left alone to recover with the help of their 'stiff upper lips'. The truth, no doubt, will appear in the course of time as to what, if any, approach should be taken, although clinical experience already suggests that, as with any clinical procedure, there should be a careful sifting of victims to see who is most likely to benefit from counselling. Statutory agencies, charities and commercial organisations often automatically offer their services to victims following traumatic events. Fearing litigation, some companies require their employees to undergo 'debriefing' following certain incidents. More promising are studies which show good results when the intervention was not offered to everyone indiscriminately but only to a minority with acute stress disorders who are at a higher risk of developing subsequent psychiatric disorders. The interventions in this successful situation involved multiple sessions and were based on a cognitive-behavioural model. Another study involved work with the Marines. All ranks had been offered simple training so that when disasters happened the 'therapist' and 'patient' shared a common culture and outlook which gets over the problem of using strangers unknown to the patient and invariably coming from another 'culture'. What form any mental disorder following trauma has taken is a matter for detailed clinical analysis rather than short hand diagnostic descriptions such as PTSD. What treatment, if any, should be given to the patient in these cases will depend on the precise delineation of symptoms present, the past history and an evaluation of the patient's previous personality, and not on any diagnosis alone. A study undertaken among service personnel found that PTSD and post-traumatic stress symptoms were not associated with consequent disability. Rather, it was the co-morbid symptoms of depression that were significantly associated with disability. The clinical importance of PTSD and post-traumatic stress symptoms may therefore become questionable if they are not a cause of disability.

The prognosis for stress reactions is in general good. An impaired prognosis is associated with delay in treatment, where there is misuse of substances following the reaction to stress and where there has been a delay in rehabilitation when in common with most psychiatric conditions of this type, a disabling secondary handicap can supervene.

Stress reactions can cause risk-associated behaviour to arise in many situations involving the law. The criminal law, family and child law, employment law and, of course, personal injury law may all become involved. These behaviours may involve aggression and violent conduct and it appears usually to be the case that it is the underlying anxiety that is responsible for the 'acting out' behaviours.

6.12   HYSTERIA

History justifies the inclusion of hysterical reactions in a book of this nature in that it has historical sanction and the condition, in its way, helped to define both neurology and psychiatry. The disorder involves unconscious mechanisms which, perhaps as a result of their subterranean presence, are far from clearly understood despite several years of study. There is undeniably a strong cultural and social background to the condition because gross examples of hysteria are now rare in the West, although still observable in many parts of the developing world and also in migrant communities in the developed world. Hysterical symptoms are usually diagnosed in the absence of so-called 'organic' features of illness. These symptoms, subdivided into dissociative symptoms and conversion symptoms, are therefore diagnosed by exclusion. Dissociative symptoms are believed to represent a loss of normal correspondence between different mental processes. Conversion refers to the translation of anxieties into physical symptoms. The short explanation to be proffered in seeking an understanding of this condition is to say that when a patient is confronted by unbearable and unresolvable anxiety as a result of some inner conflict, the unconscious mechanisms at work translate this conflict into physical symptoms, thereby giving the patient what is called primary gain through relief from anxiety. Secondary gain may then arise from any practical advantage to be accrued by sporting the symptom to the world. The symptoms in question are manifold and may include amnesia, wandering (the fugue state), stupor, trance and possession states, motor paralysis and sensory loss and, in extreme cases, multiple personality disorder. The other symptom of note is *la belle indifference* which refers to an apparent lack of concern shown by some patients towards their symptoms and is often regarded as being characteristic of conversion/ dissociative states. Recent studies, in fact, have shown that true 'organic' illness may underlie conversion symptoms and that this finding of indifference actually discriminates poorly between 'organic' and 'functional' symptoms. In fact, serious physical illness such as multiple sclerosis may initially present with symptoms which, as they often nonplus the clinician in the early stages of the disorder, are not uncommonly damned as being hysterical. Treatment is by way of intensive psychological investigation for which relatively few of these patients are suitable. Notwithstanding this, the results in the acute state ie where symptoms are short-lived may be surprisingly good, although recurrence is not uncommon.

6.13   SOMATOFORM DISORDERS

In this category exist those conditions where patients present with somatic or physical symptoms which have no obvious basis in a known physical disorder and which cannot be explained as being features of other psychiatric conditions such as depressive illness or anxiety states. The cultural background of the patient must be taken into account for, as stated before, it is common for patients from African and Asian communities to present with physical symptoms even when the underlying condition is one such a depressive illness.

The concern about physical symptoms may involve the presence of an illness or deformity or may involve only preoccupation about a symptom or some group of symptoms. By definition, these concerns or symptoms must have no basis in some obvious physical condition or be disproportionate in relation to some actual condition. Other psychiatric conditions involving mood changes, delusions or hysterical reactions need to be excluded. also. These conditions may appear to have a strong environmental bias in that deprivation or abuse in childhood or an upbringing by anxious parents may be risk factors.

Patients with hypochondriasis are preoccupied with the idea that they are suffering from a serious physical condition. Recurrent complaints of physical symptoms yield little or nothing by way of physical investigation which, in some of these cases, can be extensive and prolonged. There is no alternative to full investigation of these symptoms for the elusive 'real' cause of the symptoms; the skill comes in knowing when to put a stop to investigation and to resist the entreaties and importunities of the patient. Closely related to this condition is another where the preoccupation is with bodily appearance (dysmorphic disorder). The patient's life may become very restricted as a result of preoccupation with, say, the notion that one's nose is grossly misshapen and demands may be made for a referral for cosmetic surgery.

Closely related, at any rate in appearance, is the condition referred to as the chronic fatigue syndrome. The main complaint here is that of a persistent and disabling mental and physical fatigue. One cause of this condition appears to be myalgic encephalomyelitis (ME). As said repeatedly throughout this book, all these conditions are likely to have their origins in some form of brain dysfunction but present day knowledge does not as yet allow any formulation in those terms. This outcome appears to be especially upsetting to ME sufferers who, caught up in mediaeval distinctions between body and mind, actively resent and resist any suggestion their symptoms are 'all in the mind', implying that they are second class patients. Treatment of all these conditions is difficult. There appears to be some scope for antidepressant treatment although results with CBT, if and when accepted by patients, are often better. The prognosis is variable, better results being obtained in hypochondriacal states (where the patient may at least be persuaded to remain socially active despite the symptoms, with the help of apt references being made to public figures who discharge their functions despite suffering apparently disabling conditions) than with sufferers of the chronic fatigue syndrome where the preoccupation with proving a 'physical' basis is often associated with a poor outcome. For what it is worth, the overriding approach should be to encourage patients to lead as full and active a life as is possible.

6.14 SUMMARY

1.   The risk of developing any of the neurotic conditions is that they are due to, and their natural history is heavily influenced by, the personality of the individual concerned. As personality is for all practical purposes beyond any fundamental correction, treatment in many cases may only have a limited impact. A simple method for understanding these disorders is to consider them to be the result of an interaction between an individual's personality and his reaction to some stressful event. Where the personality is stable, and the impact of some discrete stressful event a relatively powerful one, the results from treatment appear to be appreciably better.

2.   Although the neurotic conditions are described as minor psychiatric
     disorders, their consequences can be serious. Both depressive illness
     and anxiety states are well known to lead to misuse of alcohol and
     illicit drugs, resulting in the individual's behaviour impinging on the
     subject matter of both the criminal law and family and child law.
     Chronic neurotic conditions may prove so disabling that sustained
     employment could be compromised. Obsessive-compulsive states
     could also become disabling with implications for an individual's
     overall functioning. The somatoform disorders may prove wasteful
     of resources including clinicians' time. Anxiety and depression, in
     particular, may be associated with aggressive and violent behaviour
     involving the patients suffering from the conditions described in this
     chapter. Whatever the diagnosis might be, if there is underlying
     anxiety, there may be scope for aggressive and violent conduct.

CHAPTER 7

DISORDERS OF DEPENDENCE AND APPETITE

Alcohol and illicit drug misuse have a clearly established relationship with aggressive and violent behaviour and must be studied in some detail. An entire work has previously been devoted to the psychiatric aspects of the misuse of these substances (Mahendra, 2008b). Substance abuse, the term used to collectively designate misuse of alcohol and illicit substances, is much misunderstood, which is paradoxical given the prominence the subject attracts in the media. One reason for this is that, despite the vast resources given to the study of the problem, objective scientific evidence in respect of many aspects of the difficulties concerning these substances is still sparse. We begin by considering some general aspects of substance misuse before dealing in turn with the individual substances.

7.1 SUBSTANCES AND THEIR MISUSE

The role of substance misuse in precipitating or contributing to aggressive and violent behaviour can hardly be denied. The issue of substance misuse must, however, be studied in a wider context if any impact is to be made in terms of public health. Mahendra (2008b) has given detailed consideration to the issue of substance misuse in psychiatric practice. In later sections of this chapter, individual substances of abuse will be considered but the importance of the subject is such, and so complex are the interactions between mental disorder, personality factors and the misuse of substances, that some general principles are discussed in this section in detail. Part of the difficulty faced with any campaign of information and control of these substances is due to the mixed nature of the substances that are commonly misused. Substance misuse is a worldwide problem. There is probably no country in the world, including those which prohibit alcohol for religious or cultural reasons, where there is no measure of difficulty with alcohol involving some individuals. It was ever thus. While the more glamorous substances of misuse may dominate the headlines, in every generation the greatest public health problems have arisen out of alcohol misuse and, indeed, the problems due to other substances often pale into insignificance compared to what is caused by alcohol, though alarm and despondency are caused in the public mostly by the abuse of other, often less well understood, substances.

There used to be a fashion to make a study with a view to determining those who might be most at risk of developing dependence on the substances of misuse. Groups were drawn up by social class, income, occupation, even religion and nationality. If there was any validity for these classifications in the past, there is none now, for all sections of any given community are now well represented in the ranks of those given to the misuse of substances. The control of substances has only been a legislative preoccupation for about a century. Before that there was generally a free and easy attitude to many of these substances (at any rate what the public was acquainted with for some of the substances discussed in this chapter had not been discovered or invented then) to the extent that they could form the basis for Imperial policy and also be fashion accessories in the *beau monde*. As will be seen, many of these substances, derived from wildly growing indigenous plants, had been consumed by the natives of those regions for centuries until civilisation discovered both these peoples and their substances. Cannabis, cocaine, mescaline and khat, among other substances, came to our attention in this way. As the world opened up, prosperity grew and boredom with existence became a luxury many, rather than the few, could afford, and substances began to be taken for recreation. It is true to say now that the study of substance misuse is one area where distinctions of class, colour, race and nationality have now more or less been eliminated.

Yet, there are individual variations. Some individuals have a clear predisposition to substance misuse. How much of this is genetic and how much could be due to the immediate environment is as problematical to unravel with substance misuse as it is with many other disorders. Twin studies (involving two individuals with the identical genetic endowment who have been separated at birth or soon after and brought up in different environments) have indicated that there is a definite albeit small component due to genetic factors accounting for later misuse, especially of alcohol. But the influence of the environment cannot be wholly ruled out. Every individual is affected for better or worse by influences arising from the home as well as the world outside. In the clinical situation, trying to separate out these effects is mostly a futile exercise. For every patient who misuses substances as his family has done before him, there is another in whom the family had particularly strong views against substances including alcohol with several forbears even engaged in the Temperance movement or its equivalents.

The control of substances is now, of course, a major political issue. As with all transactions there is a supply side and a demand side to the equation. Much has been said about the supply side with attempts to control supply through law enforcement. Some radical views have even been expressed about the possibility of abolishing all control and leaving the market to determine the nature and scope of transactions. These matters were discussed briefly by Mahendra (2008b) when it was shown that superficially attractive though some of these notions might be, the matter is complex and not without further risk and complications. The demand side is less often in the headlines, but a few moments of thought will remind one that it is perhaps the more important side of this equation involving supply and demand. If there was no demand there will be no supply. It is not easy nowadays to find an abacus for purchase when the world is dominated by personal computers and pocket calculators and anyone needing to undertake arithmetical calculations has access to these. There have been laudable attempts to educate the public and inform them of the risks of substance misuse but the results have not been commensurate with the efforts made. Except for those cases where dependence has been caused by inappropriate (usually) medical treatment, most cases of substance abuse which have reached problematical dimensions arise out of some persistence of use. It is rare to find dependence arising out of single use of any substance, although the opiate drugs have long been believed to carry the risk of this phenomenon. Some persistence of use is therefore necessary and the essential question is why individuals are drawn to such persistent use. Many explanations could be offered, including those concerning the relatively low cost, ready supply and social pressures. But rarely is an individual forced to use a substance which must mean there must be internal factors driving problematical substance use. It seems from clinical observation that if an individual finds greater satisfaction from the use of a substance and greater enjoyment of the social settings in which these substances are often used than in the usual forms of emotional satisfactions and the pleasures of the senses, then he or she will persist in the kind of use that could lead to harmful results concerning his or her functioning. This matter often comes up in family and child practice where surprise is often expressed that a spouse, partner or parent could find greater satisfaction in a substance than in family life, or at any rate is unable to give priority to the latter over the use of a substance. Some families find a *modus vivendi* in relation to a substance that is being misused, although it is not wholly satisfactory when a marriage becomes crowded involving as it does a husband, a wife and the bottle. These brief few words can do scant justice to the greatest challenge facing those attempting to control misuse of substances, namely, the emotional make up of individuals who are vulnerable to misuse. Unless we can do something about the inner satisfactions of individuals and the means by which these are expressed or sought, measures of control are likely to prove futile, for even the most repressive of regimes have failed to eliminate the misuse of substances.

7.2 SUBSTANCE MISUSE – CLINICAL AND BEHAVIOURAL FEATURES

A book of this nature will, of course, dedicate most of its space to a consideration of matters of clinical interest and this is duly done in the sections that follow. How these effects arise is still not known for certain.

They must originate in the brain, of course, for there is no other source of origin. We cannot, however, be sure which parts of the brain are definitely involved but we do know that neurotransmitters – those chemicals which help mediate mood and other functions – are affected in diverse ways when substances enter the system and reach the brain. It also appears to be the case that the chemicals involved in the brain are also those which have been implicated in common forms of mental disorders such as schizophrenia and depressive illness. That is useful to know and helps explain the overlap between the behaviours arising out of use of substances and the symptoms due to naturally occurring mental disorders. We shall later speak of 'depressive equivalents', a phrase which indicates, especially when it comes to the misuse of alcohol, that an individual who could have taken to drink has instead become depressed and, of course, *vice versa*. This phenomenon is easy to understand if chemicals common to both conditions have become aberrant in their functioning. The situation is complicated by the finding that substances such as cannabis may carry within them not only the chemicals which are believed to cause the well known effects due to this substance but also, so to speak, the antidote by way of other chemicals. It appears possible that it is the proportion in the substance of the more toxic element that determines the severity of the symptoms arising, in the case of cannabis this element being tetrahydrocannabinol (THC).

7.3   ASSESSMENT AND INVESTIGATION OF SUBSTANCE MISUSE

The assessment of substance misuse and the disorders arising is essentially a clinical exercise. What one looks for are not merely the signs and symptoms that follow misuse of one or more of the relevant substances, but also the impact these substances have made on all aspects of an individual's functioning. Where the civil law is concerned, its usual interest, in cases involving the individual as spouse, partner, parent or employee, is how such an individual's levels of functioning could have been impaired through the misuse of substances. The criminal law may be interested in the mere fact of use (or of possession, preparation or distribution) and also in knowing how the mental state in terms of the *mens rea* required to commit an offence could have been affected. An individual's habitual day-to-day functioning is not usually the criminal law's concern; it is much more interested in specific incidents. The clinical assessment of substance misuse is usually undertaken in the overall context of a comprehensive clinical psychiatric assessment.

There is considerable – some may say, even on occasion, an uncritical – interest in the laboratory investigations of the evidence for substances in the body as an indication of their consumption. Substances, once ingested or otherwise administered, will be metabolised and then excreted from the body, usually through the breath or urine. They will upon use find their way into the blood stream and then onto the brain where they exert their effects. A residue of the substance may be stored for shorter or longer periods in tissues such as the hair. They may, therefore, be of considerable forensic interest, especially in the criminal law where the absolute values found in the breath or blood are of capital importance in cases of driving a motor vehicle under the influence of substances. The law has set limits for the lawful presence, say, of alcohol in the breath and blood and any excess would normally form the basis for a conviction for an offence. For some years now the presence of levels of substances found in the breath, blood and hair have been admissible as evidence in the courts, both criminal and civil. The presence of substances in the hair is of particular interest, as this presence may be prolonged when compared to the transient presence of the substance in the breath, blood or urine. The evidence of the consumption of a substance may be traced back up to a year if the length of hair used in the analysis is adequate for this purpose. It is more usual to try to detect use over 90 days and 180 days.

Laboratory investigation of substance misuse has other uses. Hair strand analysis, as it is called, was first used in sport in 1998 for drug testing at the Tour de France, an event now notorious for drug-related scandals and also for drug-related deaths among the participants. Drug misuse is now a major concern in most sport. However, as will be discussed below, the sporting authorities do not appear to be at one when it comes to the mode of testing for drugs, in particular regarding the standing of hair strand analysis.

The procedure employed in the laboratory for hair strand testing is an essentially simple one. The strand of hair, collected from the individual who is the subject of the assessment, is washed to rid it of any contaminants. It is then placed in a solvent and the substance under investigation is then extracted from this solution and subject to analysis. The analytical procedure used is gas chromatography/mass spectrometry. The results obtained find widespread use in the criminal law and also in family and child practice where parents, involved as parties in both public law and private law Children Act 1989 cases, are routinely subject to hair strand analysis for evidence of misuse of substances. It is also finding increasing use in the sphere of employment where employers seek the use of this device to screen employees before and also in the course of employment. Hair strand analysis has been called by its advocates the 'gold standard' for cases coming to the courts, especially those involving children. However, this enthusiasm is apparently not shared by others including, it seems, the World Anti-Doping Agency (WADA) whose rules govern international sport including the Olympic games. In their view hair testing is not considered to be of sufficient reliability for application as part of anti-doping measures employed in sport, according to the experts they have consulted.

Clinicians also remain sceptical of the value of any free-standing laboratory test to detect substance misuse. As will be discussed later, their primary use is an adjunct to the overall clinical assessment and management of any patient. While they have an obvious place in the criminal justice system, their status is less clear in family and child practice where it is not so much the presence of the substance or the amount used as the impact of the use on the individual that is of crucial importance. These tests may also have value in the therapeutic management of substance misuse but saliva, urine and blood tests, which are substantially cheaper to use, are preferred to routine hair strand testing in this setting. With all laboratory testing, the issues of reliability and the possibility of false positive and false negative results must also be borne in mind. It is a matter for concern that many of those involved in the interpretation of laboratory findings, especially in family and child practice, have so little by way of any scientific background. As a general rule it could be said that no one who has not had experience of even a few days in a laboratory should attempt to interpret any finding coming out of a laboratory.

7.4   MANAGEMENT OF SUBSTANCE MISUSE DISORDERS

The term management is infinitely more accurate than the word treatment when it is applied to the help given to those suffering from the substance misuse disorders. There is, in fact, very little specific treatment to be offered to those misusing substances. When complications due to substance misuse arise, there may be scope for offering treatment in the usual way to control these symptoms of some complicating psychiatric disorder, but drug treatment is generally reserved for the treatment of the withdrawal states arising on cessation of use of substances on which an individual has become physically dependent, for maintenance treatment such as by methadone or in attempts at prevention of relapse as may be tried in cases of alcohol misuse. Management, on the other hand, involves a wider ambit of therapeutic involvement. Any estimation or evaluation of the form of therapies offered in cases of substance misuse disorders is bedevilled by the fact that so much turns on the using individual's motivation to come off and stay off these substances. In the last analysis no one else can decide whether an individual is to use or refuse substances. Apart from the prohibitions the law provides generally against the possession, preparation and distribution of illicit substances, there is no compulsion available unless a court imposes a sanction on conviction which makes treatment and rehabilitation a necessary part of the sentence or in the occasional case where substance misuse has led to mental disorder which brings an individual's condition within the scope of the compulsory provisions of the Mental Health Act 2007. As far as alcohol is concerned, there is very little available by way of preventing consumption even in excess; indeed, in recent years access to this already freely available and lawful substance has been further eased by the liberalisation of controls and regulations.

There is small evidence that professional therapeutic involvement with those individuals misusing substances could bring some benefit. There is controversy as to which form of these psychosocial interventions could be of greatest value. It seems possible that it is the fact of contact rather than anything more specific by way of therapy that could be the crucial element. An individual who goes to the trouble of maintaining contact with his therapists – even attending at some local centre is often beyond the capabilities of many of these individuals – may well lead to such individuals being more receptive to advice and exhortation. Rehabilitation through organisations such as Alcoholics Anonymous and similar organisations is of proven benefit in some cases. Those who are committed to helping themselves through such organisations are already self-selected and are usually also of a cast of mind which can be influenced by the atmosphere of the confessional such organisations exist in. Some 30 years ago a study showed that in cases of alcohol misuse plain advice given to individuals who had been abusing the substance was as good as any involved therapeutic endeavour. It cannot be said with any great conviction that matters have moved further ahead in the generation that has followed.

7.5 PROGNOSIS IN SUBSTANCE MISUSE

The term 'prognosis' when applied to cases of substance misuse is probably even less meaningful than the term 'treatment'. 'Prognosis' is strictly a concept which is attached to some disease condition which has a natural history which can be altered to some extent by the efforts of a therapist who deploys some specific treatment directed at that condition. The crucial requirement is that a patient's attitudes to treatment – apart from, of course, refusing to co-operate with treatment – must not play such a part that it comes to determine the course of the condition itself. It is easy enough to see that a depressed patient, provided he takes the medication given to him, could have some hope of some physical agent influencing the course of that illness. In cases of substance misuse the greatest influence on the condition of misuse is the personality and the attitude of the individual engaged in the misuse. So great are the imponderables involved that it is virtually impossible to predict how any individual presenting for treatment will fare with the regime. One may never see him after the first day when the initial assessment of him was undertaken or he could turn out to be a faithful attender at sessions and one who goes on to achieve abstinence and its successful maintenance. Clinicians play safe by demanding a period of abstinence (or of controlled drinking) before essaying any kind of prediction concerning the outcome, being safely of the knowledge that the longer the period of abstinence, the greater the likelihood of a successful outcome after a period of, say, two years. But these are only probabilities and an individual can relapse at any time. This raises two issues which are of value to appreciate. The first of these is that a patient's personal circumstances are beyond the reach of even the most skilled and dedicated therapist and these circumstances can often have an overwhelming influence on substance using habits. Little can be done with even the most promising of candidates being offered treatment if they lose their employment owing to an economic downturn or they are beset by separation, divorce or bereavement. It is a not uncommon finding that achieving a settled life is the pre-requisite to achieving abstinence in respect of misused substances, a finding also made in cases of personality disorder where the mental state usually reflects the storm or calm affecting the individual's life. The second point to make is that there are respected workers in the field of substance misuse who hold that a tendency to substance misuse is a life long affliction and that one can only speak of exacerbations and remissions affecting any individual who has become dependent on these substances. In other words, however fair the weather has been and for however long, a tempest can break out in these cases at any time and wreak havoc again.

7.6   RISKS ASSOCIATED WITH SUBSTANCE MISUSE

The risks arising to the physical and mental health of individuals who engage or persist in the misuse of substances will be discussed in detail in the succeeding sections of this chapter. But there is now also growing concern with the untoward incidents that may involve the substance-misusing individual. The overall functioning of these individuals may be substantially impaired by the misuse. Their functioning as spouses, partners and parents may be so adversely affected that it becomes an issue in proceedings concerning family and child law. Their duties as an employee may be so compromised that disciplinary sanctions and even dismissal may follow. These patients also have a calculable tendency to precipitate accidents in a variety of settings. The role of alcohol as a factor in road traffic accidents has been long studied and interest in the subject of substance misuse-related accidents now also encompasses other substances. A study of the possible role of cannabis in causing fatal road traffic accidents has led to these risks being better appreciated and it must only be a matter of time before other substances are also studied in a similar vein. The risk of violence involving individuals engaged in the misuse of substances is also a matter of concern to the public and those who govern them. There is very little doubt that indulgence in most substances can lead to an increased incidence of violent acts, but it is too simplistic to seek the sole cause of violence in the nature of these chemicals alone. There are very powerful personal, social and cultural factors also in play and which must be studied with care if a full understanding of the problem is to be achieved. If a man having consumed alcohol, perhaps in excess, attacks another man, it is no doubt correct to say the disinhibiting properties of alcohol have been at work, but although alcohol is a necessary cause it is by no means a sufficient cause in producing violence. Two men who have drunk the same quantities of alcohol do not necessarily behave in an identical fashion. It is their personalities and their social and cultural backgrounds that determine how they will behave in particular situations when under the influence of any disinhibiting substance.

7.7   MEDICO-LEGAL SITUATIONS INVOLVING SUBSTANCE MISUSE

The substances commonly misused are all psycho-active substances and will therefore have effects on the brain and through that organ on behaviour. The law's concern is with any individual's behaviour resulting from the use and misuse of these substances. Both the civil law and the criminal law can be engaged by this behaviour. Among matters of interest to the civil law is that concerning the capacity possessed by these individuals to make proper decisions regarding what the law refers to as 'their property and affairs'. Substance misuse may lead to mental disorder but mental disorder not uncommonly also leads to the misuse of substances, it being well-acknowledged that mentally disordered individuals commonly resort to substance misuse. The criminal law's interest is somewhat in a different dimension. There is no general exculpation offered by the law to any individual who has committed an offence while under the influence of substances. In general terms, using these substances, especially on a voluntary basis, while committing an offence will constitute an aggravating circumstance surrounding the offence. Conversely, if use has been involuntary – by means of 'spiked' or 'laced' drinks or through using prescribed medication – even if an offence has been committed these circumstances may provide significant mitigation. The key special issue for the law is whether the *mens rea* required to commit an issue has been impaired in some way by a defendant's misuse of substances so as to suggest that the individual concerned could not have been fully responsible. The law does not proceed by means only of logical analysis in these situations but takes into account matters of public interest and safety by way of public policy. Broadly speaking, the law is prepared to grant that an individual who is intoxicated or is otherwise under the influence of a substance could have been impaired to such an extent that his capacity to form specific or ulterior intent may be lacking. That leaves the capacity to form basic intent intact and this still allows an impressive range of offences to be committed with a corresponding range of sentences available to the court.

7.8   ALCOHOL

Alcohol is easily the most widely used of the common intoxicants. Some 90 per cent of the British public use the substance while the figure for the United States is around 60 per cent, a preliminary indication of the differences between cultures in the use of alcohol. While alcohol-related problems are far commoner than those associated with illicit substances, the extent of alcohol misuse is not known with any certainty. Up to 10 per cent of the British public are perhaps heavy consumers of alcohol, if one takes the recommended 'safe' limits (see below) as being 21 units per week for the adult male and 14 units per week for an adult female as the guide. An example was given (Mahendra, 2006) of how even a teetotaller or novice could get caught up in a variety of complications associated with even a one-off heavy use and come to display the features of alcohol-related problems. The example also illustrated the importance of looking at the facts in any individual case. It is not always the quantity of alcohol or drug abused or the prolonged history of misuse that may be in point, but the behaviours engaged in by the individual and which are recorded in the facts of the case. A practical definition, based upon one given by the World Health Organization itself, is that abuse of alcohol occurs in those who drink excessively to such an extent that alcohol use has attained a degree which shows noticeable disturbance or an interference with their bodily and mental health, their personal relationships and smooth economic functioning or who show prodromal signs of such a development and, therefore, require treatment.

7.9   ALCOHOL – THE EFFECTS

There are various categories of misuse of alcohol. The simplest to understand is intoxication which is an acute effect of consuming too much (for a particular individual). There is then 'at risk' consumption where physical, mental or social harm may follow from persistently exceeding the recommended 'safe' limits. This may also be called hazardous use of alcohol. Then comes harmful use where, in the absence of dependence or addiction, there is misuse associated with health and social consequences. Thereafter comes true addiction. Alcohol can cause physical dependence. By this is meant tolerance has developed, in other words, more and more needs to be drunk to obtain the same behavioural effect. This also means a hardened drinker can consume considerable quantities before showing signs of intoxication whereas someone like the novice mentioned above needs only a few drinks before showing obvious changes in behaviour. Next, there may be withdrawal effects in the absence of sufficient alcohol in the system which include tremor, agitation, sweating, nausea, irritability and feelings of anxiety and panic along with a craving for more drink. These withdrawal symptoms can be quelled by drinking a sufficient quantity of alcohol which leads to a vicious circle being brought into operation. Regular drinking to avoid the symptoms of withdrawal sets in, the individual becomes preoccupied with drinking and drink-related behaviour. Soon, if measures are not taken to curb the consumption of alcohol, drinking becomes the primary activity in the individual's life at the expense of all others.

Physical and mental effects follow persistent drinking. Bodily effects include damage to the liver. At first, fat infiltrates the liver cells. Later, the liver shrinks with the onset of cirrhosis. Alcoholic hepatitis may present itself. If drinking continues in these circumstances the liver may fail altogether in its functions, and coma and death supervene. If abstinence can be brought about, and sustained, repair of the liver can take place for the organ has remarkable powers of recovery and regeneration. Effects may also be seen in the gastro-intestinal system with oesophageal and peptic ulceration. Bleeding from oesophageal varices leads to the well-known symptom of vomiting of blood in these patients, who also eliminate dark coloured faeces (melaena) as the blood present in the gut helps turn it in the course of its passage through the bowel. Heart and circulatory problems may also follow with an enlarged heart and elevated blood pressure in consequence. Considerable disturbance may also be seen in both the central and peripheral nervous systems. Effects on the brain may lead to blackouts, amnesia and fits. Peripheral neuropathy may give rise to motor and sensory deficits along with paralysis later on. It is no exaggeration to say that every bodily function may be adversely affected through persistent alcohol abuse.

Running in parallel are the mental complications due to persistent alcohol abuse. The symptoms due to states of withdrawal have been noted above. Fits may follow as well as the dangerous and potentially lethal condition called *delirium tremens* in which consciousness fluctuates and, classically, visual hallucinations involving usually small animals (rats or insects) but occasionally larger creatures ('pink elephants') are seen. Fleeting persecutory ideas may be present. Alcoholic psychosis of a more sustained kind may also be seen later. There is a notorious connection between alcohol and depression. Alcohol is a depressant, a fact not always recognised by those who see mainly its disinhibiting properties. The depression it induces leads usually to more drinking in an attempt to dull the senses and, thereby, more depression ensues which means there is another vicious circle also in operation. About 10 per cent of patients with alcohol dependence commit suicide. Sexual dysfunction ('it provokes the desire but takes away the performance') and deterioration in personality and social functioning are common consequences. The impact on social life can prove considerable. Apart from involvement with the criminal law, there are also consequences for employment, and accidents are commoner in these individuals. The impact on family life may also be substantial. The risks involved with misuse of alcohol will be taken up later.

7.10   ALCOHOL – THE RISK FACTORS FOR MISUSE

Despite many years of intensive study, those at risk of developing alcohol-related problems cannot be pinpointed with any accuracy. There is a clear genetic factor, but this generally shows a predisposition not only to alcohol abuse but also to depressive illness, in other words there may be 'alcohol equivalents', a predisposed individual going on to suffer depressive illness rather than having problems with alcohol. Environmental factors are dominant influences. Cultural influences may also play a part. In rural communities alcohol was used for the purpose of celebration, especially at the time of the gathering in of the harvest. As society industrialised, grew more urban and prospered, the form of alcohol-related problems became more uniform. There may also be racial differences in the way alcohol is metabolised and in the occurrence of phenomena such as hangovers and withdrawal effects which could lead to excessive drinking in some communities. There seems no doubt that the ready availability of alcoholic beverages in the community can contribute significantly to an increased prevalence of problems concerning alcohol misuse. Economic factors are also important. It has been shown that alcohol has become cheaper in 'real terms' over time, making its routine use within the reach of most pockets. Thus, there seems to be a close relationship between *per capita* alcohol consumption and alcohol-related problems and an inverse correlation between the 'real price of drink' (as a percentage of average disposable income) and national *per capita* consumption of alcohol. Finland is among several countries where relaxation of previously restrictive licensing laws had been shown to cause significant increases in alcohol consumption. As the recent debate on the relaxation of the licensing laws showed, there are also quite considerable cultural and sub-cultural influences at work. As has been repeatedly pointed out, the patterns of drinking in Continental Europe are appreciably different to those found in Britain. In those countries there is still much stigma attached to public drunkenness (whose manifestations, even without disorderly conduct, attract official sanctions in those parts) and there appears to be an altogether socially more appropriate and responsible to the consumption of alcohol compared to the excesses which habitually mark and disfigure British life.

There is no hard and fast rule pointing to any community or group that may be preferentially at risk of developing alcohol-related problems. Social change had rendered out of date the assertions that certain occupations – bar staff, journalists, manual workers, mariners – were preferentially at higher risk. Clinical practice reveals virtually all trades and professions now represented, not to mention those who have no occupation. The professional bodies concerned with both doctors and lawyers have expressed their alarm at the prevalence of alcohol-related problems among their members and have established forms of assistance for those affected. One striking social change is the presence now among problem drinkers of women and, increasingly, younger children, among the ranks of the problem drinkers. The advice, which is somewhat conservative in its import it has to be admitted, as to what might constitute 'safe' drinking allows 21 units of alcohol per week for adult males and 14 units of alcohol for adult females. Common observation shows that large numbers of individuals comfortably exceed the conservative limits proposed and suffer no discernible harm. Even the consumption of a bottle of wine a day – easily achievable in the circumstances of modern life – may mean the individual concerned may be consuming more than three times the recommended limit if a man and up to five times the limit if a woman. What constitutes a unit of alcohol is not without controversy. A half pint of standard bitter beer, a measure of spirits or a glass of wine were conventionally deemed to make up a unit of alcohol. But this assumption has been undermined by the growing alcoholic strength of beverages and also by social and cultural change such as the growing preference for New World wine and lager beer which may be much stronger in alcohol strength than the counterpart beverages. It seems a matter of urgency that more realistic advice is proffered to citizens if mass disobedience, seemingly openly practised, is to be corrected.

7.11 ALCOHOL – TREATMENT

The actual treatment is more problematical than allowed for by many lay persons. The truth is that there is little by way of any specific treatment for alcohol-related problems. What there is is advice and support to assist such a person to bring his problems under control. It is *par excellence* a problem which requires self help. It follows that the single most important determinant of success in treatment is the motivation and attitude shown by the individual. Without this, all help will be futile and will fail. The patient must accept with true insight – mere lip service is insufficient – that he or she has a problem with alcohol and has to take steps to counter this problem and bring it under control. This means the patient must also feel he or she has the necessary incentive to turn over a new leaf.

Results of treatment of alcohol misuse are far from satisfactory. Where dependency exists, the first requirement is detoxification, by which means alcohol is leached from the system through abstinence. This can be achieved in the community but a hospital setting is favoured when community detoxification has previously failed and in cases in which intercurrent physical or psychiatric conditions are also found. Detoxification may be supported through treatment with benzodiazepine drugs such as chlordiazepoxide. Vitamins are prescribed as ancillary agents to forestall some neurological complications that may follow withdrawal. That, in most cases, is the easy part of the management. The altogether more challenging task is to maintain the state of abstinence or of controlled drinking. Some drugs may be of use – disulfiram and acamprosate are two of the agents used – but the treatment at this stage is predominantly psychological. Support and advice are the key elements. Cognitive behavioural therapy, social skills training and motivational enhancement may assist.

There appears also to be considerable interest in objective indices of alcohol abuse. Liver function tests are commonly utilised for this purpose. As a snapshot of current heavy drinking they may have some use but their limitations must be understood. Increased liver enzymes, in the absence of liver disease or concurrent medication, may be indicative of heavy persistent drinking. But the liver, as we have seen, has substantial powers of recuperation and regeneration and absence of disordered liver function may denote little more than a temporary period of abstinence. There is little alternative to taking a holistic view in relation to any patient suspected of heavy drinking, clinical observation being supplemented by the reports of witnesses. Heavy drinking, in itself, can be concealed but its effects – on domestic life, child care, social activity, occupation – can rarely be kept hidden over any period of time. Any deficiency in behaviour will usually be apparent if observation continues long enough.

Too much emphasis is often laid on the 'treatment' aspect of management of alcohol-related problems. In truth, specific help by means of pharmacological treatment is very limited, being reserved for some select and exceptional cases, and has no application in the vast majority of cases seen in practice. Treatment therefore ordinarily means counsel, advice and support deployed through community-based agencies. Counselling provided by public agencies may be complemented with attendance at Alcoholics Anonymous, an organisation that is sometimes mocked but which has a useful ancillary part to play in assisting the motivated patient with his rehabilitation.

7.12   ALCOHOL – THE PROGNOSIS

Since the disease concept of alcoholism is largely a matter of form and convenience, and the specific medical element in any treatment is so small, it is a somewhat artificial exercise to talk of prognosis in any accepted medical sense. However, over a period of years, clinicians have utilised their experience of these cases and the accumulated knowledge to arrive at a 'rule of thumb'. It is believed two years usually have to elapse – involving either abstinence or controlled drinking – before one can sign off a patient as being 'cured' of the disease of alcoholism, albeit perhaps only for the time being. The danger period is in the early phase of abstinence. Nobody knows for certain how many fall off the wagon – that is, they drop out of treatment – but it is believed that in the first six months following abstinence some 50 per cent of patients will relapse. There are those who argue that a tendency to alcohol misuse is a life-long affliction and that as a result one can only speak of remissions and exacerbations. Be that as it may, the patient has to show evidence that he has attained mastery over drink, however temporarily. Whether he can aim for controlled drinking in the future rather than settle for the somewhat monastic existence (probably a misnomer as monks have traditionally been enthusiastic brewers of beer and, no doubt, also consumers of the product of their labours) involving total abstinence is usually determined entirely on an individual basis, by trial and error in most cases, and there can be no hard and fast rule as to who could aim for moderate social drinking and who should aim for abstinence for life. Some individuals will not be able to touch another drop, others may be able to develop a much more socially appropriate *modus vivendi* with alcohol. It is one of those decisions that patient and counsellor need to work out following a course of treatment.

Once alcohol has been defeated, on however short term a basis, the patient needs to be reassessed in terms of his mental state. Alcohol can mask many problems and once it is out of the picture one may be able to see if there remain difficulties such as depressive illness, anxiety states, chronic pain etc which might have induced, or contributed to, the original bout of heavy drinking. It is obviously more rational to treat any underlying condition which might have been a significant causative factor in the previous drinking in its own right rather than leave the patient at risk of relapse into further drinking. More ordinary social repair work can also be contemplated for such matters as marital or relationship difficulties, financial problems, poor housing or occupational concerns.

In the ultimate analysis, any prognosis to be given, as might be expected, is very variable. The only valid point to make is that if there is any underlying problem, and if this remains or recurs, the danger of relapse could be high. In the end one is reduced to saying that if the patient derives greater satisfaction from alcohol – or, at any rate, greater relief from emotional pain from drinking – than from more normal social pursuits and satisfactions, then he may have greater incentive to take or return to drinking. On the other hand, if the physical and mental well being associated with a freedom from excessive drinking enables him to pursue worthwhile and rewarding social goals, it is likely the balance will shift in the opposite direction. The concerned professional, confronted with a patient or client with alcohol-related problems will do well to see how the balance sheet in respect of these matters reads.

7.13   ILLICIT DRUGS

There are many drugs that are in common use. Greater detail as regards their properties will be found in Mahendra (2008b, *op cit*). Some of these drugs include those which are legitimately prescribed and have genuine medical properties for use in those for which there is a need for them to be prescribed but which, occasionally, find their way in large quantities into the hands of patients (whether those for whom they were originally prescribed or others). We are not here concerned with these prescribed drugs. Rather, we shall concentrate our attentions here on cannabis, the opiate drugs, the amphetamines and cocaine which, in the public eye and in respect of public health, are the illicit drugs, so to speak, of substance. The problem involving illicit substances is not at all uncommon. It has been estimated that at least three per cent of the population, that is about two million people in Britain, will take illicit drugs at any given time. In the nature of things this figure is likely to be an underestimate. Apart from causing the mental and behavioural consequences of misuse in their own right their association with mental disorder (co-morbidity, as it is called) is significant. More than 40 per cent of patients managed by community mental health teams reported problem drug use and/or harmful alcohol use among the patients in the previous year. The implications for aggressive and violent behaviour are obvious. The general perception among professionals is that co-morbidity has a much greater impact on services than its single components with increased psychiatric admission, violence and poor treatment outcomes.

7.14   CANNABIS

This is probably the most commonly used of the illicit drugs. It is used as marijuana, hashish and ganja and consumed on virtually every continent on the globe. It is imported from the tropics (an area said to be increasing in extent on account of climate change) although *cannabis sativa*, the hemp plant from which these substances are derived, can be grown with success in Britain and *aficionados* of the drug relish the superior quality of the home-grown product. The main psychoactive component is delta-9-tetrahydrocannabinol (THC) which acts on susceptible receptors in the brain. Cannabis is usually smoked neat or combined with tobacco, but can also be eaten on its own or after being baked into cakes and biscuits. Its fumes have a distinctive odour when smoked, nowadays to be considered as part of the smells of the street. It has been a drug which has been used in some cultures for centuries and has the status of a staple recreational agent much as tobacco used to have elsewhere. Its effects are very variable and dependent on the purity of the source, the amount taken, the route through which it is absorbed, the personality of the consumer and the social and cultural expectations in play. In cultures where its use is traditional it is accepted as a relaxant and as an aid to social intercourse and conviviality. It has a tendency to exaggerate the mood existing at the time of consumption – the calm become mellow, the forceful more aggressive. There may be a tendency to distort space and time and judgement may be impaired in relation to many matters including motor performance (the word used in its widest sense to include vehicular propulsion). In some users, increased anxiety may progress to agitation and even paranoid behaviour. However, it has long also been associated with apathy and lack of motivation, and debate has raged as to whether it is the laid-back individual who is drawn to its use or if the drug itself induces feelings of relaxed indifference and insouciance. These effects are deemed to be psychological and it is not clear whether physical dependence can also arise as with alcohol or the opiate drugs.

There have been reports of pulmonary complications following prolonged use, though confirmation of this is awaited. However, what is of renewed psychiatric interest is the implication of cannabis in cases of psychotic breakdown where it has been alleged that the drug can precipitate or induce psychotic symptoms in a predisposed individual. Similar claims have also been made for the precipitation of violence following its use. Neither the inducement of psychosis nor the production of violence is a universal feature and it appears to be the case that a susceptibility, probably of the genetic kind, is required as a pre-condition for psychosis and/or violence to arise. Concurrent other substance misuse may also be a contributory factor. Nevertheless, it is probably true to say the drug is by no means as benign as claimed by those who campaigned for its decriminalisation, a revised point of view now seemingly accepted by the authorities who fear another problem drug may have fallen into their hands and are now preparing to advance its status back to being a Class B substance, the category it occupied until it was relegated to being a Class C substance.

7.15   THE OPIATE DRUGS

Like many drugs that are now abused socially, the opiates have had a parallel history of having been very valuable weapons in the medical armamentarium for decades. Morphine, heroin (diamorphine) and codeine along with synthetic derivatives such as pethidine and dextropropoxyphene continue to have legitimate medical use. Opium has, of course, been used and abused for centuries and a sub-culture of abusers, some intellectuals, others mere addicts, has existed probably in every age and in every society. The most important illicit use nowadays concerns heroin which finds its way into the streets of Britain from origins in Afghanistan and Pakistan (an important reason for the maintenance of the current war in the former country). As with cocaine, commerce is difficult to control in large part because of the importance of the substance to the local economies; intricate networks of supply supplemented by the financial infrastructure needed to support the trade are in place. The effects of the drug are virtually indistinguishable from those seen when it is used in some form in legitimate medical practice, save for the complications due to contaminants. Purity is variable and when a pure supply of the drug occasionally hits the streets many deaths not uncommonly occur as users do not allow for the strength of the uncontaminated product when they unwittingly consume it. The drug may be smoked, inhaled or injected. Dependence of the physical type can supervene – sometimes following single use – and withdrawal effects are similar to those seen in alcohol deprivation with an added element of more intense craving, a state in which the individual is prepared to sacrifice everything, including his liberty and even his life, in the pursuit of the drug. The feelings experienced on use include euphoria. With chronic use there could be malaise (which may lead to repeated use in an attempt to regain the experience of euphoria), loss of appetite and interest and libido, constipation and the tell-tale sign of pinpoint pupils. Tolerance is usual as in all substances leading to physical dependence. The euphoric feeling which follows its immediate use is difficult to replicate with the same repeated dose, so the amount taken needs to be increased, resulting in the phenomenon of tolerance. Death follows overdose which leads to respiratory depression. Other complications include the high risk of infections and thrombosis following intravenous use. The use of needles also leads to the risk of contracting hepatitis B and C and HIV infections.

In general the severity and length of withdrawal depends on the nature of the drug being abused, shorter acting drugs tending to have more severe withdrawal symptoms over shorter periods as compared to longer acting drugs. The symptoms noted on withdrawal may include anxiety and agitation, sleeplessness, sweating, muscle pains and cramps, diarrhoea and vomiting, dilated pupils, a running nose and a sense of feeling cold. The onset of withdrawal symptoms is usually within 8–12 hours of the last dose, with the most intense withdrawal symptoms experienced over 24–48 hours and subsiding over 7–10 days.

The opiates, when used outside of medical supervision, are as socially destructive as any substance that can be imagined and life expectancy used to be drastically reduced in untreated cases, quite apart from the complications arising from infections due to contaminated needles, intercurrent infection and concurrent medical disorders. Two thirds of heroin users have had drug overdoses and a third of them have done so in the previous year. Part of the reason attributed to this is that, as we have seen, the purity of heroin can vary so that, especially when injecting, the exact dose being taken is unpredictable. It has also been suggested as an alternative explanation that a near-death experience may form part of the desired euphoric effect due to heroin. Methadone overdose has also been reported to be on the increase.

7.16   AMPHETAMINES

These drugs also had legitimate medical use in the days before standard antidepressant drugs came into being to elevate the mood in depressive illness and more recently for conditions such as attention deficit hypercativity disorder (ADHD) and narcolepsy. It is freely available on the streets nowadays – methyl amphetamine use is now said to be the biggest public health hazard in terms of illicit drug use – and its commonplace nature sometimes leads to these drugs being treated with disdain and contempt among the authorities. Its effects are initially to produce euphoria along with the appearance of increased physical and mental energy. However, persecutory ideas along with paranoid states (indistinguishable from the usual run of paranoid disorders) may also be seen and convulsions are not unknown. The actions of the drug are short-lived – no more than a few hours – and, if the effect is not sustained by repeat use, there is the 'downer' element in which depression and lethargy supervene. Sleep and appetite, both suppressed with use, may remain permanently impaired.

7.17   COCAINE

This drug has effects similar to the amphetamines. It is derived from the coca plant in South America and the substance is a mainstay of the economy of countries such as Colombia. A more powerful part-synthetic derivative is called 'crack cocaine', which is notoriously even more addictive than native cocaine. The substance is conventionally inhaled, or snorted, or 'piped' (a form of inhalation using glass vessels in which holes are drilled to convey fumes drawn from cocaine which has been ignited on top). Its effects, though more dramatic than those seen with the amphetamines, last an even shorter time than the amphetamines and repeat use has to be resorted to. There is an increase in physical and mental energy and feeling of euphoria following use. As with the amphetamines, a complication of recurrent use can be paranoid psychosis and there may be present a combination of psychological and physical dependence. A stimulant dependence syndrome – usually involving the amphetamines but increasingly also cocaine and 'crack' cocaine – has been mooted.

7.18   SOME OTHER ILLICIT DRUGS

Ecstasy is a synthetic amphetamine derivative (3,4 methylene dioxymeth-amphetamine) which is in part stimulant and part hallucinogen. Its use is commonplace among significant numbers of teenage children part of whose 'clubbing' experience the drug provides. Its adverse effects include hyperpyrexia (elevated body temperature) and acute renal failure due to dehydration as well as water intoxication following attempts to compensate for water loss. Acute psychotic conditions may also be seen. Concern has been expressed that long term emotional and cognitive effects could persist even after cessation of use.

Hallucinogenic drugs include 'magic mushrooms' and the synthetic preparation lysergic acid diethylamide (LSD). Hallucinations and other sensory distortions are the usual feature following use of these substances with distorted sense of time and space and changes in body image. Dependence is psychological but there is the possibility of 'flashback' phenomena, that is, the sensations due to the drug being re-lived even after a good deal of time has passed since the drug was last consumed.

7.19   ILLICIT DRUGS – TREATMENT

The assessment and treatment of illicit drug abuse follows the principles set out in regard to the treatment of alcohol misuse. In general terms there is little by way of an underlying medical reason – save those cases where opiate dependence has followed therapeutic use of these drugs – for becoming dependent on or abusing these substances. Social conditions are now such that problematical abuse of these drugs now mostly follows the casual or recreational use of these substances. Medical complications may, of course, follow their use. Dependence in the physical sense is common with the opiates and is occasionally probable with amphetamine and cocaine use but only psychological dependence is normally seen with cannabis use. Psychological dependence means, broadly speaking, the

patient feels he can take or leave the substance, but its effects being such –
the sense of relaxation, increased sociability, confidence and well being –
that the patient is drawn into continuing use of the drug. It may be
thought that a distinction between physical and psychological dependence
in these circumstances is little more than academic.

The actual medical treatment of cases of misuse of illicit substances is
limited, being restricted in the main to the management of opiate
dependence. Detoxification may be carried out in an in-patient setting or
in the community. The former is probably the preferable option as control
is easier to maintain and there is the added bonus that concurrent physical
and mental disorder can be investigated and, where possible, treated.
Maintenance (or substitution) therapy is now a common feature of long
term treatment of opiate misuse, although not all practitioners are
convinced of the efficacy of maintenance treatment. The purpose of
maintenance drug treatment is to achieve some control over the patient's
drug use by prescribing him maintenance drugs rather than leaving him to
seek these or other drugs on the street. By such means his use of the drug
may become stabilised, he may be able to give up such hazardous means
of consumption as injecting himself, with all the complications that could
follow such a course, and be able to divert himself from criminal conduct
which he usually has to engage in to fund his habit. The majority of
patients with opiate dependency tend to be managed, at least at some
point, in a maintenance programme. It is said that maintenance treatment
of this kind retains patients in treatment, reduces illicit drug use,
diminishes criminal activity and may also lower the incidence of HIV,
hepatitis B and hepatitis C infection. It may also improve the chances of
resocialisation. The substitute prescribing usually involves oral methadone in a dose necessary to control withdrawal symptoms. The aim
generally is to reduce the methadone over time and cease its prescription
altogether but there will always be patients who will need long-term
substitution drug prescription and dispensing. Buprenorphine (Subutex)
is an alternative drug used on similar principles.

The rest of the treatment consists essentially of advice, support and
counsel. A variety of treatment approaches have been tried with little by
way of consistent results. The time scales used in measuring prognosis are
as for treatment of alcohol misuse. The prognosis in the short term is
probably comparable to that achieved in cases of alcohol misuse, the
longer term prognosis could be worse, though sharp individual variations
are to be found. Motivation is the key to the stopping the use of all
substances when misused and for keeping away from them. Progress in
treatment may be monitored with the aid of objective measurements such
as by testing hair strands for the presence of illicit substances. These
measures are most useful when a patient is under treatment and regular
hair strand testing for drugs can be undertaken to see if progress is being
made in respect of controlling the use of the drug and, later, to ensure
abstinence is maintained. Random drug tests are occasionally undertaken

in family and child proceedings and are of limited value, whether positive or negative values are obtained. It cannot be overemphasised that, as in the case of alcohol misuse, what is really in point in these proceedings is the actual behaviour of an individual. As will be readily appreciated, the matter that normally concerns the law is the actual behaviour of an individual, not simply the extent of his substance misuse.

An important aspect of alcohol and drug use is the social scene in which these substances are indulged, in other words the social relationships and networks fostered among users, along with the sense of camaraderie which follows any involvement in what could be seen to be daring and unlawful activity. This may mean breaking away from the illicit drug scene is difficult – conveying also perhaps a sense of betrayal or treachery in respect of one's comrades – even when the patient is otherwise motivated and has the incentive to desist from further use.

Untreated, the picture can be dire. Apart from accidents and suicide, intercurrent infections and those complications directly attributable usually to intravenous drug use, there is the ever present risk of entanglement with the criminal law as these substances remain unlawful to possess or distribute and the cost of their consumption is not negligible. Apart from medical and legal complications, there is always also the risk of social and personal degradation involving the patient. However, all is not lost if the patient seriously engages in treatment. Recent studies have shown that some hope is permissible in cases of opiate dependence. On a 30-year follow up of patients who had suffered injected heroin abuse, 42 per cent of patients had been abstinent for at least ten years following treatment. Ten per cent of patients were continuing to take methadone and 22 per cent of patients were dead.

7.20 PATHOLOGICAL GAMBLING

A few words need to be said about this condition in view of the social and legislative changes that have led to the easing of previous restrictions on gambling. There is a potential for violence when gamblers fall into debt and also when their vice makes an impact on their personal and family life. The association with aggressive and violent behaviour is therefore more indirect than with the substances already discussed. Pathological gambling is a hidden menace for indulgence in gambling, at any rate in Britain, is not unlawful, is seemingly encouraged by the state and its effects are not as obvious as may be, say, with problematical alcohol use. There are believed to be about 300,000 persons who could be described as problem gamblers in Britain and their numbers are believed to be growing. Problem gambling, in the clinical sense, does not usually involve such glamorous activities as playing the roulette wheel or engaging in the activities of well-appointed clubs in Mayfair. It normally involves an impecunious individual who has become pathologically dependent on such humble activities as playing the lottery and scratch cards besides engaging in the more traditional pastime of backing horses and dogs. Other areas of dependence are found increasingly through activities of gambling on the internet. It is as pernicious a form of addiction as any other mentioned in this chapter and the personal and social cost can be immense and lead to the destruction of a not insubstantial number of individual lives and those of families. The poor are selectively more afflicted because they are the least likely to afford the inevitable losses associated with gambling. The point made earlier about the self-absorption and the relentless pursuit of personal gratification at the cost of all else in respect of alcohol and illicit drug use applies equally well here, helping to bring the subject within the purview of the family and child lawyer and occasionally the criminal lawyer, for gamblers need somehow to finance their activities and may need to resort to unlawful means. Treatment is entirely by psychological means – unless there is some underlying medical condition such as mania or bipolar affective disorder predisposing the individual to pathological gambling – and success of any therapeutic endeavour depends, once more, on the motivation and the desire for change exhibited by the affected individual.

7.21 SUBSTANCE MISUSE – THE RISKS OF AGGRESSION AND VIOLENCE

It is easy to see how affected individuals may come to interest various areas of the law. Broadly speaking, the risks involve the direct result of the misused substances as may be manifested by physical, mental or behavioural changes. Secondly, there are also risks associated with the pursuit by these individuals of the means by which these substances of abuse are acquired. Pathological gambling usually only involves the second of these aspects of dependence behaviour. One way or another the criminal law becomes involved in cases of substance abuse. Such is the impact of the behaviour of these individuals on others, including those who are members of their families, that the subject is of lively interest to practitioners in family and child law. Employment may, of course, be affected and nuisance behaviour may be engaged in the form of antisocial conduct. As far as aggressive and violent conduct are concerned, as was seen earlier in this chapter, the effects of substances could be direct as well as indirect, namely, through the disinhibiting properties of various drugs, most particularly alcohol.

7.22 DISORDERS OF APPETITE

These disorders are included in this chapter for completeness and as they appear to have at least a superficial resemblance to the kinds of perverted appetites found in the cases involving alcohol and illicit drug misuse. There is an appreciable risk of suicide involving these patients and that alone justifies a brief consideration of these conditions. We leave obesity from any consideration here. This is no doubt a subject of considerable and expanding medical importance but here we shall concentrate instead on anorexia and bulimia nervosa while also noting that there are several forms of atypical eating disorders which, while not meeting the diagnostic criteria of the conventional disorders, may yet be of clinical significance.

Anorexia nervosa is a condition that has been known for some centuries, although it has come into greater prominence in more recent generations. There is a 'fear of fatness' in the individuals who suffer from these disorders – the vast majority adolescent girls and young women – which leads to their imposing a low weight threshold upon themselves. The disorders are characterised by the refusal of the individual to maintain a minimum normal body weight, often to the point of starvation. The core feature is an intense fear of gaining weight. This lower body weight is maintained at least 15 per cent below the standard norm applicable to such an individual. The behaviour aimed at achieving this self-imposed target includes the avoidance of high calorific foodstuffs, self-induced vomiting, self-induced purging, excessive exercise, and the use of appetite suppressants (the attraction of these properties of amphetamine drugs is obvious) and diuretic agents. There may also be a loss of the menstrual cycle. The medical consequences of starving may be serious and not uncommonly life threatening in graver cases, especially if the unwillingness to consume food is compounded by the simultaneous use of laxatives and diuretics and the effects of vomiting. There may also be some features of depressive illness including obsessional symptoms and irritability. Social withdrawal follows in the wake of the preoccupation with eating behaviour.

A variant of the condition is bulimia nervosa involving binge-eating, which has some similarities to the episodic heavy alcohol intake or dipsomania. There is a history of anorexia nervosa in many who later become bulimic and indeed patients may move from one condition to the other. One of the features in this condition is that normal body weight may be retained, indeed some subjects can be overweight. Binges of eating may be followed by the use of laxatives, diuretics and excessive exercise and vomiting. Complications could arise as a result of the abuse of substances.

7.23   EATING DISORDERS – CAUSATION

The onset of the condition is in early adolescence and a feature is the preoccupation with food in all its aspects apart from eating it. The condition may go unnoticed for many years for a preoccupation with figure and weight is otherwise considered normal in young girls. The female predominance in anorexia nervosa is notable and there is no doubt that, at present, this is a condition found primarily in the developed world. The eating disorders, as conventionally understood, have been viewed as a culture-bound disorder, rare or absent except in Western cultures, where there is pervasive pressure to diet to obtain a socially desirable weight and/or shape. There is a tradition of self-starvation in some cultures but the motivation of individuals undertaking this ritual is quite different. An intriguing recent study from Ghana questions, however, the Western view of these disorders. Firstly, it says, there are historical descriptions of cases of self-starvation without concerns about weight in cultures in which there is no emphasis on slimness. Secondly, cross-cultural comparison has suggested that the eating disorders do not necessarily follow the accepted Western form. Starvation in these cultures may be an end in itself, often undertaken for purposes of religious devotion. Weight concern as in the usual case of anorexia nervosa may become more common as the degree of Westernisation increases. The Ghana study suggests that anorexia nervosa may take different forms in different cultures and the patients studied there had a form of anorexia nervosa without concerns about weight. Studies examining eating disorders in developing countries seem to have assumed that the psychopathology of anorexia nervosa follows the recognised 'Western' form. The authors of this study suggest that a unifying theme of the diverse cultural presentation of the disorder is morbid self-starvation which may be driven in many ways and that self-starvation may, in fact, be the core feature of anorexia nervosa with the attribution for the self-starvation behaviour varying between cultures. However, there is also evidence that the incidence of conventional cases of eating disorders is rising in those parts of the world where the major preoccupation has traditionally been with finding enough food to eat. An interesting phenomenon awaits us if, with growing prosperity and the advances towards globalisation, these disorders became as common in those parts of the world as other psychiatric disorders have usually done.

There may also be growing parity between the sexes as roles become blurred as between men and women and the former also start becoming preoccupied with appearance and weight, a feature also believed to be on the increase (one has already noted that the behaviour concerning alcohol consumption in women has approximated that seen in men in recent years). This does not make these conditions solely those of social and cultural origins for an intriguing involvement of the brain is found in some of these cases. It is believed, at least in some of these cases, the problem is primarily one concerning body image, that is, of the view that one comes to achieve of one's body, a matter of perception and therefore capable of being traced back to the brain. Social and cultural factors – such as the pictorial depiction of the desirable female form and build – may well provide the raw material for the brain to work on. It has also long been known that complex endocrine changes associated with such symptoms as the loss of menstrual periods are found in this condition, and aberrations in the levels of hormones have also been noted. Whether these are causal phenomena or are effects secondary to the disorder are not always clear. There is a genetic influence that can be seen but the effects of this are not pronounced. Family conflict is often elicited. Childhood trauma, especially involving sexual abuse, has been discovered in a minority of cases. Bullimia nervosa is rarer than anorexia but shares many of the aetilogical features of the other. The major difference between the two conditions appears to be the greater genetic risk present with bulimia nervosa.

7.24   EATING DISORDERS – TREATMENT

Treatment of these conditions is far from satisfactory or indeed from finding a consensus among therapists. Measures include both practical steps – a regime of controlled re-feeding – and psychological treatment. The latter may involve individual or group psychotherapy and also family therapy. Cognitive behavioural therapy may have some merit and has its advocates. The aim with psychological treatment is to attempt to alter the individual's attitude to weight and body shape. Drug treatment is of limited value. Severe weight loss may necessitate in-patient treatment which may also be required if the risk of suicidal behaviour or medical complications becomes appreciable. The prognosis is variable, dependent as it is on so many factors peculiar to each patient and on account of the poor understanding as yet achieved of these disorders. The severity of the occasional case involving the eating disorders is often underestimated and it is believed that five per cent of these patients will die, either through starving themselves or by suicide. Severe cases may need to be treated in hospital and specialised units now exist in an attempt to achieve the best possible result. The prognosis of bulimia nervosa appears to be better.

7.25   SUMMARY

1.   Substance misuse, other forms of addictive behaviour and the eating disorders appear to be heavily influenced by prevailing social and cultural conditions and attitudes. Depending on the substance involved, physical or psychological dependence could be encountered. The complications arising out of these conditions could be considerable, involving physical and mental disorder and also impairment of relationships within the family and the community.

2.   Substance-misuse behaviour may lead to involvement of the individual with the criminal law (through behaviours involving the substances directly as well as in the attempts made to fund use) and family and child law and is also a major consideration in personal injury and employment practice. These conditions are also implicated in changing mental states and with nuisance behaviour. Thereby, they involve every form of risk that is considered with aggressive and violent behaviour. The possible mechanisms underlying these behaviours have been considered in some detail in Chapter 2. The absence of any reliable form of treatment for the common forms of addictive behaviour compounds the problem.

CHAPTER 8

DISORDERS OF PERSONALITY AND PSYCHOPATHY

Where aggressive and violent behaviour are concerned, the disorders of personality match the effects of substance misuse in their impact. The mechanisms responsible for untoward behaviours due to these disorders have been considered in Chapter 2 and Part III further considers the effects of the disorders of personality on public and political violence. No other condition in all psychiatric practice leads to such confusion, disagreement and dissent as do those conditions making up this category of mental disorder. The essence of personality disorder is a failure on the part of an individual to adjust to the norms and standards of society. Many definitions have been given, though no single one is satisfactory. The ICD-10 defines personality disorder as 'deeply ingrained and enduring behaviour patterns, manifesting themselves as inflexible responses to a broad range of personal and social situations. They represent either extreme or significant deviations from the way the average individual in a given culture perceives, thinks, feels and particularly relates to others. Such behaviour patterns tend to be stable and to encompass multiple domains of behaviour and psychological functioning. They are frequently, but not always, associated with various degrees of subjective distress and problems in social functioning and performance.' Not surprisingly, these difficulties often spill over into the law, in particular the criminal law, but family and child law as well as other branches of the law also consistently encounter these patients, hence our current interest.

8.1   PERSONALITY DISORDERS – GENERAL FEATURES

Some points may be made in trying to break down the kind of compendious definition of personality disorder such as the one given above.

1.   The abnormal behaviour pattern is persistent and enduring, in other words it is not episodic as may happen with most forms of formal psychiatric illness. Even in saying that we must utter a word of caution for chronic illness, such as some forms of schizophrenia or depressive illness, may itself lead to personality change which may be difficult to distinguish from the disease process, although the history may suggest normal development up to the first onset of the illness.

While personality disorders amount to mental disorders, conditions
such as schizophrenia and depressive illness are considered to be true
disease entities and, as such, are forms of formal mental illness.

2.   Personality disorders are mental disorders in their own right but
      these are to be seen separate from formal mental illnesses such as
      depressive illness to which many personality disordered individuals
      are subject. Similarly, the alcohol and illicit drug misuse these
      individuals frequently indulge in may found a diagnosis of mental
      disorder in their own right and must be kept separate from
      personality disorder as far as one can do so.

3.   The crux of the problem is the element of 'rule breaking' in relation
      to the norms and standards of society. This lack of harmony with
      their surroundings and the inability to conform may be due to
      several elements in their psychological functioning, eg their poor
      impulse control, their often high levels of anxiety and arousal, their
      ways of thinking and perceiving, their view of another person etc.

4.   It follows that the abnormal behaviour pattern may be pervasive and
      may lead to maladaptive responses in many areas of personal and
      social behaviour.

5.   Although the diagnosis is not to be made until maturity is reached,
      at least in chronological terms, problems of adjustment and conduct
      are invariably seen in childhood and adolescence and persist into
      adult life.

6.   The condition is usually associated with significant problems in the
      social and occupational spheres.

7.   The disorder may lead to significant personal distress, although this
      may happen only later in its course and may not always be detected,
      especially if contact with the patient has not been made by
      professionals.

The distinction to be made between the personality disorders and formal
illness, briefly touched on above, may be usefully expanded upon along
with a discussion on the inter-relationship between the two conditions.
Firstly, personality disorders can predispose formal mental illness. An
anxious or obsessional personality is more prone to suffer the
corresponding neurotic condition than an individual with a more normal
personality. Secondly, personality disorder and formal illness may
co-exist. This state is commonly found in situations involving misuse of
alcohol and illicit drugs where the mental disorder due to substance abuse
may be found alongside a personality disorder which may make the
patient vulnerable to other disorders. This is an example of the state of
co-morbidity. Thirdly, as already noted, personality changes, sometimes

amounting to disorder, may follow from illness. As we shortly shall see, personality deterioration may follow head injury and there is the possibility of adverse personality change in cases of chronic schizophrenia. Fourthly, the features of formal illness and the behaviours associated with it can be modified by a personality disorder. Violence (that is, suicidal behaviour or violence directed against others) involving the mentally disordered is commonly suspected to be the result of some mental illness *per se* but, in fact, may actually flow from the underlying personality of the individual concerned.

8.2 PERSONALITY DISORDERS – CLASSIFICATION

We consider here a practical psychiatric classification of the common forms of personality disorders. A psychological approach to the classification of these conditions is considered in Van Rooyen and Mahendra (2007). Given the state of current knowledge, personality disorder is only amenable to description and the classification of subtypes – themselves subject to change over the course of years as diagnostic methods become refined – are based on clusters of descriptive features. Many sub-types are recognised and we consider briefly here only those commonly seen in medico-legal practice.

1. One such type is the *dependent* personality disorder, referring to an individual who encourages or allows others to make most of one's important life decisions, subordinates one's own needs to the wishes and demands of others, has a feeling of helplessness, is insecure on account of fearing desertion and requires excessive amounts of advice and reassurance from others. It has an association with borderline personality disorder and the aetiology is thought to be the outcome of early social processes within the family environment.

2. Closely related to the *dependent* type is the *anxious (avoidant)* type who has persistent and pervasive feelings of anxiety and tension, believes one is socially inept, physically unattractive and inferior to others, is over sensitive to being criticised or rejected in social situations, unwilling to become involved in situations unless certain of acceptance, leads a restricted lifestyle in order to have security and avoids social or occupational activities that involve significant interpersonal contact because of fear of criticism, disapproval or rejection. It is also associated with phobic disorders, specifically social phobia which has similar clinical features.

3. The *histrionic* type of personality disorder involves an individual given to self-dramatisation and exaggerated expression of emotion, is suggestible and easily influenced by others, is shallow with changeable emotions, is continually craving excitement, appreciation of others and the need to be the centre of attraction, is inappropriately seductive in appearance or dress and is unduly

concerned with physical appearance, is egocentric, self-indulgent and manipulative. Although traditionally believed to be commoner in women, more recent studies show the gender ratio to be 50-50. It is more commonly found in divorced and separated persons and is associated with parasuicidal behaviour. It is associated also with women who suffer unexplained medical conditions and in men with substance misuse.

4.   The *paranoid* personality type is excessively sensitive to setbacks and rebuffs, has a tendency to bear grudges persistently, is suspicious and with a tendency to distort experiences through misconstruction of the words and actions of others, is combative and tenacious in regard to personal rights, has a tendency to experience excessive self-importance and is given to suspecting conspiracies in regard to personal matters as well as in the world at large. It is more commonly found in males and persons of a lower social class, and also more common among relations of patients with schizophrenia. It exists with anti-social personality disorder and is associated with violent crime.

5.   The *schizoid* sub-type is more prevalent in offender populations. It has been suggested that this category may be better classified as a neurodevelopmental disorder than a personality disorder, possibly within the spectrum of autistic disorders.

6.   The *obsessive-compulsive* type finds grouped within it 'high functioning' individuals, more commonly white males who are highly educated, married and employed. It has an association with anxiety states.

7.   An important sub-category, which may have significant implications for medico-legal practice concerning the patients within it, is the *emotionally unstable* type. This kind of personality is governed by his or her impulses without any considerations of consequences or repercussions. The ability to plan ahead is much reduced and there may be outbursts or explosions of anger, sometimes leading to violence. These individuals may be unduly provoked when they are thwarted. There are two variants of this sub-category. One is the *impulsive* type characterised by emotional instability and lack of impulse control. Outbursts of violence or threatening behaviour are commonly found here. The other is the *borderline* type which also is characterised by emotional instability, with disturbed behaviour, a chronic feeling of emptiness within and with a liability to become involved in intense and unstable relationships which are associated with repeated emotional crises which lead to violence (whether directed against oneself or others). It is not unknown for this – and perhaps subtypes such as the paranoid personality – to tip over fleetingly into displaying the features of psychosis including

delusions, hallucinations and losses of insight and a sense of reality. It is said to be more prevalent in younger age groups (19-34), white females, associated also with a poor work history and single marital status and also more common in urban areas. It is further associated with substance misuse, phobic and anxiety states and has a nine per cent suicide rate. It is associated in forensic samples with anti-social personality disorder. There is also an association with depressive illness. It is most severe in individuals aged in their mid-twenties with improvement noted in those aged in their late-thirties and beyond.

8.3 PSYCHOPATHY

Psychopathy may be referred to as the 'turbo-charged' version of personality disorder. It has achieved notoriety and invariably attracts a bad press. The highest in the land may be caught up in its coils as is exemplified by the government's seeming inability to know how to deal with some of the more violent members of this group – what is called dangerous and severe personality disorder – and the ensuing debate that held up the reform of the Mental Health Act 1983 which has now been amended rather than repealed and replaced. Traditional classificatory systems used to mark these patients as being inadequate, creative or aggressive. Sociopath is the favoured term in the United States, where intensive studies have been undertaken on them with little enlightenment forthcoming. It is believed there is a prevalence of psychopathy of 2-3 per cent in most Western societies and it is 4-5 times more common in men than in women. The highest prevalence is in the 25-44 age group. It is associated with school drop out, homelessness and raised mortality in early adult life. Prevalence is raised in inner-city areas and is lower in rural populations. It has a high association with substance misuse. The symptoms of anti-social personality disorder or psychopathy diminish in middle age but about 20 per cent of sufferers are still said to meet the criteria for diagnosis at the age of 45 years.

Most of the remarks addressed above to personality-disordered individuals will also find application to those suffering from psychopathy. The condition remains a matter for observation and classification with little by way of any objective measurement as yet feasible. Some of the features seen in these individuals include a marked unconcern for the feelings of others, a gross and persistent attitude of irresponsibility in terms of 'rule-breaking' to be discussed below, an incapacity to maintain any enduring relationships, a very low tolerance to frustration and boredom with a corresponding low threshold for unleashing aggression and violence, an inability to learn from experience including punishment (whether officially or informally meted out to them), a marked inability to accept responsibility, a tendency to blame others and the possession of a dogged capacity for rationalisation of the usually deplorable acts they have been engaged in.

As with the personality disorders, the causes of psychopathy remain largely mysterious. It is a condition found in every culture and society and even where, say, aggression and assertiveness are more socially acceptable than in cultures where restraint and moderation are the preferred approach to life it is noteworthy how denizens of the former societies can still point to individuals who have overstepped an even higher threshold. A rule breaker remains a rule breaker even when the rules may appear to have been adjusted to accommodate his like.

8.4   PERSONALITY DISORDERS – CAUSATION

These patients, as has been said, are rule-breakers. They are also abnormal individuals in the statistical sense. Truly it could be said of them, employing Thoreau's words for the purpose: 'If a man does not keep pace with his companions perhaps it is because he hears a different drummer.' Perhaps in trying to make sense of these patients a good starting point may be the normal personality, the one from which these patients are deemed to deviate. Although personality has long been studied, many gaps still remain in our knowledge. We do know there are significant genetic influences although, as with many conditions or states or attributes, normal, abnormal and pathological, the precise genetic mechanisms elude us. The genetic contribution to personality traits appears to be modest. As for personality disorder, there are widely and wildly varying figures given according to the populations and groups selected for study. There are rare chromosomal abnormalities implicated in aggressive behaviour. Brain studies have shown from time to time – through abnormal scans, aberrant electroencephalographic and blood flow studies – that there could be some abnormality in function, perhaps even in structure, of various regions of the brain but these studies are far too indefinite, and on occasion contradictory, to serve any practical explanatory or diagnostic purpose. In any event, the manifestations of these disorders are so wide ranging it seems unlikely there could be one specific lesion. A high level of autonomic nervous system arousal is sometimes posited in these individuals to account for their impulsive actions. Environmental factors, at first sight, hold greater promise for purposes of trying to explain these conditions but, once again, the available studies prove too contradictory – too much, too little, parental attention, deprivation in childhood, or, on the contrary, being 'spoilt', too comfortable or too spartan an upbringing, too much or too little caring – to have much value in terms of reliability and validity. All that can be said is that those with personality disorder or psychopathy appear able to spring from any kind of soil – social class, parental background, cultures can be of any kind. In other words, those who desire to turn out well balanced, responsible citizens have little to work with and almost never can predict with any great confidence how young persons will turn out as adult citizens. Personality disorder and psychopathy are usually diagnoses made with hindsight, as the 'back tracking' to detect childhood and adolescent misbehaviour shows. In most cases, of course, children and adolescents outgrow their years of rebellion and are transformed into model citizens.

We suspect, nonetheless, that the social as well as the physical environment very probably do play an often decisive part in moulding an individual's personality characteristics. While the definitive personality emerges at maturity – which, with some arbitrariness, for these are not matters of precise chronological calculation, we may set at the age of 18 – many of the characteristics found in adult life are found surprisingly early in life, even possibly in the first few months of life according to closely observant parents. Numerous studies have shown that persistent and pervasive aggressive and disruptive behaviours seen before the age of 11 are strongly associated with persistence of anti-social behaviours through adolescence and into adult life. The risk extends far beyond anti-social behaviours to unstable relationships, unreliable parenting and underachievement in education and at work. Furthermore, children who do not have conduct problems are very unlikely to subsequently develop anti-social personality disorder, which is rare without a history of conduct problems in childhood. The brain obviously plays a crucial role and its own growth, development and maturity appears to underlie the personality the individual comes to present to the world. Therefore, any insult to the brain, while causing also possible intellectual deficiency (see chapter 9), may also hinder the normal development of the personality. These injurious factors may include infections such as encephalitis or meningitis, head injuries, environmental toxins (one recalls the recent impassioned debate on whether or not mercury could have an impact on childhood mental development when used as a vehicle for vaccines), the foetal environment itself (subject as it is to maternal health, drugs taken etc) and more obvious socio-economic influences such as poor diet and housing. One must say, however, that the vast majority of patients with personality disorder have no discernible cause for their condition and, even when they suggest one of the above factors for their condition, the examiner remains sceptical for the precise role, if any, for any such causative agent is usually far from clear. If all children suffer infections, some of which are bound to be serious, how does one know which of these children has had its personality development adversely affected by the infection it suffered? These imponderables also affect the analysis of the psychological development of children such as the quality of their upbringing, the nature and number of their attachments etc. Children brought up in dire deprivation may turn out to be well-adjusted adults and with the ground well prepared for success in all spheres of life. Equally well, those whose lives appear to be little more than a non-ending march to and from the criminal courts and prisons may reveal they had every advantage in their upbringing. The subject of personality development therefore remains one for speculation at the present day. However, an audience of lawyers will be able to appreciate the facts in a case which involved personality change in an adult person following head injury. The case was *Miah v McCreamer* [1985] 1 All ER 367, [1986] 1 All ER 943 and the primary legal interest was on the issue of remoteness in tort. The plaintiff (as these used to be called) was an estimable member of society who, however, foolishly accepted a lift from a drunken driver who proceeded to cause an accident. This passenger suffered head injury. What is of peculiar interest was what the consequences of the claimant's head injury turned out to be. He suffered a calamitous personality change which led him to committing a series of vicious sexual assaults one of which led him into being imprisoned for life. It was held he could recover for this 'loss of amenity' (subject to a reduction for contributory negligence) and that his criminal actions following head injury were reasonably foreseeable. Another man, aged in his forties, involved in both personal injury and child care litigation, on similar facts turned from being a dutiful partner and devoted father into a drunken lout who came to lose all he had following a series of violent assaults. Fortunately, his aggression abated with time and the court could entertain a claim to his right to have renewed contact with his child with some equanimity.

While it has been said already that personality disorder (and psychopathy) can only be diagnosed after maturity, ie once personality has been deemed to be fully formed, it is still believed to be necessary to 'track back', so to speak, and look at the picture that obtained in childhood and adolescence of the individual concerned. When that is done, it is invariably the case that behavioural disorders are discovered to have been manifested at an early stage in life. Precursors of an anti-social lifestyle are said to include anti-social behaviour in childhood, impulsivity, school failure, anti-social family, poor parenting and economic deprivation. Turning points away from an anti-social lifestyle include finding employment, getting married, moving to a better area for residence, and joining the army. Weak bonds to society and individuals, self-centredness, low empathy and lack of religious belief are all associated with substance misuse and an anti-social life style. Early contact with the police, truancy, school misconduct and divorce are significant predictors of premature death. There is often a history of such activities as truanting, fighting, lying, bullying, insubordination, indiscipline, thieving and other features of juvenile delinquency to be found. In other words, personality disorders and psychopathy do not appear to arise *de novo* in adult life but have already laid down patterns considerably early in childhood. All aspects of social and personal life come to be affected in these individuals and often they may leave behind a trail of destruction. Relationships – personal as well as with officialdom – are usually superficial, brittle and unstable. Repeated marriages, along with illegitimate children from numerous extra-marital relationships are not uncommon. The occupational record is equally chequered with much difficulty shown in relationships with colleagues and superiors and much disruption in the work place as these individuals have a genius for creating chaos. Confrontations, in a repeated pattern, with the law are commonplace as these individuals often have what the law has called 'abnormally aggressive' and 'seriously irresponsible' attitudes leading to involvement with the criminal law following assaults on the person as well as property and, on occasion, for acts of dishonesty. Resort is readily had to abuse of alcohol and indulgence in illicit substances. Their career appears to be one of an individual looking back on the ruins of one relationship and contemplating the next. In early middle age it is customary for these individuals to show some signs of settling down, the convictions and spells of incarceration ease and a *modus vivendi* appears to have been reached with the world. It is often suggested that by that age these individuals could be running out of the animal energy that sustained their destructive and disruptive careers and that some measure of stability is often restored although some individuals may proceed to cause havoc in their lives and those of others right through life.

The older classification into inadequate, aggressive and creative psychopaths had some merit in helping to understand the life and works of these patients. The inadequate individual is the one commonly found to have a poor interpersonal and occupational record. The aggressive individual is the one who had entangled himself with the criminal law and the penal services. The creative individual becomes the renowned businessman or artist in occupations where 'rule breaking' is the norm, where, in fact, success and progress is not possible if existing rules are not broken, although fulfillment or stability in their personal lives do not regularly match the material or artistic success they come to achieve, a matter readily explored by a study of the biographies of many gifted individuals.

8.5 PERSONALITY DISORDERS – MANAGEMENT

Treatment of these conditions remains problematical. The Butler Committee (1975) concluded, 'the great weight of evidence presented to us tends to support the conclusion that psychopaths are not, in general, treatable, at least in medical terms.' Over three decades later that sentiment remains, by and large, true. There is no specific drug treatment available for these conditions as such although therapeutic drugs may be useful in dealing with the symptoms of formal psychiatric disorder these patients, like anyone else, may develop. It is often glibly asserted that psychological approaches by way of psychotherapy – individual, group or even institutional – may produce significant results. The results, in fact, are almost uniformly poor within any timescales envisaged in medico-legal practice. Psychotherapy is a time, labour and, hence, cash intensive treatment procedure. The Henderson Hospital (one of only two institutions in the country able to offer institutional treatment for cases of severe personality disorder) contemplates the threat of closure. There simply were not sufficient numbers of cases referred to it and bringing the necessary funding with them. Using the phrase employed in demotic usage, the money seemingly was not in the mouths of those who had clamoured for this form of intensive specialised treatment.

However, other specialist institutions such as the Cassel Hospital (the counterpart of the Henderson Hospital) have claimed reasonably positive results in cases of personality disorder. Specialist psychosocial treatment for personality disorder, they say, can show appreciable and reliable improvement in symptomatology, social adjustment and global assessment of mental health over a 36 month follow up period. Improvement is said also to continue after discharge, a proportion of patients showing stable and durable change two years after termination of treatment. A phased programme that included a community-based stage of treatment was found to yield more stable improvement than a purely hospital-based programme, as shown by the greater reduction in self mutilation, attempts at suicide and readmission rates. There is at present a co-operative venture involving the prison department, the Home Office and the Department of Health in a number of locations to see how the most irresponsible of psychopaths – the most dangerously violent – can be dealt with, if at all, therapeutically. No studies have yet emerged to show any promise. It appears there is as yet no treatment or management programme that is compatible with personal liberty in a civilised society which can yet be formulated to deal with these individuals. Secure units and special hospitals remain the institutions for those individuals with these conditions who seriously transgress the criminal law. As far as timescales normally envisaged in most legal proceedings are concerned, any real treatment of psychopathy is, it is safe to say, not yet in the realm of practical politics.

8.6   PERSONALITY DISORDERS – PROGNOSIS

The remarks made above may suggest that the prognosis for cases of personality disorder is uniformly hopeless. This is not always the case. Apart from the factor of maturation mentioned above – many of these individuals do settle down in middle age – they are also subject to circumstances that could be positive. Employment, marriage, or some other new challenge may all engage them and lead to an improvement in their functioning. It is striking how well some of these patients acquit themselves when they face a real challenge such as the conditions of war. It is also repeatedly stressed how the Empire came to be built on the backs of misfits who, while they in early life idled at home, had seemingly been undone by the mundane nature of their ordinary existence. It is invariably seen in clinical settings that the single most important factor in the improvement of the clinical functioning of these patients is their capacity to lead a settled life. As these matters remain unpredictable, and largely out of the hands of clinicians, the prognosis for these patients is mostly said to be guarded.

8.7 PERSONALITY DISORDERS – THE RISKS OF AGGRESSION AND VIOLENCE

As was discussed in Chapter 2, and will be further illustrated in Part III of this book, individuals suffering from personality disorders and psychopathy find themselves involved in many situations of risk involving aggression and violence. Consequently, they are also active participants in many fields of the law.

8.8 SUMMARY

1. How personality disorders arise is far from well understood. There appears to be an interaction between genetic factors and environmental influences but the impact of genetics appears to be weaker in personality disorders than with the formal mental illnesses. The environment, therefore, appears to play a more decisive role but it is not clear how. Head injury and systemic illness and its treatment may be occasional causes of changed personality. These conditions are usually beyond all conventional treatment, although amelioration is to be expected with age and especially if they manage to lead a settled existence. Complications include the misuse of substances.

2. Given the nature of the condition, many of these patients are actively involved in litigation. Aggression and violence involves the criminal law. These behaviours, as well as impulsive and unreliable conduct, may lead to their participation in family and child proceedings. Difficulties in interpersonal relationships, associated also with aggression, may lead to problems in employment. Delayed recovery from psychiatric injuries, including those due to injuries to the head, sustained following trauma, may complicate personal injury litigation. Changing mental states seen in some patients may be attributable, at least in part, to their personalities. Their behaviour, especially when it is tinged with aggression and violence, may be such that nuisance is caused to the public.

CHAPTER 9

LEARNING DISABILITIES AND
DEVELOPMENTAL DISORDERS

9.1 LEARNING DISABILITIES

The term learning disabilities has been some time evolving. At various periods in recent history the terms mental retardation, mental subnormality, mental handicap or mental impairment have all been employed to describe this phenomenon and some of these terms still find favour with official sources such as the International Classification of Disorders (1992, mental retardation) or the Mental Health Act 1983 (mental impairment). At an earlier period in history the terms used included those such as idiocy, imbecility and feeblemindedness which nowadays are considered to be too pejorative. The primary problem in this disorder has long been considered to be one of an intellectual shortfall, although the more enlightened attitudes of today also give proper attention to the more social and emotional aspects of the processes of learning whose deficiency is now believed to be the core handicap. The ICD defines these conditions as being characterised by 'arrested or incomplete development of the mind, which is especially characterised by impairment of skills manifested during the developmental period, which contributes to the overall level of intelligence.' Intelligence, therefore, still remains a central issue with learning disabilities. The conventional measure of this is the IQ (intelligence quotient) test. Intelligence in the ordinary populations is said to have a normal distribution by which is meant that with a modal score of 100, and a standard deviation of 15, two standard deviations from the mode in either direction would cover 95 per cent of the population. In other words, all but 5 per cent of the public would score between 70 and 130 on an IQ test. A borderline score is about 70, mild learning disabilities would cover scores between 50 and 70, moderate learning disabilities will be found between 35 and 50, severe and profound learning disabilities involve lower scores. The practical difference between those with higher scores – involving the vast majority of patients with learning disabilities – and the lower scores is that the former can hope to live in the community with some support while the latter may come to require institutional care of some kind. There are other distinguishing features found between those suffering from mild, moderate or severe handicap. Those with mild handicap or disability – who account for some 85 per cent of the total number with learning disabilities – may have reasonable language skills with a measure of literacy, possess ordinary social skills, hold down employment (usually involving jobs of an unskilled or semi skilled nature) and have conditions rarely associated with physical illness. In other words, these individuals are little different from members of the normal population. Those with moderate or severe deficits have, however, generally limited language skills, are employed, if at all, in unskilled or sheltered employment, may be deficient in social skills and suffer more often from associated physical disorders.

For historical reasons the study of learning disabilities has fallen, in the medical sense, to the specialist psychiatrist. It is a condition which is distinct from formal mental illness, although associations between learning disabilities and other mental disorder are not uncommon. Learning disabilities, of whatever origins, always arise in childhood. A distinction needs to be made between these conditions and dementia, where intellectual impairment is acquired in adult life.

These conditions may first attract the attention of those involved with the education of the individual or those called upon to deal with the behavioural problems of childhood, at which stage problems involving conduct may at first mask the intellectual deficits that may also be present.

9.2   LEARNING DISABILITIES – CAUSATION

The prevalence of learning disabilities within any population is about two per cent, with a slight male preponderance. Despite some of the commoner causes of intellectual handicap having been tamed – for example, childhood infections being better controlled through programmes of immunization – prevalence appears to have remained stable. It is probable that mild forms of handicap are constant the world over. These are usually associated with socio-economic factors, less easy to eradicate than infections. In many undeveloped rural communities learning disabilities, as commonly understood, may not even be seen to be an obvious handicap whereas in complex developed societies it is only all too clear that such an affected individual may be at substantial disadvantage in coping with ordinary existence. This is especially well seen in the sphere of employment. An agrarian society has a supply of work and a supporting social network for individuals at all ranges of intellectual functioning while a modern industrialised society demands increasing skills and may exclude even those who are only mildly impaired in intellectual terms.

The disorders leading to learning disabilities show clear evidence of both genetic and environmental influences. Plainly, the brain must ultimately be affected in some fashion to bring about disability and impairment. As a general rule, the more severely afflicted tend to have a known genetic cause for their condition while the mildly disabled have no obvious genetic causation but are believed to be affected to a greater or lesser extent by socio-cultural influences. There are obvious exceptions to this rule for severe brain damage due to a clear environmental cause, eg trauma or infection can lead to grave affliction while a condition such as Down's syndrome can lead to variable levels of intellectual difficulties.

The causes, where known, of learning disabilities are numerous. An example already given involving chromosomal abnormality is Down's syndrome. Genetic disorders include phenylketonuria (involving the metabolism of phenylalanine). More than 1000 genetic causes of learning disabilities are known to exist. Other causes include maternal infections in the course of pregnancy (eg rubella) or other complications of pregnancy and it is also believed the maternal consumption of alcohol, tobacco or prescribed drugs could be important, though as yet unquantifiable, causal factors. Birth injury and childhood infection such as meningitis are well established causes, as are later head injuries. One area whose causative potential is as yet little understood involves the role of adverse social and cultural factors such as poor diet and material deprivation. How these elements affect the developing brain remains unclear for there are children developing in conditions of extreme poverty and privation who yet emerge, as far as can be ascertained, normally into the world with their intellectual inheritance intact.

9.3   LEARNING DISABILITIES – MANAGEMENT

As the modern term learning disabilities suggests, the disabilities of individuals suffering from this condition go well beyond intellectual difficulties and may include also those problems associated with social and educational functioning in a wider sense. The assessment of the needs of these patients is a complex exercise and may involve a variety of agencies including the educational services, the local authority and the health authority. The modern trend is to have these patients functioning as far as possible in the community with appropriate support, which may include supported lodgings. The days of traditional institutionalisation are long over, the older institutions now believed to have significantly added to the handicaps suffered by these patients by adding secondary disabilities due to the institutions themselves. Even when some form of residential care may become necessary, emphasis is placed on encouraging independence and fostering self-sufficiency among these individuals.

Intervention may become necessary when a patient with learning disabilities develops a formal mental illness. Assessment needs to be made of the requirements of the service needs of each individual. Care for these individuals, where needed, is usually shared between the local authority and the health service, as the learning disabilities need to draw on the services of both, occasionally a source of tension as scarce resources and budgets are jealously protected.

9.4   LEARNING DISABILITIES – PROGNOSIS

The prognosis is invariably poor as the underlying conditions causing learning disabilities are usually beyond any treatment available today. However, improvement in the functioning of the individual patient can be brought about through successful treatment of some co-existing physical disorder such as by the control of epilepsy or by the treatment of depressive illness. Appropriate social support eg the instruction given in budgeting their finances or settling these patients in appropriate supported lodgings can increase confidence and self esteem and thereby improve functioning as well as protecting these often vulnerable patients from exploitation.

9.5   LEARNING DISABILITIES – THE RISKS OF AGGRESSION AND VIOLENCE

Given the pervasive nature of their disabilities, many of these individuals find themselves in various situations of risk. They respond poorly to stress, often a precipitating cause of aggression and violence involving these patients. Learning disabilities may be associated with mental disorders of the more usual kinds and the aggression may then be related to mental disorder rather than the learning difficulties themselves. There is also in some cases misuse of substances, which further enhances the risk of violence occurring.

9.6   OTHER DEVELOPMENTAL DISORDERS – CHILDHOOD AUTISM

Intellectual deficits as found in the learning disabilities are due to one form (though involving many varieties) of developmental disorder. Another form could preferentially lead to impairment in personality development resulting in the personality disorders and psychopathy which we dealt with in the previous chapter. Here we take up a form of developmental disorder which leads to problems of behaviour, emotion and social interaction called the autistic spectrum disorders. These conditions have been prominent in the public mind in recent years on account of the controversy surrounding the triple MMR vaccine (used for protection against measles, mumps and rubella) administered in childhood. It was being alleged in some quarters, with little or no scientific foundation in fact, that the MMR vaccine had led to an increase in the incidence of these forms of autistic disorder. This was plainly not the case but it is still legitimate to ask whether the seeming increase in the incidence of these disorders is real or apparent. There is no conclusive answer forthcoming as yet. It has been suggested that it is the increased awareness of the condition among the general public as well as among the professionals, along with more refined diagnostic methods that had caused the apparent rise in numbers. Disorders that had previously been considered as being the usual forms of behavioural problems in childhood were now being dignified, it is said, by the diagnosis of autistic spectrum disorder. As so often happens – with attention deficit hyperactivity disorder (ADHD) when medication became available for its treatment, bipolar or manic depressive disorder when lithium treatment first became established – the advent of new therapeutic possibilities raises awareness and leads to a reconsideration of previous diagnoses. In those situations there may be a tendency to overdiagnose some conditions that might previously have been underdiagnosed. The curious feature with the autistic spectrum disorders is that there is as yet no specific treatment available and the greater awareness (and possible overdiagnosis) therefore does not appear to have any pressing therapeutic impetus behind it. For once the pharmaceutical companies could not be convincingly blamed for attempting to raise awareness of a condition so as to promote and be able to sell their therapeutic products.

Childhood autism has been known to exist for a long time and was formally recognised in 1943. It is a condition of childhood and is recognised before the child is three years of age. It has a male preponderance in its prevalence. It afflicts all social classes and the earlier suggestion that it had a preferential higher social class distribution is now known to be false. In fact, this previous assertion was cruel in its further implication that it was 'cold' parents – mostly professionals, some academics – who, by their somehow repressed methods of child rearing, had caused the condition to arise. Looked at now, this suggestions sounds as absurd as it was offensive. There is little doubt that the condition – or the spectrum of disorders – is likely to be shown to be caused by brain dysfunction, the brain being in some way disrupted in its normal development. Several findings have been made on studies of autistic brains though no result is conclusive. Brain size appears to be larger early in life of autistic individuals and abnormalities in brain microstructure as well as in neurochemistry have been proposed as possible accompaniments of the pathology.

The cardinal features of the condition include a solitariness or aloofness found in the child, what is referred to as 'autistic aloneness'. Intimacy is difficult to achieve with these children who appear from early on to have an impaired capacity to form social relationships. So unresponsive can these children be that deafness or learning disabilities may at first be suspected. They lack the playfulness usually associated with children. The second feature is an impaired ability to communicate. This may be manifested by delayed speech, sometimes in a complete failure to talk. Speech, when it appears, is of poor quality and may be repetitive and incorrect in form and content. Comprehension of speech is also poor and language skills such as reading are imperfectly acquired, even then often in a mechanical way with little or no understanding. There is poor eye contact and non-verbal communication is also affected. The third diagnostic feature is the desire for sameness shown by the child with rituals and routines adopted with repetitive patterns of behaviour which, when thwarted, can lead to much distress being demonstrated. There is a mechanical element to play and social communication with little imaginative creativity or fantasy, which reflects the rigidity in the thought processes of the child as well as in his or her behaviour. Associated features may include intellectual impairment (found in some three quarters of affected individuals), epilepsy (found in about a quarter) and behavioural problems which may include a tendency to aggression and violence. Abnormal movements are not uncommonly seen and other severe behavioural problems including self-mutilation may be observed. Seizures, as noted, are found only in a minority of cases.

These abnormalities are associated with other intellectual and behavioural deficiencies. Many autistic children are also intellectually impaired and have the kind of learning disabilities previously described. However, the range of intellectual ability is variable and some autistic children are of normal abilities and in some cases celebrated examples of isolated areas of high accomplishment emerge. These areas of excellence usually involve mathematical or artistic abilities eg being capable of undertaking prodigious feats of calculation which are usually in the province of advanced computers, accomplishing astonishing feats of memory, rising to incredible precision in drawing architectural structures after a mere glance at the building etc etc. These being isolated oases of high performance in an otherwise barren desert of serious disabilities, the term *idiot savant* has come to be applied to these perversely gifted individuals.

There is evidence of some genetic influence, although the impact of the environmental component in causation is suspected to be far greater in most cases. There is no specific treatment available for the condition and the best results are achieved through the deployment of specialised educational techniques. In fact, it has been said the only worthwhile advance in the management of autistic conditions in the past two generations has come by way of improved educational techniques. Residential care may have to be considered in the most severe cases of behaviour disorder. As might be expected, the prognosis is often poor, another indication that intractable forces in the brain are behind the condition. It is probably rare to see an individual suffering from the average case of childhood autistic disorder growing up to become a passably normal member of society. This makes the education and support of parents and teachers all the more important. The abnormal behaviours and the associated medical conditions may be amenable to more successful symptomatic treatment.

9.7   ASPERGER'S SYNDROME

Childhood autism exists at one end of the scale in the disorders of the autistic spectrum. Many atypical or less well defined cases of autism inhabit the rest of the spectrum which leads to, at this other end,

Asperger's syndrome. It may be considered to be a milder version of childhood autism. There may be a similar impairment in social communication with repetitive and isolated behaviour, the child remains aloof, solitary, clumsy and eccentric. However, unlike in the classical case of autism, intelligence and linguistic ability may appear unimpaired. It is rare also to find the associated medical complications such as epilepsy. What the causes are remain mysterious and its resemblance to classical autism in some aspects may only be coincidental. There is no specific treatment and the best hope lies in attention being paid to the improvement in social responses and communication. Individuals with this condition grow up to become not unlike those individuals who have developed some forms of personality disorder.

This is also a condition that seems to have caught the public imagination. Any mental abnormality in an otherwise reasonably successful individual appears capable of being attributed to Asperger's syndrome, as anyone with experience of family and child law, not to mention other branches of the law, knows. A galaxy of persons are now included among the suspects, in some cases posthumously with the help of tendentiously written (or interpreted) biographical studies. In fact, it is an uncommon form of disorder at the other end of the scale from childhood autism. There is no shortfall of intelligence (in fact, the opposite is usually true, as the public's view shows) and no difficulties with ordinary communication. The diagnosis turns on difficulties these individuals have in social and interpersonal interaction.

In view of the widespread misunderstanding of the condition it is well worth considering the diagnostic criteria. These suggest the following as being required, firstly, there may be marked impairment of nonverbal behaviour such as involving eye contact, facial expression, bodily posture and gestures, failure to develop appropriate social peer relationships, a lack of social or emotional reciprocity, possessing a restricted and repetitive stereotyped pattern of behaviour, interests and activities such as involvement with routines and rituals, stereotyped and repetitive behaviour, the disturbance must cause clinically significant impairment in social, occupational or other important areas of functioning, there is no clinically significant general delay in language, there is no clinically significant delay in cognitive development or in the development of age-appropriate self help skills, adaptive behaviour (other than social interaction), and curiosity about the environment on childhood, and that criteria are not met for another pervasive development disorder or schizophrenia. There may be a risk of aggression and violence on account of the poor social responses and inadequate skills in social interaction.

As is evident, there are strict criteria to be met before a diagnosis of the condition is arrived at. There is no place, it would appear, for casual suggestion that an individual could be suffering from the disorder. In one case the estranged female partner of a 35 year-old man suggested in private law childcare proceedings that he could be suffering from Asperger's syndrome. On examination, the only findings were that he was highly qualified, was rather concerned with household security (he lived in North London in an area notorious for crime and was following police advice given to householders) and was somewhat of a stickler about things and detail. He had been to university which, when the relationship had run into difficulties, had been a point apparently used by the female partner's father as a possible foundation for the diagnosis (inevitably the man occupied a higher social position than the woman's family). A second case involved a 20-year-old woman, a mother in childcare proceedings, who had developed a schizophrenia-like illness and had suffered numerous breakdowns over the course of years. She was known to abuse illicit substances extensively and was non-compliant with medication. The urgent clinical question was whether or not she had true schizophrenic illness with all the implications for having the condition (see previous discussion on schizophrenia) or this was a drug-induced schizophreniform state. However, it became known that she had a half-brother who had severe childhood autism. Asperger's syndrome as being suffered by her became a preoccupation during the proceedings.

9.8   SUMMARY

1.   Learning disabilities, although they may involve most or all functions in a patient, are conventionally attributed to intellectual handicap. Minor forms are far commoner than severe affliction and involve predominantly environmental factors in the form of personal and social deprivation of some kind, whereas a clear genetic influence may be discernible in severe cases. While the condition is untreatable in conventional terms, support can enable patients to lead reasonably successful lives in the community. There is no place now for institutional care of the traditional kind.

2.   The provenance of the autistic disorders is still unclear, although almost certainly some form of maldevelopment of the brain is involved. This spectrum of disorders contains individuals who may be near normal to those who suffer severe physical and mental disability. The condition is untreatable, the best results being obtained by special educational and behavioural measures.

3.   The nature of the handicap suffered by those with learning disabilities and autism leads them into various situations concerning the law. Offending may involve the criminal law while parental incapacity of various kinds interests family and child law practitioners. The intellectual shortfall is a consideration in employment while nuisance behaviour due to a lack of social awareness is not uncommon. The impaired social and emotional responsiveness is usually the source of aggression and violence involving these patients. They may also be unduly suggestible, a

matter of interest to the criminal law when they become suspects, and they may also be at risk of abuse and exploitation.

CHAPTER 10

SPECIAL SITUATIONS AND UNUSUAL DISORDERS INVOLVING PSYCHIATRIC VIOLENCE

Some psychiatric conditions with a bearing on the potential for aggressive and violent behaviour, although they could be accommodated within the diagnostic categories already considered, would benefit by separate treatment.

10.1   POST-PARTUM PSYCHIATRIC DISORDERS

This refers to mental disorders suffered in the period following childbirth. These conditions, at any rate in their clinical aspect, are indistinguishable from mental disorders suffered at any other time but for many reasons, including their importance in medico-legal situations, they will be taken up separately here.

The distinction to be made between physiology and pathology applies here as it does in all clinical psychiatric, indeed all medical, practice. Physiological states – such as unhappiness, uncomplicated grief reactions, psychological shock – are deemed normal responses. Up to 70 per cent of women suffer some changes in mood in the post-partum period, say within the first six weeks. These are the well-recognised 'maternity blues' with an onset normally in the first week following childbirth. Apart from this mood change in the direction of depression, there could also be anxiety, irritability and insomnia. Some negative feelings in respect of the newborn may be the result. These changes in the mood state are normal and do not require any active treatment. All that is usually required is reassurance (it seems to be commoner after the first episode of childbirth) and support. As with the distinction to be made between normal unhappiness and a clinically significant depressive illness, the differences between 'maternity blues' and post-partum depressive illness appear to be quantitative, the psychotic depressive state being rare, however.

The physiological changes which, in part, cause the 'maternity blues' and other normal phenomena may be due to the hormonal changes occurring after the birth when the body begins the process of readjustment towards the normal physical state for the mother.

10.2 POST-PARTUM DEPRESSIVE ILLNESS

This is a clinically recognised condition, meaning it satisfies the criteria required for a depressive illness to be diagnosed with the only additional element being it happens to be found in the post-partum period. This period is variously defined, but up to six months is usually allowed, although most cases of depressive illness appear to have their onset within the first three months, in particular in the first month after the birth of the child. Up to 15 per cent of mothers are noted to have this illness. The full significance of the clinical picture and, hence, the diagnosis could be missed because the symptoms come to be attributed to 'maternity blues' or a mother's natural anxiety in the care especially of a first born child. Tiredness and exhaustion following childbirth could also mask the clinical picture. Otherwise the clinical picture is as it is found in depressive illness afflicting women, and for that matter men, at other times. The treatment is also broadly similar although there is an additional urgency brought about by the need to ensure mother and baby can bond without too much disruption in their relationship. More severe cases are treated in 'mother and baby' units which are dedicated to treating mother and holding baby so that the processes of bonding continue even as the mother receives treatment. The prognosis, as with modern treatment of any depressive illness, is generally good. Post-partum depressive illness is common in mothers with a history of psychiatric disorder and in those in whom adverse personal and social factors operate. Social isolation, relationship difficulties and worries concerning finance and housing are commonly to be found. The obvious risk emanating from the mother is to the baby, an issue to be addressed in the second part of this book.

10.3 POST-PARTUM OR PUERPERAL PSYCHOSIS

Like depressive illness, the psychoses may also make an appearance in the post-partum period. The first months following birth are the time when women appear to be most at risk and a significant proportion of these (up to 25 per cent) give a history of previous mental illness. Women with bipolar disorder are at particularly high risk of puerperal psychosis, with episodes following 25-50 per cent of deliveries. In addition to a history of bipolar disorder, other important risk factors include having experienced a previous episode of puerperal psychosis, having a first degree relation who has experienced an episode of puerperal psychosis and having a first degree relation with bipolar disorder. It is, however, a far less common condition than depressive illness in the post-partum period. Only about one in 500 women is affected in this situation with this condition. The onset can be fairly sudden and acute with features of schizophrenia, a schizo-affective disorder, mania or psychotic depression all being possible. There is little or nothing that is distinctive in the symptoms seen in this period as opposed to a condition presenting at other times. There is obviously greater urgency with treatment and it is usual for admission to be sought to a 'mother and baby' unit. Some care has to be taken with medication as the mother may continue to breastfeed and many drugs are known to be transmitted through breast milk. Treatment through modern drugs – and the judicious use of ECT in appropriate cases in the past – is generally successful and a good result may be anticipated. The prognosis is as good as in the non-puerperal case and when there is a protracted or chronic course run by the illness the adverse factors determining this are as for any other illness. Nothing specifically pathogenic or conducive to a poor prognosis has been conclusively shown to exist in the post-partum period in itself. However, as stated, women with a prior history of mental disorder are more vulnerable to mental illness of all kinds in the post-partum period and, if they have suffered one bout of post-partum mental illness, it is usual to predict they could be at higher risk after any subsequent childbirth. The chances of recurrence of illness after the next childbirth appear to be about 1 in 4.

The aetiology of the post-partum psychiatric disorders remains unclear. The obvious potential causative factors are the significant hormonal and chemical changes that occur during pregnancy and persist into the post-partum period. But these changes are common to all women in this condition and no convincing differences in endocrine or biochemical changes have been established between those women who fall ill and those mothers who do not. The prior history of the mental illness and the persisting risk in any future post-partum period has been noted already. Emphasis has been laid on psychosocial factors such as marital or relationship difficulties, ambivalence towards the pregnancy and the newly born child, and more general factors such as housing and financial worries. In fact, considering the available evidence as a whole, one must conclude the post-partum period (and the preceding pregnancy) probably act as a stressful life event to susceptible women. The fact that childbirth may generally be a desirable event in the minds of most women is not a particularly relevant consideration; a much looked forward to move of house is known to be one of the most powerful adverse stressors to individuals. Prevention makes use of the fact of prior vunerability in those who have suffered previous mental ill health. Careful monitoring during pregnancy and in the puerperium should be able to prevent the onset of more severe illness and disability. The obvious risk posed by these women to the newborn child is a consideration.

Practitioners in family and child law are occasionally drawn into situations involving these cases. A mother previously in difficulty in looking after a newborn may be deemed to be at risk after any subsequent pregnancy. Liaison between local and health authorities may mean information comes to be shared more sensibly. Prejudice is, however, to be avoided. Although there is evidence that a mother who falls ill once is at a higher risk of becoming ill again in the course of a subsequent puerperium, it can never be the case that a mother's childcare abilities should be deemed automatically to be at risk of becoming impaired. In fact, the degree of illness and disability may vary widely and each situation needs careful consideration and analysis in its own right.

10.4   CULTURAL INFLUENCES

At first sight it may appear odd to separate culture from the general description given to psychiatric disorders, for no disorder is free from the influence of culture, the term used in its broadest sense. In Chapters 1 and 2 we dealt with the part that culture played in the extent and manifestations of aggressive and violent behaviour. We have also considered the impact of culture and subculture in the study of alcohol and illicit substance misuse. In this section, however, we shall use the term culture in its narrower meaning. With so many communities now displaced from their places of origin, it is widely accepted that diverse cultural influences may be in play when mental illness presents itself for examination and study. The subject is vast and here only the common influences with some impact on medico-legal situations will be taken up. Also, only those possible influences of psychiatric ie medical interest will be considered. Some further remarks will be made on the possible cultural aspects of aggression and violence when this matter is touched on also in the next part of this book.

Mental disorder, like all disease conditions, is universal and the signs and symptoms of disorders, at any rate in their technical aspects, are now increasingly studied according to standard criteria. It is, therefore, in the interpretation of these signs and symptoms that the challenge of culture-bound influences resides. We have already remarked on the cultural influences operating in any study of delusions in the chapter on psychotic disorders. A delusion, it will be recalled, is not merely a false belief that is unshakeably held despite evidence to the contrary, it is also a belief which is out of keeping with the social and cultural beliefs of the patient. Thus, one finds persisting in many cultures beliefs in such phenomena as witchcraft and 'the evil eye' and an individual from such a culture may express a view that neighbours or family or some person in or outside of his culture has evil designs on him, has taken steps to put such designs into practice, that this person should be thwarted lest he succeed in his aim for illness or misfortune due to the machinations of such an individual may otherwise come to afflict him. If within the culture of such an individual such beliefs are commonplace, it may not amount to a persecutory delusion and, therefore, is not a symptom of mental illness. Careful analysis of the facts, apart from the possession of a sound working knowledge of the culture in question, is required before one comes to this conclusion for persecutory delusions can, of course, arise in such an individual in the course of schizophrenia or some other psychotic condition. The test, as we have seen before, is to see how any persecutory beliefs an individual possesses might have originated, what form the finished product has attained and, most importantly, what the interpretation or explanation given by family members or others in the community is for this phenomenon. As a rule of thumb, anything deemed abnormal within the family or the community is more suggestive of a true delusion than any belief accepted with equanimity by others within that community.

Two examples of apparently delusional beliefs have been discussed previously (Mahendra, 2006). One involved a 26 year-old woman from Rwanda who had suffered horrific experiences including acts of multiple rape in the course of the civil war then prevailing in that country. She had become involved in childcare proceedings in England after the child conceived as a result of a rape and born to her showed serious disabilities. It transpired she held strong cultural views on those who might continue to harm her and these beliefs were based on her experience of tribal rivalries. She had also spent time in Uganda where many of her compatriots had been displaced with her. Seeking asylum in Britain, she had also made contact with an evangelical church. She naturally sought comfort among the black community in Britain but her specifications for association with members of the black community were rather strict – she was prepared to trust and work with black Americans and those whose origins had been in the Caribbean or the West Indies but she continued to have the liveliest suspicion of any person originating from Africa.

Another example was an 18 year-old girl, of Bangladeshi origins but brought up from infancy in Britain, who also became involved in childcare proceedings on account of her very young child. The girl's lifestyle, notwithstanding the strict constraints of her native culture and the location she found herself in (which was predominantly Muslim) as a teenager and adolescent, could have been, on first impression, that of a certain type of native young girl of today – she drank alcohol and got drunk, she freely abused illicit substances and engaged in casual and, for a while, underage sex. Closer inspection showed, however, a more serious disturbance of conduct along with some psychotic features such as auditory hallucinations. In fact, there appeared to be much disruption to a still evolving personality in her case and although it was probably too early yet to arrive at a diagnosis of personality disorder the signs of such a condition were suggestive. What was, however, even more interesting from the clinical point of view, was her belief that her troubles – in particular the symptoms of mental disorder – had been brought about through consuming foodstuffs given to her by the 'the many enemies of the family.' She now took extreme care to examine the provenance of any food she consumed and shunned food that had been sent to her family from abroad. Thus, the outlook and attitudes of a thoroughly modern (if somewhat disturbed) young girl, whose behaviour was to all intents and purposes those of many denizens in the West, could co-exist with beliefs which are commonplace within the Bangladeshi culture. That is why her auditory hallucinations were clearly recognised as being features of a mental disorder but her persecutory ideas had not been.

Where psychotic illness is concerned, the presence of some recognised symptoms of illness may be found in some cultures while being absent in others. Moreover, symptoms of illness may also show a change over a period of time. Until about a half century ago there was present, universally as far as one can judge these matters, a symptom of schizophrenia called catatonia. This involved both the phenomena of mutism (mute by visitation of God, in medico-legal parlance) and stupor, that is a severe psychomotor retardation. So common was this condition that a sub-category of schizophrenia called catatonic schizophrenia came to be recognised. Over some generations this condition has shown a dramatic decline in incidence in the nations of the West, so much so that the diagnosis (which is still in existence in the ICD-10 Classification of Mental Disorders) is largely made only in the developing parts of the world. This also means the condition may still be found in immigrant communities in the West. Why this decline should have taken place so selectively remains something of a mystery although there have been suggestions that an infectious process might be involved – a virus, perhaps, that mutated into innocuousness in some parts of the world. Whatever the explanation, catatonia remains a condition where a physical symptom appears now to be determined by a cultural influence of a more tangible kind.

In a similar vein, the influence of known infection, especially in the causation of acute confusional states, including delirium, which could have been acquired in the cultures of origin is not to be disregarded when it comes to the evaluation of mental disorder in migrants. Other physical illness, now rare in the West, as possible causes of mental disorder, should also be borne in mind when dealing with these patients.

In Chapter 5 we noted the need to consider the patterns of presentation of depressive illness in various cultures. In those patients originating especially from the cultures of Asia and Africa it is customary for them to emphasise the physical aspects of symptoms (such as the insomnia or the aches and pains associated with depressive illness) and deny or play down the psychical element such as the low mood or the reduced capacity to enjoy oneself. It is usual to ascribe this emphasis on the physical to the stigma still believed to prevail in many parts of the world against mental disorders. Notwithstanding this, it is important to recognise this cultural bias, for it has a bearing on the issue of the kind of insight the patient possesses in respect of his disorder. In evaluating the presence of insight it is usual to seek evidence that the patient recognises that he or she is suffering from a mental or psychological problem. It can be readily appreciated that in a patient from these cultures denial of psychological causation or manifestation of disorder is not necessarily a sign of lack of insight as the term is understood. Further, given the apparent prominence of physical symptoms as reported by these patients, there is also the risk of over-investigation in the pursuit of supposed physical causes of the disorder. Unnecessary radiological or laboratory investigations are to be deprecated in the management of psychiatric disorder as they tend to reinforce the impression the patient may already have that what underlies his feeling of being ill is possibly something grave which could be identified if more energetic (and expensive) investigation were only undertaken. One runs the risk of converting someone suffering from a straightforward disorder such as a depressive illness into someone with a somatoform disorder or hypochondria.

This leads us naturally into considering the hysterical or conversion/dissociative disorders which were briefly dealt with in the chapter on the neuroses The grosser manifestations – once very common and which helped to make the reputations of Freud and other psychoanalysts – are now rare in the West. However, the more florid examples of this condition – paralysis, blindness, trance states etc – are still to be found from time to time in persons from communities drawn from the developing world. Hysterical conditions are believed to be due to a neurotic reaction to stress which may be perceived or only unconsciously expressed. In many cultures gross mental disturbance in the form of psychosis – reactive or stress-related – may also be found. These are usually short-lived episodes of illness proximately related to stressful events, reasonably easily treated through symptom relief by anti-psychotic agents and the treatment does not need to be prolonged. The prognoses of these conditions does not depend on any underlying disease process (as may occur with schizophrenia or the bipolar affective disorders) as such but in the capacity the individual possesses to deal with and cope with future stressful events.

There are many culture-bound, as opposed to culturally influenced, psychiatric disorders which are of little relevance to everyday psychiatric practice in the West. We mention here only '*amok*' which has entered the language by way of such phrases as 'running amok'. This is a condition occasionally manifested in South East Asia and which is marked by extravagant behaviour in the face of stressful events and which may lead to homicidal or suicidal acts being committed unless the patient is restrained, usually with the help of a traditional local healer.

We are more interested here in a few otherwise uncommon disorders which nevertheless may have an impact on legal practice. The first of these is morbid jealousy.

10.5   MORBID JEALOUSY

This is referred to also as the Othello syndrome. The main symptom involves a state in which the patient may show a variation between demonstrating excessive suspicion of a spouse or partner's fidelity (males are more commonly afflicted) to possessing full blown delusions, having symptoms in other words which make up a psychotic condition. There is often present an inadequacy in the personality of the sufferer even before the illness sets in and there is also an association with abuse of alcohol. The behaviours engaged in may be unreasonable, even extreme or bizarre. One recalls a middle-aged man who worked as a commissionaire at the doors of a financial institution in London. He sported colourful livery as his uniform. His jealous wife forbade him to wear this uniform on the underground, which he used to reach his place of employment, lest it turn women passengers' heads. There is usually a relentless pursuit of the truth the patient has become convinced of, namely that the spouse or partner has been unfaithful and all that is necessary for the evidence to emerge is to leave no stone unturned in looking for that proof. Investigation, interrogation and cross examination may reach extraordinary levels with spying on movements, checking credit card slips or telephone bills, following the spouse wherever she goes, and examining her underwear and bed linen for evidence of sexual activity. Violence is not uncommon and it is one of the psychiatric disorders where in a small minority of cases the killing of a spouse or partner becomes a rather more predictable eventuality than in the usual run of psychiatric cases. Treatment is difficult, for the interference of the personality is usually strong and the best results are probably obtained when morbid jealousy is a symptom of another condition such as schizophrenia, depressive illness or alcohol misuse rather than as a free standing paranoid illness in its own right. The protection of the spouse or partner may become a matter of urgency. The subject is of obvious interest for consideration of risk of aggressive and violent behaviour which in these cases is very real.

10.6   EROTOMANIA

Another condition, once believed to be a rare curiosity, has come into prominence on account of an association, at least in a few cases, with the phenomenon called 'stalking'. In its traditional form – called erotomania or De Clerambault's syndrome – spinsters of a certain age used to be affected. She would become deluded that a man, usually of exalted social status or distinguished standing, was in love with her. She would proceed to arrange her life accordingly and could remain chaste and faithful while waiting for him to come definitively into her life. At this stage things remain fairly innocent but the behaviour could extend to harassment and pursuit which could lead to social, personal and professional embarrassment for the victim (some male doctors have been hauled up before the GMC following a complaint by a spurned female patient suffering from this disorder that there had been an improper relationship between them). The criminal law could also become implicated. Injunctions, their breaches and ensuing incarceration are not unknown. Treatment is rarely straightforward unless, as in the case of morbid jealousy, the delusional belief is a symptom of another psychotic illness amenable to treatment when there is a reasonable prospect of success, although relapses are common. The free-standing psychosis is a form of paranoid disorder or a persistent delusional disorder. More recently, the phenomenon of stalking – a form of nuisance behaviour – with a male preponderance, has become recognised although few of these individuals involved in it have any recognised mental disorder in them. There is no conclusive explanation for the phenomenon though it could be suggested that the easy familiarity with the lives of and imagined intimacy with celebrities – encouraged by the media – makes it appear that anyone, however high, is now accessible to someone, however low. Treatment, if actually merited, is difficult and the law's protection may have to be sought by the victim. This condition, too, has obvious implications for the study of risk that may involve the victims of these deluded individuals.

10.7 MUNCHAUSEN'S SYNDROME

This topic has made several sensational appearances in connection with the law, especially by way of its alleged variant, Munchausen's syndrome by proxy, and therefore it seems appropriate to make passing reference to it in these pages. The syndrome in its classical form owes its name to an eighteenth century figure. Baron von Munchausen (sic) (1720-1797) was a real enough person, a German soldier descended from ancient Hanoverian nobility. He served in military campaigns and was noted for his ridiculously exaggerated exploits. A collection of stories was attributed to him. However, much of the final form of the stories was due to the work of Erich Raspe (1737-1794), a scholar and curator of gems and medals at a museum. Accused of stealing and selling the medals, he fled Germany for England. Here he engaged in further swindling and had to flee, in turn, to Ireland where he died.

The symptoms displayed in the classical form of the disorder have as much foundation as the baron's stories but display a more humdrum character which, paradoxically, succeeds in fooling doctors. Young men are preponderantly affected. They show the features of pathological lying, exaggeration (or manufacture) of symptoms and the presentation at various hospitals, especially in their casualty departments. Their symptoms may be described with such skill that extensive investigations may follow. The features of an acute abdominal emergency may be so convincingly described that they may come to have numerous operations and they walk about sporting 'criss cross' patterns on their abdomen as stigmata of their adventures. Apart from the lying there is often also the skilful acting complete with the necessary props eg simulation of bleeding, self-injury with swallowed objects and the convincing portrayal of physical and mental illness. They are deemed nuisance patients for they waste so much resource (while also putting themselves at risk of iatrogenic illness or injury) and their details may be transmitted across the land so as to alert hospitals to their existence and possible attendance at their doors.

The syndrome is probably best understood as a form of severe personality disorder although a hysterical basis cannot be ruled out (see case described below). A severe personality disorder is probably the most likely explanation also for the variant Munchausen syndrome by proxy which has achieved such notoriety that the diagnosis has been discredited. In this situation a parent (most usually the mother) repeatedly seeks medical intervention for a child by making up symptoms of disease or by deliberately inducing same in the child by any means including causing injury. In other words, the child is being made an instrument of the parent's psychopathology. Gross disorder of mental functioning may be seen in such parents. A 30 year-old woman with a young child – hence their involvement in childcare proceedings – not only made up symptoms of illness for herself and her child but also consistently denied usually impeccable sources of factual information – the details on her birth certificate, marriage certificate, pictures of her wedding, letters written about the child by doctors and other documents in similar vein. She would not accept her recorded age or that for the child even when these had been established through official documentation. When the paternity of a second child was brought into question, she tampered with a sample being taken for DNA analysis and very nearly earned a conviction for attempting to pervert the course of justice. The diagnostic category most closely fitting her behaviour appeared to be mixed dissociative disorders (F.44.7 of the ICD-10). The condition, whether in its classical form or its variant, is untreatable for practical purposes.

These conditions often have strong associations with matters genuinely involving health and the care of patients. A notorious case which made public headlines was that involving the paediatric nurse Beverley Allitt (another case involving a nurse recently was that of Benjamin Geen, a nurse in Oxford convicted in similar circumstances) who was convicted in May 1993 and sentenced to 13 life sentences for murder, attempted murder and serious assault. She was a nurse aged 24 who was said to have craved approval, attention and sympathy from colleagues and senior staff by raising alarms and helping to save the lives of child patients whose lives she had placed in jeopardy through her own actions. She had later shown no remorse, indulged in pathological lying and attention-seeking behaviour and had sought to be a member of the medical resuscitation team. It turned out she had herself made numerous visits to the casualty department of a local hospital in the course of a three-year period. She had been treated for various self-inflicted injuries and had made false complaints of pregnancy, gastric ulcers and brain tumours. She also alleged she had been sexually assaulted at knife point and also had had treatment for anorexia nervosa.

10.8   SUMMARY

1.   Post-partum mental disorder is not uncommon, although frequently missed on account of 'maternity blues' being so common. Various risks including a failure of attachment between the newborn and the mother and physical risk to the newborn may arise. Results with prompt and vigorous treatment are satisfactory. There is an increased risk of recurrence following future childbirth.

2. Culture, the term used in its widest sense, influences the presentation of all mental disorders, in some cases conditions being confined to particular cultures. In some cultures the physical symptoms are given greater emphasis, which does not indicate loss of insight but is a manifestation of cultural belief. Treatment is influenced by beliefs of the individual affecting his attitudes to medication and psychological treatment.

3. Morbid jealousy, a form of psychosis, is a potentially dangerous condition, a spouse or partner being at appreciable risk of being a victim of violence. Protective measures need to be taken in all cases. The results of treatment depend on whether the condition is a symptom of another condition when results may be relatively good or is a free-standing psychotic condition when results are usually poor. There is a strong association with alcohol misuse. The risks of aggressive and violent behaviour are high.

4. Munchausen's syndrome and any of its variants are to be seen as forms of severe personality disorder. The preoccupation these individuals have with matters concerning health may lead to harm being caused to themselves and also to those with whom they are intimate, especially their children or other persons being cared for by them.

PART III

VIOLENCE – SOME SPECIAL SITUATIONS

CHAPTER 11

DOMESTIC VIOLENCE

11.1 DOMESTIC VIOLENCE – GENERAL CONSIDERATIONS

Domestic violence belongs to a special category of aggressive behaviour and may be deemed to be a sub-species of violent behaviour in its general aspect. At the outset we need to define what is meant by the term domestic violence for the purposes of this book. In many studies undertaken now the term used is intimate partner violence which, as is suggested, involves violence between spouses or those who are in a quasi-matrimonial intimate relationship. This chapter has a wider ambit and considers all violence that could take place in a domestic context. In other words, violence involving the children of a family, that between siblings or an extended family including the issue of forced marriage and violence involving also employees in a household also form part of the subject matter that is studied here. Many of the points already made in regard to violence in general are applicable when studying this special case from a psychiatric point of view. However, some preliminary points may be made in respect of this issue. Firstly, while all criminal statistics are far from reliable, domestic violence is probably in a league of its own for unreliability. We have to resort to anecdotal evidence and personal professional experience when writing about this issue but it seems true to say domestic violence is far from uncommon. It is found in the most unlikely of situations, no age and neither sex is preferentially favoured among victims, and it cuts across every social class and every community. Social and, especially, cultural factors play a decisive role in determining the level of domestic violence that is found within any given community. There are some communities now established in Britain where cultural practices inform behaviour that leads to domestic violence which, in fact, may not even be recognised as such. Much bewilderment and even offence may be caused to these individuals by investigating such behaviour which, in some communities, may be seen as the norm. Chastising one's wife or child (the wife also joining in the latter activity) is time-honoured and sanctioned by long-standing cultural practice in some communities. Forced marriage is an example of a culturally sanctioned practice. It is one of the challenges faced by the family and child practitioner to deal with such behaviour which comes into conflict with the much more enlightened attitudes which now find reflection in English law. One of the insights to be gained from studying practices which are habitual in migrant communities is that they also offer an understanding of behaviour which may be found in native sub-cultures, e g those involving persistent criminal activity especially involving gangs associated with the use also of illicit substances where the constituent populations of those marginal communities may be entirely of native origins. It is a conclusion one draws from studying domestic violence, at any rate from the psychiatric point of view, that aggressive behaviour may stem not only from the actions of individuals but also as a reflection of the dynamics and shared values of a particular family or community.

Whether special cultural factors are present or not, one still needs to study the mental states of the members of the family who are involved as victims of violence. Where illness or disorder is present (depressive illness, an anxiety state, perhaps dementia in the spouse or partner, or some behavioural disorder involving a child) the provoking factors for violence may be clear enough. But often there may not be overt mental disorder present but rather the presence of personality difficulties or defects in the spouse or partner which tend to make him or her a readier victim than would have been the case if such an individual had possessed a normal, well adjusted personality. The remarks made concerning the aggressive, anxious or dependent individuals who may become victims of repeated violence apply *a fortiori* to cases of conflict in the domestic situation. There is also apparent collusion on the part of the victim with the acts of violence being perpetrated against him or her, who conceal or deny these acts and also show ambivalent behaviour where criminal proceedings are concerned, making and withdrawing complaints and first supporting and then drawing back from prosecutions. A full assessment of incidents of domestic violence involves the examination of both parties. There are obviously other factors besides those of personal emotions operating in families – financial difficulties, debt, housing problems, and physical factors such as disability and age. An individual who is trapped within a domestic setting for whatever reason is at greater risk of continuing violence – physical as well as emotional – than one who has the independence of spirit and body and the means to assert himself and, where necessary, effect an escape. Desperation may make one a victim, or renew one's status as a victim. A 35-year-old woman of uncertain immigration status was trapped in a marriage with a man who was said by her to be a brute and a bully, causing her to flee to a refuge with her son. They separated and the child resided with her. Unfortunately, she suffered a bout (her second) of a stress-related psychotic illness and had to yield the son to its father. She was not entitled to housing or social benefits on account of her unsettled immigration status and was rendered both homeless and penniless. She was reduced to accepting lodgings with a relation of her ex-husband and to accepting money from the ex-husband. In formal childcare proceedings she consented to the child living with his father and accepted sessions of contact left to the discretion of the father to arrange. The portents for renewed domestic violence were not good.

As all the studies show, there is a high risk of repeated violence in a domestic setting and it has been estimated that there are at least two murders each week involving spouses or partners. Risk involves both parties to different degrees for, in a minority of cases, the abused partner, in a case of the worm turning, may kill the abusing partner. This is the extreme case. Far commoner is the involvement of both parties in routine acts of violence committed on one another. The term 'battered wives' syndrome' has sometimes been applied to the mental state a chronically abused spouse or partner suffers as a result as a result of repeated beatings. The term is obviously a misnomer for a growing number of husbands or male partners are also found to be victims. Further, it is not as yet a recognised psychiatric syndrome and there must be doubt if a special category is needed for violence occurring in a domestic context as opposed to non-domestic situations. Where murder comes to be charged it could be argued in most instances the facts could satisfy the partial defences of diminished responsibility or provocation, the domestic circumstances merely forming the backdrop to these partial defences.

Mental disorder in the perpetration of domestic violence is relatively uncommon, though recognised psychiatric illnesses such as schizophrenia, depressive or bipolar illness may predispose to violence, especially in the acute phase of psychotic illness. Morbid jealousy, as already discussed, is known to produce risk of battery or worse suffered by spouse or partner. By far the commonest type of mental disorder involved in these cases is personality disorder where the spouse or partner suffering from this condition acts out his aggressive tendencies in the face of domestic stresses, or following no provocation at all. Mental disorder, as mentioned, may also be exhibited by the victim when it takes on a similar presentation. In the absence of obvious mental disorder on the part of the assaulting partner or spouse, one is reduced to looking at a situation of bullying translated to the domestic context, cultural or subcultural factors, and any previous experience the perpetrator has been exposed to, especially childhood physical abuse. Many abused spouses or partners show anxiety (avoidant) or dependent personalities. The inability to escape – for whatever reason, be it emotional or financial – may be a factor in exposing such an individual to further violence. Other factors noted in the literature include immaturity, lack of adaptability, and emotional conflict suffered by the abusing spouse or partner. Some victims, by repeatedly returning to situations of violence, are believed to have masochistic tendencies along with feelings of being needed. Aggression may also be provoked when the assailant spouse or partner finds himself unable to satisfy the needs of a spouse or partner for excessive dependence on the other. Some men have sadistic tendencies with sexual connotations in that they do not feel fully potent unless they can establish their authority over a helpless female, in the absence of which he cannot give or receive affection in a manner which is emotionally satisfying to him. There is also an element of learned behaviour which contributes to situations of domestic violence. Some individuals have learned in childhood that violence had helped them to achieve their desires and this tendency to aggression might have been reinforced by parental example. This learned violence is carried over into his own relationships when domination is sought to be created over his spouse or partner. Cultural constraints such as the stigma attaching to the separating party, especially when female, in some communities also exposes the victim to recurrent acts of violence. In many cases one is left musing upon that notorious phrase – 'he or she does it because he or she can' – when trying to explain why a violent spouse or partner appears to be getting away with repeated acts of violence. Single mothers appear in general to make up a vulnerable group. They are significantly more likely to have psychiatric disorders and poor mental health outcomes, particularly anxiety states and substance misuse. Lone mothers are also more likely to have experienced physical and sexual violence and these severe traumatic experiences are more strongly associated with the presence of psychiatric disorders than either single parent status or other socio-demographic characteristics.

The role alcohol and illicit drugs play in the victim may also be a crucial element in situations of continuing violence. If both spouses or partners engage in the misuse of alcohol or illicit substances, they may together also inhabit a subculture from which neither feels free to withdraw. One partner may well be dependent on the other for the supply of substances, and the craving associated with the need for alcohol or illicit drugs may make them more literally dependent on the other to ease them out of a withdrawal state. There are other explanations proffered for why spouses or partners – usually women victims but an increasing number of men caught up in these situations as well – continue to accept violence and abuse, but most of these (eg a perverse desire to improve or 'cure' a violent partner) are beyond the scope of ordinary clinical observation and consideration. Similar considerations apply to situations concerning forced marriage.

An individual's personality is formed in the context of his childhood spent within his family and it is well accepted (though not yet provable in any quantifiable fashion) that formative experiences are vital to the shaping of any personality. What could be positive experiences and which are negative are not all known by any means, but there is sufficient evidence that childhood experiences of abuse – physical, emotional or sexual – do come to play an important part in the psychological make up of the adult individual and if such adverse experiences do influence the finished personality in relevant ways, the stage may be set for the behaviours determined by such a personality to make an impact on those with whom such an individual comes to have relationships with in adult life. Where children are concerned, such difficulties involving the personality may be transmitted to yet another generation. The saying that the abused become abusers has some truth where, at least, physical violence is concerned.

11.2 DOMESTIC VIOLENCE – THE EFFECTS

As domestic violence has grown in recognition, the mortality and morbidity concerning the victims of domestic violence are now altogether better appreciated. Surveys have shown that at least two adult spouses or partners die each week as a result of being victims of domestic violence. At least three children are said to die each week as a result of violence or neglect in the home. Golding (1999) showed that the prevalence of mental health problems among battered women was nearly 50 per cent, that suicidal behaviour was found in 18 per cent, post traumatic stress disorder was found in 60 per cent, alcohol misuse in 19 per cent and illicit drug misuse in 9 per cent. Itzin et al (2008) have summarised the studies undertaken on the nature and extent of domestic violence and abuse. Child sexual abuse is said to involve 21 per cent of girls and 11 per cent of boys while child physical abuse concerned 21 per cent of children with 7 per cent being the victims of severe physical abuse. Further, a third of sexual offenders in contact with the criminal justice system annually are said to be adolescents. Domestic violence involves 25 per cent of women, with, as already mentioned, two killed each week and one-quarter of all violent crime is found in a domestic setting. Pregnancy appears to be an especially traumatic period for women with 30 per cent of cases of violence directed against them starting or escalating in that period. Cases of rape and sexual violence in the domestic context involve 7 per cent of women and 0.5 per cent of men. Over 50 per cent of the perpetrators of this form of sexual violence are current or ex-partners while 35 per cent of other assailants are known to their victims and only 11 per cent of these offences are committed by strangers. These authors also summarise the effects of childhood violence and abuse on health and mental health. The long-term mental health effects of childhood sexual abuse include depression, anxiety post-traumatic stress disorder, psychosis, substance misuse, eating disorders, self harm and suicide. Other adverse health effects of childhood sexual abuse include higher rates of behaviours involving health risks such as smoking, alcohol and drug misuse, risky sexual behaviour (including prostitution), sexually transmitted disease and gynaecological problems.

11.3 DOMESTIC VIOLENCE DIRECTLY INVOLVING CHILDREN

The physical abuse of children which, of course involves violence, has been the subject of several studies. What kind of parent is likely to abuse children in this fashion has been subject to research. Some studies have shown that in cases of physical abuse the parents need not belong exclusively to any particular social class, level of educational attainment or occupational group but are to be found everywhere in the community. But other studies have found an association between physical abuse of children and deprived areas which held parents belonging to lower socio-economic classes and also a higher number of mothers who were of less than average intelligence. These parents also showed frequently personality disorders which involved high levels of emotional conflict and anxiety with difficulty in tolerating frustration and controlling impulsive behaviour. Most, though by no means all, had had a history of unsatisfactory parenting themselves and poor childhood experiences. These individuals were emotionally deprived, felt rejected and their need for a dependent relationship frustrated. Their self-esteem, confidence and capacity for trust were correspondingly low. Many had been punished excessively as children and themselves subjected to physical abuse and they, in turn, tended to repeat the styles of parenting and child control to which they themselves had been subjected. They lacked adequate knowledge of the practicalities involved in childcare and failed also to understand or accept the needs and dependence of immature children.

One study has suggested there may be three styles of family relationships associated with the physical abuse of children.

1.   The severely hostile, aggressive parent who appeared to suffer almost continual anger, had uncontrolled outbursts of temper and violence at any irritation or frustration, including those provoked by the child.

2.   The passive, inadequate parent who looked desperately for opportunities to be dependent, and competed with the children for the attention and support of the spouse or partner. These parents were highly anxious and frequently became depressed. They were capable of neglect as well as abuse of the child.

3.   The rigid, compulsively controlled and orderly parent, who lacked warmth and tended to reject the child. Their own need for success and order made it difficult for them to accept the demands and mess created by the child who was expected to show excellence in behaviour and development to assuage the parents' doubts and fears about their parental ability.

Psychiatric disorders are relatively uncommon to find in cases involving physical violence directed against children. But psychological disturbance of the kind noted above is a commonplace occurrence. The subject has been discussed by Van Rooyen and Mahendra (2007). Among the issues of interest for the purposes of this book are some of the risk factors that have been identified. Risk of violence is said to be higher with younger children, where there has been developmental delay in the child, frequent illness in the child and where the child has a difficult temperament and itself is aggressive. Parents who pose a high risk usually also have an unrealistic, even fanciful, expectation of the child, little knowledge of child development and poor mood and anger regulation skills along with deficient skills in showing empathy with a child. An additional area which raises risk involves attachment problems involving the child, marital discord and poor social networks available for the parent.

11.4 DOMESTIC VIOLENCE INVOLVING CHILDREN INDIRECTLY

A child does not need to suffer direct violence to show emotional or behavioural effects due to the harm caused to it. While it is usual to focus attention on the individual parent, occasionally on both, the family as a dynamic system may be causative of harm suffered by the child. Both parents may play a contributory role in causing harm to a child, a situation which indicates bi-parental failure in some cases. In cases where a troubled relationship with one parent is offset sufficiently by a more positive relationship between the child and the second parent, this could serve as a buffer of protection against the development of the consequences of harm. The bi-parental failure occurs where both mothers and fathers show significant impairment and a failure to carry out properly their parental functions. Characteristics of families showing disturbed functioning which could lead to emotional harm to the child include those where there is or are:

1. Frequent separations and disruptions within the family.

2. Violent arguments witnessed by the child and serious marital discord.

3. An atmosphere in the home of turmoil and impending violence.

4. Lack of adequate role models to identify with.

5. A degree of neglect and parental rejection.

6. Unstable and inconsistent mothering.

7. Continuing abuse of the child making him or her feel helpless and angry.

8. Psychiatric disorders present in family members.

Children from families in which both parents suffer from psychiatric illness may be at a double disadvantage. Not only could they inherit the illness of one or both parents but they are also made vulnerable by separation, whether physical or emotional, due to the disorder suffered by the parents and in the course of the treatment of these disorders. However, it is by no means the case that whenever there is disorder in one or both parents one finds a child at emotional risk. Many, perhaps most, parents in a situation involving dual pathology on their part are perfectly capable of offering adequate parenting. Every case needs to be studied in respect of the parenting jointly or severally offered to a child and the child itself investigated for signs of emotional harm suffered.

Psychopathology in the parent may also lead to poor attachment between it and the child. Many emotional difficulties faced by a child in its growth and development are said to be due to the poor or even non-existent attachment between it and the parent. We have already stressed in the section on post-partum psychiatric disorders the urgent need to treat the mother in these circumstances and also the need to be mindful of avoiding unnecessary separation between a mother and her newborn child. Any psychiatric disorder carries the potential to compromise the processes of attachment. Those where the emotions could be impaired such as the chronic schizophrenic states are commonly found to be a cause of malattachment. But chronic or recurrent depressive illness, an uncorrected anxiety state, personality disorders with emotional distur- bance and, of course, the misuse of substances may all lead to the impairment of the process of attachment. But, as with everything else involving parenting, there can be no fixed rules about the effects of mental disorder on any aspect of parenting. Attachment, in particular, appears to be a complex process and what the requirements are for parent and child leading to a satisfactory attachment between them are far from completely understood. In other words, there cannot be any assumption that mental disorder on the part of the parent, by that fact alone, will necessarily lead to poor or non-existent attachment. Once again it is a matter for investigation in every case where poor attachment is suspected.

11.5   DOMESTIC SEXUAL VIOLENCE

This subject, too, may be regarded as another sub-species of general violence, though, of course, some special factors also apply. The subject is vast and controversial and the observations made here are only those which have some relevance to family and child practice. Marital rape or quasi-marital rape is now to be treated like any other act of rape or sexual assault although evidential problems concerning consent may present difficulties above the usual when trying to get a conviction. Domestic sexual violence is usually present in the context of circumstances where non-sexual violence also takes place. Mental disorder is as uncommon as in any other area of domestic violence although periodic sexual violence against a spouse or partner may be a characteristic of manic illness which may feature an increase in levels of libido, energy and aggression. Far more likely are personality factors (involving both parties) and a tendency to bully and intimidate a vulnerable partner. Morbid jealousy, either as a symptom of another psychotic illness or as a paranoid disorder in its own right, may be associated with sexual violence against an allegedly unfaithful spouse or partner, along with non-sexual violence. The difference usually observable between domestic and non-domestic sexual violence is that in the latter case personality problems associated with inadequacy and antisocial tendencies may be commoner than in cases involving domestic sexual violence. This is only a general observation but it does appear that persons engaging in domestic sexual violence do so because, in the words of George Bernard Shaw's dictum on marriage, 'there is a maximum of temptation with a maximum of opportunity.' Many individuals, especially men, involved in domestic sexual violence appear to be only too conscious of their rights and, as may readily be appreciated, cultural forces applying in some communities may also especially endow the husband or male partner with rights he feels at liberty to enforce irrespective of the consent of the other party.

11.6 SEXUAL VIOLENCE AGAINST CHILDREN

A distinction needs to be drawn between sexual activity, which is by definition unlawful, carried on with children in a public setting as opposed to such activities in a domestic atmosphere. Family and child law practitioners are naturally concerned with cases involving the latter type, but it is in general true to say that mental pathology is more likely to be found in those cases involving children in a public setting rather than in a domestic context. Formal illness is not common although any form of disinhibition – which tends to loosen social restraints – may also affect sexual conduct. Thus, with the psychoses, in cases of dementia or head injury, inappropriate sexual activity with children may occur. In fact, it is not unknown for dementia, whether senile or pre-senile, to present with uncharacteristic behaviour which may include also sexual misconduct with children. Alcohol and illicit substances also have a tendency to disinhibit normal, socially approved behaviour. Far more likely is a personality problem on the part of the perpetrator which may make normal sexual relationships difficult to achieve. Inadequacy of personality is notoriously common. Paedophilia itself is classified (F.65.4 – ICD-10) as a disorder of sexual preference. In one American study involving child sex offenders it was seen that those who committed new sex offences had previously committed more sex offences, had been admitted to correctional institutions more frequently, were more likely to have been diagnosed as being personality disordered, were more likely to be single and had shown more inappropriate sexual preferences on initial assessment than those who did not reoffend. Behavioural treatment did not seem to affect the rates of recidivism.

Domestic sexual violence against children takes on a different colouring. Mental disorder is still uncommon where parents are concerned as perpetrators, although it may exist among acquaintances outside the family committing the abuse. More usually there is a dysfunctional relationship within the family, commonly involving the parents, and the children could be sucked into this maelstrom. There is also the case where the parents are feckless and are also into the abuse of alcohol and illicit substances when the general air of neglect pervading the household is conducive also to sexual abuse of the children. Personality problems are not uncommon and add to the inadequacy most often observed in the dependent personality who (most often the wife or female partner) attracts and sustains the type of partner who may proceed to the abuse of children, hers or perhaps even theirs. It is notorious in the nether world of paedophiliacs that certain men (and some women) are known to prey on vulnerable individuals so as to gain access to their children. The parent with a dependent or inadequate personality may through psychological weakness brought about by their need to be cared for by someone at all costs, however unsatisfactory such an individual may be, sometimes perhaps through the incapacity brought about through misuse of alcohol or illicit substances, may leave the child unprotected. In many cases incidents of domestic sexual abuse are traceable to a poor relationship between the parents and the seeking of revenge against spouse or partner, a tendency to bullying and a failure to control impulses, aggravated on occasion by alcohol and illicit substances in the context also of a rather disordered and structureless life.

A 35-year-old man with a long history of personality inadequacy had been convicted of a sexual assault on his five year-old niece. He fully accepted his guilt and did not dispute the facts, merely proffering the explanation that he 'loved' the child. He had poor adjustment generally and was virtually incapable of forming normal adult relationships. In time he fathered a child. This child came to make equivocal complaint of possible sexual interference. The man strongly denied he had been responsible in any way for inappropriate behaviour with the child. His seriously inadequate and abnormal personality, however, was sufficient to put him in the high risk category of sexual offending in respect of children – for his previous behaviour could be deemed reasonably likely to recur – whether his child's allegations were proved to be true or not. Only supervised contact with the child was deemed to be appropriate.

The assessment of risk in respect of child sexual abuse involves several stages. At a basic level, the assessment concerns historical and factual data such as the individual's age, past convictions for sexual or violent offences and the characteristics of previous victims. These are the 'static' elements referred to previously in the assessment of risk in general. The second stage of assessment involves the intrinsic features of individuals that are relatively stable over time such as psychological characteristics, personality, cognitive processes and behaviour patterns. Although these elements are stable, they do have the potential for change with or without treatment. Characteristics of these second level risk factors include features such as sexual interests and sexual drive. Thinking processes, cognitive patterns, emotional management, ability to regulate impulses and the management of lifestyle are all considered. As said before, an important area of assessment is victim empathy. Where this is lacking it may suggest that there may be a lack of emotional intimacy, lack of emotional congruence with children (that is, identifying with them and feeling more comfortable in their presence) and thereby could be an indicator of a high risk of re-offending. Cognitive distortions, which are thought patterns, processes and beliefs associated with offending such as, for example, believing that a young child has enticed an adult into a sexual relationship (thereby also revealing a lack of insight) need to be assessed alongside levels of victim empathy.

The final stage of risk assessment concerns acute factors, that is, those behaviours and circumstances that are ongoing. These are liable to change over short periods of time and could be associated with short-term high risk. It could be considered a situation of high risk if the offender's behaviour and interests were to bring him into contact with potential victims, or if such individuals were to engage in hobbies, interests and employment that brought them into contact with potential victims, or if such individuals were to demonstrate a deterioration in their lifestyle such as breakdown of relationships, loss of accommodation, loss of employment, change in mood state and the perception that the individual is suffering from stress. Where supervision and treatment of the offender are involved, missed appointments, lying, deceit and rule breaking would in general indicate heightened risk.

Van Rooyen and Mahendra (2007) reviewed the research that indicated possible prognostic indices in the risk assessment of offenders who had been engaged in the sexual abuse of children. Good prognostic factors included the offender attending treatment sessions, not preferring children as sexual partners, the index incident being situational (eg occurring while the usual partner was away), abuse was relatively minor (eg confined to touching), the offender referring himself for treatment rather than being ordered to attend, the history of abuse was of recent onset, the offender displaying many areas of appropriate parental functioning, genuine guilt and remorse being expressed, there being empathy with the child and a full acceptance of responsibility for his conduct.

Poor prognostic features included a desire to leave treatment, the preference for children as sexual partners, the abuse not being limited to specific situations, the abuse being serious in itself, the offender being ordered to attend treatment in the face of his reluctance, there being a long history of abuse involving several children, there being a lengthy history of antisocial behaviour with substance abuse, the offender's guilt being related rather to apprehension felt about consequences, blaming others, the use of physical force in the abuse and a history of sexual abuse experienced by the offender himself.

What the long-term effects on a child suffering sexual abuse are, remains to be fully established. A recent study clearly demonstrated that childhood sexual abuse is associated with increased rates of a range of mental disorders in childhood and adult life. Male victims of childhood sexual abuse seem as likely as female victims to show subsequent psychopathology. Conduct disorders are significantly more frequently found in both male and female victims of childhood sexual abuse but males have significantly higher rates than females.

11.7 SUMMARY

1. Domestic violence is invariably under-recognised in both its frequency and gravity. There are said to be at least two killings each week associated with domestic violence involving spouses or partners. Three children are said to die each week as a result of abuse or neglect in the household. Social and cultural factors play an important part although no social group seems spared from this form of violence. As a rule, formal mental illness is uncommonly found among perpetrators of domestic violence. The commonest disorder met with in these cases is personality disorder, which in turn is strongly associated with the misuse of alcohol and illicit drugs. While the characteristics of any victim in a situation of violence are important to study, the issue takes on special importance in cases of domestic violence where there may be an appreciable presence of personality difficulties, if not disorder, in the victims who may also be vulnerable for other reasons of personal or social weakness.

2. Violence directed against children is also underestimated. Many of the factors concerned with domestic violence involving adults also affect children. Personality disorder and the misuse of alcohol and illicit drugs is especially important to consider. Children are also at risk of being adversely affected by the effects of indirect violence when they are witnesses to adult violence. As much social behaviour is learned, the impact on children of situations of violence may be considerable.

3. Domestic sexual violence, whether or not involving children, is not usually associated with mental disorder but appears to have its roots in the personal and social characteristics also linked to domestic violence in general. Misuse of alcohol and illicit drugs is common in these situations and there may also be much domestic turmoil.

CHAPTER 12

SERIAL AND SEXUAL VIOLENCE

We consider serial and sexual violence together here for convenience. It is, of course, the case that serial violence often involves a sexual element. However, acts of serial violence may be lacking in a sexual component as happened notably in the killings of his patients by Dr Harold Shipman, a Manchester general medical practitioner. It is also clear enough that sexual violence may involve merely a solitary act, behaviour that is then not repeated. Any work on the psychiatry of violence is bound to consider these behaviours but it has to be said that it is comparatively uncommon for formal mental illness such as schizophrenia, the bipolar affective disorders or the neurotic disorders to afflict the perpetrators of this form of violence. Yet, behaviour of the kind involved in this form of violence is obviously abnormal in any statistical sense. The question then arises as to how much and to what extent this form of behaviour could be deemed pathological. We need to divert our attention for a few moments to a consideration of the normal, the abnormal and the pathological to give the subject matter of this chapter a preliminary context.

12.1   NORMAL, ABNORMAL AND PATHOLOGICAL

A pervasive problem in all psychiatry is to determine the line between what is normal and what is abnormal, and also what demarcates abnormal from the pathological. What is normal is in these situations a contentious question. It could be reduced to manageable proportions for our purposes by taking a statistical approach to the issue. Biological features such as height or intelligence are amenable to such an approach. These have what is called a 'bell shaped' distribution in any given population, that is to say the ends are truncated while the middle is expanded. This means the vast majority of the population will be found congregated in the middle. This is obvious enough when one considers parameters such as height or intelligence. Very few persons are excessively short or tall; more are what is called of being of 'average' height. This kind of understanding is useful to have when considering a psychological phenomenon such as the mood. Most people are of a neutral temperament, some may be perpetually cheerful while others may be given to pessimism and are disposed to take a dark view of themselves and the world they live in. However, it is by no means clear that anything that may lie beyond the 'average' is necessarily pathological. In this respect mood is a particularly useful parameter to explore for an excess of mood in either direction may indicate pathology, being a feature of depressive illness or mania. Unhappiness, on the other hand, is merely a part of the human condition, which seems obvious enough to state. It is not so obvious when one considers the mood changes that are found in what are deemed to be normal forms of human behaviour such as found in ordinary grief, the premenstrual state or the 'baby blues' which commonly affect the mothers of the newborn. The challenge for the psychiatrist – in the present state of knowledge where no objective indices of measurement exist – is to see where normality ends and where abnormality/pathology begin.

At first sight it may be thought that psychotic phenomena involving hallucinations or delusions will provide clear-cut distinctions between what is normal and what is not for, in the popular mind, these phenomena are associated with mental disorder. But this is not always a clear-cut matter. As we shall see, auditory hallucinations are common in schizophrenia. They are usually found to be distinctive and have particular characteristics such as the voices being clearly heard from outside one's head, voices referring to one in the third person and so on. But there are phenomena also called 'pseudohallucinations' which emerge from within one's head and are not at all uncommonly found in states of grief and other situations where the individual is in need of comfort and solace. The bereaved, those with learning disabilities or with personality disorders may be subject to them. Some individuals invent imaginary persons and conversations to stave off isolation and loneliness and may say they hear voices, often within, sometimes outside of, the head. Delusions are clearly enough understood in most cases involving pathology but some individuals do have odd ideas – the earth being flat, the literal truth of religious texts and so on – which while being odd are far from being pathological. Apart from the personal element there are, as was discussed in Chapter 10, essential social and cultural considerations to be taken into account before one can establish a delusion. Many cultures have a persecutory tinge, no doubt an essential element in assuring survival of their communities. Thus, to be suspicious of one's fellows, even suspect them of potential malevolence and blame them for causing misfortune, may be perfectly normal behaviour in some cultural contexts and these beliefs cannot, by themselves, be taken to amount to delusions. Within any given culture these ideas are not even abnormal, using the crude statistical approach we have taken above. When these communities are transplanted in another society these beliefs may become, in the statistical sense, abnormal, but they are not necessarily as yet pathological.

Psychiatry, in the present state of its development, is therefore hard put to determine when the abnormal has become pathological. Objective evidence of the kind feasible in the rest of medicine is still not forthcoming. Radiological and laboratory investigation are only undertaken to detect concurrent systemic conditions which may or may not have a causative bearing on the psychiatric condition or, sometimes, to find out if there are complications of the mental disorder eg liver function tests to detect liver damage due to heavy alcohol use or to monitor treatment eg recording of serum lithium levels in the course of treatment with these drugs. What therefore psychiatry is left with is trying to give descriptions to symptoms and gather a cluster of symptoms which go to make up a disease entity. The procedure is almost entirely clinical and may be thought arbitrary but that is all that seems possible in the present state of knowledge.

The psychiatric disorders that come closest to describing most of the individuals who engage in serial and sexual violence are probably the severe personality disorders or psychopathic disorders.

12.2 SERIAL AND SEXUAL VIOLENCE – GENERAL CONSIDERATIONS

Gekoski (1998) has surveyed nine offenders of this type whose careers ran in Britain in the five decade period from 1950. The author provides a useful corrective to the view not uncommonly held that serial and sexual violence is a modern phenomenon. In the fifteenth century there were at least two specimens for study. A French nobleman by name of Gilles de Rais is reputed to have raped, tortured, killed and eaten the flesh of some 800 children. His counterparts in Edinburgh in the same century were the 50-member Beanes family who were a brutish, inbred lot who inhabited a cave and killed and ate passing travellers. In the nineteenth century Fritz Haarman of Hanover is said to have raped and killed dozens of young boys and in the same period in the USA Hermann Mudgett built a mansion for himself containing a torture chamber in which it was believed more than 200 victims perished.

As Gekoski pointed out (the book was published in 1998, some ten years before the conviction of Robert Napper whose case changes this view somewhat and will be further considered later in this chapter) in the last 50 years in England, among the subjects surveyed, no serial killer had successfully pleaded insanity or even manslaughter by reason of diminished responsibility. One of the more plausible reasons suggested for the unsuccessful outcome of these pleas is that the Crown and juries are apparently reluctant to accept them for fear of being accused of not giving sufficient heed to the public revulsion against these heinous offences. It is apparently widely believed that anything less than a verdict of murder – carrying a sentence of life imprisonment which in these cases would invariably attract a whole life tariff, the convicted individual being ordered to die in prison – would somehow be a soft option. Where especially a plea is made which is founded on mental disorder there is also the fear that the convicted killer could successfully claim to have completed a course of treatment and that attempts could then be made to rehabilitate him in the community. The public, gullible though it may be in many other matters, does not trust the claims of psychiatrists and psychologists to be able to successfully treat the men and women who have entered the public demonology and whose actions are believed to be due to evil, thereby lying in the province of metaphysics, not physic.

The one serial killer in that time who did have a diagnosable clinical condition at the time of his offending was Kenneth Erskine, the so-called Stockwell strangler, who had killed seven elderly persons in south London. He had a mental age of 11 and was therefore obviously suffering from learning difficulties or mental subnormality.

One of the points regularly made by those who have encountered these individuals (in the safety of the prison cell or at court) is that many of them not only appear sane but are also lacking in the features or behaviour which would decisively set them apart from ordinary members of the public As a rule there is nothing grotesque to be observed in either appearance or behaviour. It is perfectly in keeping with the ordinariness of their existence that, when employed, they follow occupations such as being a general medical practitioner like Dr Harold Shipman or a nurse such as Beverley Allitt or Benjamin Geen (whose cases were noted in Chapter 10).

Serial killing (what number constitutes a series of murders is not defined but ranges from three to five, the former number finding favour in Britain, the latter the criterion used by the Federal Bureau of Investigation in the USA) is to be distinguished from mass killing which involves a number of individuals as victims in a defined geographical area who are killed by a lone assailant within a short space of time. The most recent British example of this phenomenon involved Thomas Hamilton who in March 1996 in Dunblane shot dead 17 individuals, including 16 primary school children, before killing himself. The primary motivation of serial killers is not the slaying in numbers but the gratification of some impulse or fantasy. Thus, they may come to range over a much wider geographical area and their actions may thereby be diffused over space and time. It appears also to be the case that there could be a build up of tension with time within them which requires urgent release from time to time in the killing of and the sexual assaults on their victims. The attacks are therefore compulsive acts done to gratify some impulse or fantasy. The association of serial killing with perverted sexual behaviour is common but not invariable. A further distinction that could be made is between sexual assaults, where the assault is the primary motivation driving these individuals, and where any associated killing is undertaken usually in an attempt to silence the victim of the assault. This behaviour differs from those killings involving a sexual element where the killing itself is the primary motivation, not the sexual gratification due to the sexual element in the offence.

It is not at all uncommon for these assaults and killings to be reported in the media as being motiveless. This is far from being correct. In fact, there are no actions or omissions that are truly motiveless. Psychoanalysis has invested even unconscious or subconscious actions with a motive. A perverted or deranged motive is still a motive. An impulse or a fantasy provides a motive for the offence.

The motive in very many of these cases appears also to be the need to assert control or domination over the victim. This was most clearly seen in the murders carried out by Dr Harold Shipman, whose actions have been subject now to numerous investigations including a criminal trial, a coroner's inquest and a public inquiry. There appears not to have been any sexual violence in his actions and no obvious material gain (although, ironically, it was an attempt at material gain by means of forging the will of one of his victims that led to the investigation which led in turn to Shipman's capture). What there was usually was the power Shipman held over his victims. He was their medical attendant. He was the trusted individual summoned to the patient's bedside. He had lawful access to opiate-based drugs which would prove lethal beyond the usually prescribed dose. He was thus able to assert complete control and domination over his victims. It has been suggested that even in cases involving sexual assault the desire for power and control over a victim could be as great as a desire for sexual gratification

12.3   SOME CASE STUDIES

John Christie

John Christie was hanged in July 1953 aged 54. He had been convicted of the murder of his wife. He had, in fact, murdered at least 6 women and was morally responsible for the death of an innocent man, Timothy Evans, who had been executed three years previously for the murder of his wife who had, in fact, been killed by Christie. Christie's origins were in a lower middle class family in Halifax, Yorkshire. Always a nervous child he had grown into an anxious and insecure boy who was friendless and solitary. He was in awe of his father who had been a petty domestic tyrant despite (or perhaps because of) his apparent respectability (he had founded the Conservative association in the town and was diligently involved in a variety of good works). There had never been any doubt about Christie's intelligence which was at least average, probably higher, but despite this he never achieved formal qualifications or regular employment. He drifted from job to job and became a petty thief, graduating in time to more serious forms of dishonesty, and was repeatedly imprisoned. During the last months of the Great War he served as a soldier in France and was the victim of a mustard gas attack by the enemy. He sustained no physical injuries but suffered a bout of hysterical aphonia, that is, a stress-related loss of voice. During the Second World War he had served as a special constable.

The roots of his later criminal excess were laid down in adolescence. He had found himself impotent when attempting sexual intercourse with a local girl. He had then become an object of ridicule within his school and wider community as the girl proceeded to broadcast the news of his disgrace. Thereafter Christie appears never to have achieved normal sexual relations except with passive, undemanding and submissive women, most notably his wife. He demanded a passive sexual partner and it was only a matter of time before his predilections led him to women who had been rendered unconscious by him and, in the ultimate expression of passivity, dead. He, in fact, raped comatose women whom he had made unconscious by the use of gas and other inhalants, and after their death had sexually interfered with the women he had killed.

He was also a notorious hypochondiac, host to a bewildering variety of ailments for which the cause was never found and, in time, began to take an even unhealthier interest in medical matters. His knowledge of matters relating to health and the human body enabled him to masquerade as a health practitioner, even as a doctor, and some of his victims had been drawn to him as a repository of medical knowledge. At least one, the wife of Timothy Evans, sought to procure an abortion from him.

At his trial the defence floated the idea of insanity on the ground that he must have been mad to commit the offences he did (a not uncommonly held lay view in these circumstances). Some attempt was made to suggest that he could have suffered injuries from the mustard gas attack during the course of the Great War. An attempt was also made to show that he could have suffered head injury in the course of a road traffic accident he had been involved in. In the event the jury returned a verdict of murder. The evidence suggests that what he could have suffered from was a personality disorder in which the symptoms of anxiety were prominent.

12.4   Peter Sutcliffe

Some of the oddities and idiosyncrasies associated with psychiatric practice came to the fore in the case of Peter Sutcliffe, the Yorkshire Ripper. He was aged 35 when convicted of the murder of 13 women. In all there had been at least 20 attacks on women attributable to him. He was born in a small town near the city of Bradford into a family which could be regarded as being lower middle class. The father of this family was seen to be a pillar of the local community when showing his public face but, as is often the case, was a domestic tyrant responsible for much physical violence visited on Sutcliffe and his five siblings. Their mother appears to have been passive, submissive and a kindly spirit. As we shall see, her own later actions could have contributed to the kind of man he turned out to be and possibly to his later notoriety.

Sutcliffe's early life appears to have been unpromising in that he was a weakling from birth. Socially isolated and lacking in confidence, he was a solitary child wrapped in his own thoughts. Bullied at school, and by his father, he became closest in childhood to his mother. One of his brothers turned out to be a violent thug, often in trouble with the police. Sutcliffe's academic record was poor and he shone neither at work nor at play. Indeed, he was anonymous and unremarkable in his existence at school. At 15 he left school when a change became apparent in him as he gained in confidence and began to develop interests in such fields as motor bicycle riding. Perhaps of later significance, he took up the occupation of grave digger and it was noticed that he had an interest in death and dead bodies that went beyond the call of duty. In fact, he had become fascinated with death and all that was associated with it. The impression given to observers was that of a strange and odd fellow.

He had by now met his girlfriend, a woman who was of Czechoslovakian origin, and who would later become his wife. They appear to have been well matched, not least in their strangeness. She would later develop paranoid schizophrenia and Sutcliffe became adept at recognising the symptoms of schizophrenia. A series of events concerning her, his mother and a prostitute at this time set the scene for some of the most significant experiences he was to have in his early adult life. His girlfriend had been spotted in the company of another man, although how close this liaison was had been unclear. Furious when told of this news, Sutcliffe attempted to extract revenge for this perceived infidelity by visiting a prostitute. But disaster was to follow. Not only did this woman cheat him out of his change, she later taunted and publicly humiliated him. At about the same time, his saintly mother had been discovered having an affair with a local policeman. Sutcliffe's father had detected this bout of infidelity and had proceeded to publicly humiliate his wife by summoning her to an assignation in the guise of her lover and then confronting and denouncing her there in the company of all their children, including Sutcliffe. This business is said to have profoundly shocked Sutcliffe who had, in short order, been betrayed by three women, two of whom he had trusted.

His association with prostitutes, however, proved to be of long duration. Not satisfied with visiting them, he would drive around shouting abuse at the street walkers in his town. Despite this he constantly consorted with them and, by all accounts, began to develop an unhealthy interest in them.

In all, his criminal career lasted five years. In 1975 he had attacked a woman, hitting her on the head, rendering her unconsciousness and then mutilating her. She, however, survived. He then attacked another woman and then, in the course of his third attack, succeeded in killing his first victim. In all he would kill 13 women, but seven would survive his attacks. Luck appears to have been on his side as a series of bungles, diversions, hoaxes and simple good fortune on his part protected him against detection. He was finally arrested, when in the company of a prostitute, after he had given a false name to a curious police officer and his car had been found to be sporting false number plates. When confronted, Sutcliffe admitted his offences and made a full confession. The case appeared to be an open and shut one at this point but there were more complications and hazards to come.

Some months later Sutcliffe informed the police that he had lied about his motivation in killing women when confessing. He had, in fact, been on a divine mission all along with orders from God to kill prostitutes. Three psychiatrists were hired by the defence and agreed that Sutcliffe suffered from paranoid schizophrenia. His defence was to plead not guilty to murder but guilty to manslaughter on the grounds of diminished responsibility. The Crown, in the person of the Attorney General who was personally in charge of the prosecution, had accepted the plea. However, the trial judge, Mr Justice Boreham, was having none of it. He questioned the factual basis for the plea of diminished responsibility. As little of fact underlying the basis of this partial defence was forthcoming, the judge ordered a full trial with a jury in attendance. The Crown's case now was that Sutcliffe was little more than a cold, calculating, sadistic murderer who had conveniently, at the eleventh hour, attempted to introduce a partial defence on the grounds of mental disorder. Among the arguments now proffered against him was that the 'divine mission' argument had not surfaced until a couple of months after he had first confessed to his crimes. Prison officers related that they had overheard, or had even been directly told by Sutcliffe that he was minded to concoct this defence. Sutcliffe, in fact, seemed to have derived his knowledge of the symptoms of paranoid schizophrenia from the genuine illness suffered by his wife. The Crown also attempted to show the 'divine mission' argument was untenable because not all the victims had been prostitutes and also that Sutcliffe had derived sexual pleasure from killing his victims. As for Sutcliffe himself, he produced the full list of psychiatric symptoms associated with paranoid schizophrenia including auditory and somatic hallucination, delusions and thought control and passivity.

The jury, however, did not agree and, in fact, returned a verdict of murder by a majority decision. Sutcliffe was sentenced to life imprisonment with a recommendation that he serve at least 30 years. There was, however, a post script to this trial, the verdict and the sentence imposed. Some time after he had commenced his sentence in prison Sutcliffe, in fact, developed what appeared to be genuine symptoms of paranoid schizophrenia. He was transferred to Broadmoor Special Hospital and will not be released during his lifetime.

12.5   Dennis Nilsen

Dennis Nilsen, convicted of 15 murders in 1983, was the child of a Norwegian soldier and a Scottish woman who had married in 1942. Nilsen was born in 1945. His father was a highly unsatisfactory one, often absent and then to disappear forever from his life following a divorce from his mother when Nilsen was aged four. He became closest to his maternal grandfather who died when Nilsen was aged five. An abiding memory carried by Nilsen thereafter was of his grandfather's body laid out in a coffin. His mother thereafter became the principal emotional support. Although an apparently well-adjusted figure at school, he never truly felt settled. He had begun to experience homosexual feelings in adolescence and at some point his images of death, derived from his grandfather's demise, and those concerning homosexual fantasies began to coalesce.

He enlisted in the army and served there for 11 years until the age of 26. He had successfully concealed the fact of his homosexuality in the army (where it was still proscribed) but despite an exemplary record in the services he did not rise beyond the rank of corporal. He then joined the Metropolitan Police force but left after a year. Then, after a brief spell of unemployment, he became a clerical officer in the civil service and had become an executive officer at a Job Centre in Kentish Town until the time of his arrest in 1982.

During this time he led the life of an unattached homosexual cruising gay bars and having casual sexual encounters with men who were similarly placed. There was a brief permanent relationship which ended in 1977. Somewhere towards the latter years of the 1970s be began to act out the fantasies he had of death and homosexual sex. On New Year's Eve 1978 he killed his first victim. Some 14 others would follow. All had been killed by some form of asphyxiation, Nilsen once boasting he had exhausted his supply of ties on his victims.

Disposal of so many bodies became problematical. He mostly dismembered them and attempted to dispose of these remains in diverse ways. This proved Nilsen's undoing for the human remains came to block the drains and it was the plumbers who first alerted the authorities. At least three psychiatrists were involved in assessing Nilsen after his arrest. They were agreed that he suffered from no formal mental illness and there appears also to have been substantial agreement that he suffered from a significant degree of personality disorder. There was, however, dissent on the issue of whether the personality disorder had substantially diminished his responsibility for his acts as is demanded by section 2 of the Homicide Act 1957 in order for a charge of murder to be reduced to one of manslaughter. In the event, the jury brought in verdicts of guilty by a majority verdict on all six counts of murder that had been charged, and both unanimous and majority verdicts on three counts of attempted murder. Nilsen was given a term of life imprisonment with the recommendation that he serve a minimum of 25 years. The testimony of the survivors – the victims of the attempted murders – was crucial in putting together the outlines of Nilsen's *modus operandi*. As happened in the case of Peter Sutcliffe there had also been blunders and chance elements which had led to Nilsen's apprehension having been delayed. Such banal details as false number plates and blocked drains, rather than superior detective work, had led to the unmasking of these offenders.

12.6 Ian Brady and Myra Hindley

Having considered a series of individual misfits we need now to turn our attention to a couple who managed to achieve what could possibly be regarded as the case gaining the greatest notoriety in British criminal history of the twentieth century. Ian Brady and Myra Hindley, one could almost say, were destined to meet one another. Brady had a most unpromising start in life having been born illegitimate in 1938, in Glasgow. He was four years older than Hindley. Brady's mother, a single parent, farmed him out to a couple in what appears to have been an informal process of adoption. It would be four years before Brady saw his mother again. From the beginning he had been a difficult child, given to head banging and temper tantrums. As he grew older he started on a career of visiting cruelty on animals. Although bright enough, his school performance was poor, he had little interest in sport and appears to have spent his time mooching about the outdoors on his own. Even after passing examinations to enter a school which accommodated gifted children, he continued to misbehave and was soon getting into trouble with the police. He had also begun to to develop an interest in Nazi lore and memorabilia and fascist literature in general. By the age of 13 he was in the juvenile court charged with an act of burglary. At the age of 16 he was again convicted of an offence of burglary but was spared incarceration on the condition that he went to reside with his mother, who had by now married and was living in Manchester. He now met his stepfather, Patrick Brady, for the first time. However, he remained a maladjusted misfit with an interest in literature of an equivocal nature, featuring sadistic and fascistic themes and including the works of the Marquis de Sade. He returned to crime but confined his involvement to property offences at this time. He came to spend a couple of years in borstal, moving later to prisons of the more usual kind. While his solitary habits and an absorption in sadism and Nazi and fascist literature persisted, he also undertook a course in book keeping which led to employment as a clerk in a company. He was aged 23 when that company welcomed a new secretary, the 19-year-old Myra Hindley.

Her early life had been altogether better settled despite a birth during the war years. The arrival of a younger sister had led to Hindley's adoption, more or less, by a grandmother. Despite possessing a higher than average IQ she failed her examinations, a fact attributed to her giving priority to her social life. Nevertheless, she managed to develop her creative side and became especially fond of poetry. She was also a sportswoman of some note. She was also much in demand, it seems, as a babysitter on account of her effective ways with children. She was aged 15 when she encountered her first tragedy when a 13-year-old boy, described as her best friend, drowned. She was to have accompanied him swimming and blamed herself for not having gone, being certain she could have saved his life if she had done so. Her response to this death appears to have been somewhat hysterical and she also converted to Roman Catholicism, the religion professed by her dead friend. Her school work, however, deteriorated as grief led to indifference and drift. She left school aged 15 with no formal academic qualifications. Aged 17 she became engaged to be married but broke off this alliance within six months. Aged 19 she met Ian Brady by going to work for the company in which he had already been employed.

Hindley became attracted to and fascinated by this 23-year-old with a sullen, aloof and mysterious demeanour that hinted at hidden depths, a man unlike any she hitherto had been acquainted with. She prayed he would reciprocate her feelings and he eventually did. They met and spent their first evening at the cinema watching a film on the Nuremberg trials. He introduced her to Nazi marching songs and associated literature which continued to absorb him. Hindley soon found herself in his clutches and came to be seen to be totally under his influence. She changed from being a somewhat simple girl with conventional modes of thought into a being who was almost perverse in her dislike of not only marriage and conventional institutions but of children whom she had previously adored. When Brady started talking of robbing a bank, Hindley took driving lessons so that she could serve as the getaway driver of the car they would use. They also procured guns. Within two years of their meeting they had killed their first victim, a girl aged 16. Four other children were to follow. There was little public interest evinced at the outset when these children disappeared.

Indeed, nothing might have come to light if Brady and Hindley had not attempted to recruit Hindley's sister's husband as a fellow killer. Brady had taken this young man, David Smith, under his wing and had lectured him on the merits of sadism, pornography and the views of the Nazis. Brady and Hindley had then picked up a 17-year-old youth and had tried to persuade Smith to become their accomplice in the killing of the youth. This youth was hacked to death. The brother in law, who was present at the scene of murder, was so sickened by what he saw that he went to the police. When the body of the youth was discovered Brady tried to implicate Smith in the murder. Hindley remained pleading innocence when she was questioned. Further, Smith informed the police of how Brady had boasted of burying bodies on Saddleworth Moor. Four other bodies were dug up in due course. Brady and Hindley were tried and convicted of these murders. Held in separate prisons they gradually drifted apart but, while Brady was resigned to ending his days in prison, Hindley became a celebrity while fighting to be released, recruiting notably Lord Longford, among others, to her cause. In the meanwhile Brady quietly went mad suffering from visual and auditory hallucinations and persecutory delusions.

12.7   Robert Napper

As this chapter was being written, news came through of the conviction of manslaughter, on grounds of diminished responsibility, of Robert Napper, aged 42. He had in July 1992 killed Rachel Nickell, a mother who had been walking her two-year-old son and their dog, on Wimbledon Common. He had stabbed her 49 times and had mutilated her body in the presence of the child. 16 months later he had raped, stabbed to death and mutilated the body of Samantha Bissett in her flat in Plumstead, south east London. Her four-year-old daughter was sexually assaulted and then asphyxiated. Napper was convicted of these murders in 1995 and sent to be held in Broadmoor Special Hospital. It would be there that he would be questioned later of the murder of Rachel Nickell and then arrested.

Long before these attacks, Napper's mother, in 1989, had reported to the police that her son had committed a rape. No further action had been taken, there apparently having been confusion as to whether this alleged rape had taken place *on* Plumstead Common (as the mother reported), where no crime had been reported at that time, or on premises *in* Plumstead Common where an offence of rape was later reported. This was one of a series of blunders alleged against the police in what was described as being one of the worst failures involving the Metropolitan Police

Napper, whose origins lay in Erith, south-east London, had a troubled upbringing with much domestic violence in the home until his mother sought a divorce from his father. Her own health had never been good and Napper and his siblings had been accommodated several times in foster homes. At the age of 12 he had been sexually assaulted by a family friend after which, it had been said, his behaviour had changed for the worse. In his teenage years he became withdrawn and obsessive and later a diagnosis of Asperger's syndrome had been entertained. However, his life until about 1989 appears to have been uneventful as he did casual jobs and managed to live alone in a bed sitting room. In that year he is believed to have shown the signs of paranoid schizophrenia which had led, in the course of five years until his apprehension in 1994, to his committing numerous sexual assaults. It is believed he could be implicated in over 100 offences committed in the course of those five years.

Observations undertaken at Broadmoor had shown Napper to be deluded, suffering from both persecutory and grandiose delusions. He believes he has a higher degree in mathematics, that he has won the Nobel Prize, that he has medals won in the course of the war in Angola, that he holds millions of pounds in bank deposits and that his family are featured in *Who's Who*. Further, he also claims to be able to transmit thoughts telepathically and that he has been 'knee capped' by the IRA.

From 1989 his attacks on women began to increase in ferocity and there were several attacks concerning him in 1992 in the weeks before the assault on Rachel Nickell. In time it became clearly apparent that a series of bungles on the part of the police had left Napper free to prey on women, among whom he singled out lone women with young children. Even after the Nickell murder Napper had been questioned four times. His DNA had been sought from him twice but he had failed to keep appointments. He hailed from south-east London, some distance away from Wimbledon Common, which is located in south west London, and the police believed Nickell's killer must be someone who was familiar with the locale. Napper was also believed to be too tall to be the Nickell killer.

Some months after the Nickell killing, in October 1992, Napper had been arrested when a search of his flat yielded a huge cache of weapons including guns, knives and a crossbow. He was convicted and imprisoned for eight weeks. While searching his flat the police had not realised the significance of some other material that had been found there – hand drawn maps of London with places marked, an annotated London A-Z and diaries. In July 1993 he had been arrested while peering through the window of a young woman's flat. One of the police officers involved in this arrest had noted, even while letting Napper go, 'subject strange, abnormal, should be considered as a possible rapist, indecency type suspect.' Yet, Napper remained uninvestigated fully for reasons which should become clear after the discussion below. It was not until May 1994 that Napper had been arrested for the Bissett murders. Even then the link between the Bissett and Nickell murders eluded the police despite much incriminating material linking Napper to the killings.

Perhaps the most powerful reason for the almost wilful denial of the facts and evidence linking Napper to the Wimbledon Common murder was that the police had in their sights another man, Colin Stagg. Encouraged by a forensic psychologist working as an 'offender profiler', the police sought the conviction of Stagg as the killer of Rachel Nickell and devoted all their energies and resources to this end. Sir Harry Ognall, now retired, was the presiding judge at Stagg's trial for this murder. After Napper had been convicted in December 2008, Sir Harry commented on his own judicial involvement. He had immediately realised that there were three issues of importance in this case – there was enormous public pressure to secure a conviction, that the evidence against Stagg was weak indeed but, if that evidence were permitted to go before a lay jury, a conviction could still result. Sir Harry noted also how the police had sought a so-called 'honey trap' confession, whereby a suspect is seduced into a confession by an undercover policewoman, but had failed lamentably in this endeavour. In the event there had been no identification evidence, no scientific evidence, no circumstantial evidence and no evidence of subsequent incriminating behaviour on Stagg's part. There had been no DNA evidence either to incriminate Stagg or to exonerate him. The judge ruled the 'honey trap' evidence impermissible to be put before a jury. The rest of the Crown's case thereupon collapsed. For his pains Sir Harry was subject to a vendetta pursued against him by some newspapers in the aftermath of this failed trial in 1994.

As was freely acknowledged by nearly all independent observers after 1994, the mischief in failing to apprehend Napper for the murder of Rachel Nickell lay in the fact that the police had become so convinced of Stagg's guilt that they had closed their minds to the possibility that any one else, let alone Napper, could be guilty of the crime. The forensic psychologist 'offender profiler' who had been advising the police had dismissed any notion that there could have been similarities between the Nickell and Bissett killings. It had been his idea that the 'honey trap' in the comely form of a policewoman be sprung to entrap Stagg. So they had got Stagg and strove mightily to pin the guilt on him. It was how their idea that Wimbledon Common being familiar ground to the killer had been born (Stagg lived nearby) and why Napper was believed to be too tall (Stagg was appreciably shorter). It was why so many leads linking the killing to Napper, including incriminating clues, were ignored. After Napper's conviction of the Nickell murder the police claimed that investigatory techniques, including laboratory analysis, had improved from 16 years ago. One could be permitted the riposte that all the investigatory improvements will avail little if one does not first grasp the significance of a clue or dismisses it as being irrelevant as a result of a closed mind.

The role of expert advice proffered to the police came once again into question. 'Offender profiling' has been relegated in its importance since 16 years ago when it was believed to be some magical method by which offenders could be tracked down to the exclusion of all other methods including the dull routines of police detective work. It is now only one of several techniques employed. The police, like may lay persons, appear to be bewitched by some technique which is superficially plausible, coming to see it as the main, sometimes the only, means of ensuring a satisfactory conclusion to a case. This could be called the 'sat nav' approach to investigation analogous to using satellite navigation as the sole aid to seeking a location while ignoring common sense aids such as reading a map, and taking note of topography and landscape. The upshot is one may end up in the small village of Lille in Belgium rather than in the major city of Lille in Northern France. There is also the phenomenon referred to as 'confirmation bias' whereby once the police have rounded up one or more of the 'usual suspects' (a time honoured police tactic) all resources, energy and intelligence (in every sense) are dedicated to proving the most likely of these subjects guilty. Often it is the 'local nutter' – to employ the phrase used by counsel for Barry George when defending him of the charge of murdering Jill Dando, a charge of which he was cleared – who is picked up and pursued for no other reason than that he is the most plausible villain who, with luck, could be proved to have been guilty. It cannot be stressed too often that there is an urgent need to equip detectives with an understanding of the scientific method, of the need for the independent testing of hypotheses and the requirement to put aside *a priori* assumptions in the face of the evidence gathered. Modern scientific detective work requires skills and methods going well beyond the ability to read off test results arising out of laboratory investigations.

12.8   Harold Shipman

We now need to say a few words about a non-sexually motivated serial killer, Dr Harold Shipman. His background, for a doctor, was most unremarkable. After his apprehension some attempt was made to try to connect the early death of his mother to his later perversions but that is a most tenuous link. By any ordinary standards, Shipman's background can only be said to be lacking in anything significantly out of the ordinary. He completed medical school and became an accomplished general medical practitioner. No criticism was ever essayed in respect of his ordinary clinical practice, a matter of irony given the regulations now imposed on doctors, to ensure they remain competent, up to date and safe in their practice, many of which came about as a result of reforms and changes made after his activities came to light. Indeed, nothing but praise was ever heaped on him when he had been a general practitioner. Even after it had been shown that he could have killed at least 216 of his patients, there were those who remained even handed in their judgment of him. As one son of a victim of Shipman's put it, 'he was a fine doctor, only he killed our mother.' Many of his victims had, in fact, been urged to join his practice by others among his satisfied patients, some of whom were later themselves to become his victims or the relations of victims. He was a single handed practitioner, a circumstance that facilitated his killing, but that is hardly a remarkable fact involving any professional who wishes to practise his occupation on his own. In fact, his very competence and devotion to duty probably protected him from the carping criticism that professionals feel they are heirs to. The only obvious point about Shipman, made after his crimes had come to light, was his love of control of others including his family who have remained loyal to him and have dismissed all the allegations. Hindsight was needed to make this observation. Shipman appears to have revelled in the domination he held over his patients, his privilege to make, literally, decisions of life and death and his lawful access to potentially lethal therapeutic drugs.

12.9   CONCLUSIONS

As one contemplates the early life and biological and social provenance of serial killers, including those who have been featured in this chapter, several common themes emerge, but in not one of these cases could a criminal career encompassing such enormity have been reasonably predicted. Many serial killers appear to spring from working class or lower middle class origins but that is hardly predictive of criminal excess.

Many also have been members of large families but that, too, is of limited value in trying to explain desperate deeds as having been born out of possible anonymity and even emotional neglect that could sometimes be associated with such families. Many also emerged out of families where the fathers were absent or were petty tyrants, visiting punishment not only on the subjects of interest to us but on their siblings and their mothers. But not every child bullied at home, or even many of them, turn to serial killing. Many of the men who feature in this chapter were attached to their mothers, might even have been indulged and spoilt by excessive maternal attention, but even that can hardly be predictive of a later career undertaken on such a breathtaking scale. Many of these men were also solitary, inadequate and social misfits which could lead to the suggestion that such characteristics could be predictive of later anti-social behaviour, but there is a palpable difference between anti-social conduct and serial killing.

Perhaps the most significant finding is that of personality difficulties often amounting to a clinically diagnosable personality disorder. These men became 'rule breakers', first at school, then in the wider community, and engaged at first in petty crime. They were protesting against the rules from early in their lives but, then, many a delinquent will outgrow his early deviancy. Several had been bullied at school and, perhaps, it is the case that resentment afflicted them from early on and spurred the extraction of revenge later on. Sexual difficulties from a young age was a feature in many serial killers in whose offending there could be discerned a sexual element, and a fairly common theme was sexual inadequacy allied to humiliation of a public kind as happened in the cases of Christie and Sutcliffe where a thoughtless young woman, either a member of a peer group or commercially procured, had proceeded to mock and humiliate the man publicly for his failings. It is uncertain how deeply rooted such acts of ridicule become and form the basis for later revenge taken against women of a similar age group to the tormentors.

A common theme is also that of persistent social and occupational underfunctioning. Apart from Shipman, who by all ordinary standards achieved a measure of professional success, many of these men did not match attainment to aspiration or aptitude. Almost all had above average intelligence which was not reflected in academic or occupational success. This is invariably a sure sign of the adverse influence of elements in the personalities of individuals and may hint at the possibility of there later building up resentment and fuelling the thirst for revenge. Hardly anyone of intelligence blames himself alone for his failures. Resentment can also be a powerful driver of the need for control and domination, a theme we shall also have cause to study in the subject matter of the next chapter.

CHAPTER 13

PUBLIC AND POLITICAL VIOLENCE

Conflict is part of the human, indeed all animal, condition. There has probably not been any period of history when war – global, international or civil – has been absent from human life. It has been said that in the six decades since the end of the Second World War the British armed services have not been deployed in any theatre of war or conflict in only one of those years. The human cost of these conflicts is immense. The World Health Organization estimated that in the year 2000 alone over 300,000 individuals could have perished as a direct result of violent conflict. According to this agency, about 1.6 million individuals worldwide died as a result of all acts of violence in that year. These acts of violence included suicides and homicides besides violent armed conflict. In other words, about a fifth of deaths due to violence each year is due to violent armed conflict.

The physical effects of conflict are well recognised. Every November homage is paid to the fallen of the two great global wars and other armed conflicts. Recognition is also given to those who were maimed in those conflicts, some of whom or their immediate relations, a dwindling number with the passage of the years, parade at the same service of commemoration. These survivors are conspicuously physically disabled. Indeed, for decades the notion that survivors could also have suffered psychiatric injuries in the course of conflict was not one that was seriously entertained. Although 'shell shock' had been recognised early enough in the course of the Great War, servicemen who 'deserted' as a result of psychiatric trauma sustained in the trenches of conflict still faced execution. Even a generation later psychiatric injuries among servicemen were still deemed second class afflictions when set besides the horrific mutilations that could result from armed conflict. Even today, when figures for the victims of the atomic bombing of Hiroshima and Nagasaki are given, also annually as part of remembrance, it is almost invariably the case that it is the number who were killed in the instant of detonation of these weapons and those who died, in the short or long term, as a result of injury due to radiation that are broadcast. While it is certainly true that psychiatric injuries do not make for easy computation, it is virtually certain that even if the numbers come to be known in only some approximation to the true figures, the psychiatrically damaged would be comparable to those who were killed or were physically injured. There is now, however, a growing recognition and appreciation of the psychiatric conditions arising out of the trauma experienced in conditions of conflict including the disorder of post traumatic stress disorder (PTSD), especially in the period after the war in Vietnam.

Despite the second class status hitherto accorded to the psychiatric victims of conflict, and even given the nature of this book, it is not our intention to consider in any detail the psychiatric *sequelae* of violent conflict. Much has been written elsewhere on individual conflicts and also more generally on the subject. Whalley and Brewin (2007), for example, reviewed the literature on the impact on mental health of terrorist attacks and have shown that there are widespread mental health effects even on communities geographically distant from these attacks. 30–40 per cent of populations directly affected by terrorist attacks are likely to develop PTSD and at least 20 per cent are likely still to be experiencing symptoms two years later. There is, however, less evidence that rescue workers and members of the emergency services are at a high risk of developing a disorder. The psychiatric features seen among victims are neither significantly nor qualitatively different from the affliction of patients in peace time or in the absence of conflict. One sees the full range of symptoms of conditions surveyed in this book. Whether these individuals have been the victims of civil or international conflict, torture or are the survivors of concentration camps, psychiatric injuries and disorder only seem to differ in quantitative terms from mental disorder in peace time.

Rather, in this chapter, we shall concentrate on some aspects of the mental health of those who provoke or participate in conflicts involving, at times, millions of civilians. While it is not our intention to survey in any detail the madness of nations or communities, we shall attempt to describe and understand the mental states of individuals who, on their own or in mobs of their fellows, visit violence of an extreme kind on those who may be of a different religious persuasion, tribal loyalty or racial description. One of the more frightening aspects of modern civil conflict is the emergence, or re-emergence, of the suicide bomber or an adherent to suicide terrorism as the phenomenon is called. Then, we need to consider the probable mental states of the leaders whose actions led to war, conflict, terror and genocide. It is commonplace to hear the names of Hitler and Stalin, and among those who are more up to date, Saddam Hussain and Robert Mugabe, being suggested as belonging to the ranks of madmen. We shall say a few words about Hitler and Stalin, who have been extensively studied and where some valid conclusions are now possible.

13.1   MAN'S INHUMANITY TO MAN

Human experience will remain incomplete if one has not been witness to the madness of crowds that is a feature of virtually all forms of civil conflict. The individuals involved are mostly citizens of the same country. They may be separated by race, religion, tribe, caste, political affiliation or none of these as may happen in the case of anarchist violence. It is usually also the case that these different communities have lived among one another for long periods of history in peace and harmony. In those settled times it would usually have been the practice for members of these diverse communities to mingle, to trade and even to marry one another. In fact, one of the many tragedies that involve these communities is that, when conflict breaks out, the participants may not even be sure where or to whom they belong for their blood might have been mixed over the years. They might together have seen, over the years, and shared, misfortune, famine, drought, misrule and even war against some common enemy. All this comes to nought when conflict among them breaks out. Sometimes it is politics that comes to separate them for unscrupulous politicians may play off one group against the other, riding the waves of sentiment born out of economic hardship or some question of land ownership or historical entitlement taken away by some colonising power and now needing to be re-established. Whatever it might be, the conflict that comes about is real, bloody and murderous.

Of one matter we may be certain. The prime movers behind a conflict of this nature rarely if ever suffer from any recognised mental illness. Whether these individuals could be suffering from a personality disorder is less certain, a matter to be considered in the final sections of this chapter. Among the foot soldiers of these conflicts – the poor bloody infantry of conflict, increasingly comprising younger and younger children – there could be some evidence of mental disorder. Some who are mentally unstable could be drawn to a cause wherein they find a purpose to their otherwise unsatisfactory lives. Some could have been rendered mentally unstable by the stresses and privations of the conflict itself. Some may be those who previously suffered from a mental disorder and whose condition could have relapsed on account of the dislocations due to the conflict which might have led to the interruption of treatment or the collapse of support networks as family and friends have died or fled.

It is also instructive to note how a conflict begins, or is rekindled after a period of quiescence. There is almost always some perceived provoking factor. It is rare for the actual differences in affiliation – despite which, as we have seen, communities can live among one another in a spirit of co-operation and peace for many years, sometimes even centuries – to set off spontaneously, due to these differences alone, conflict and bloodshed. There is usually some new fact, actual or perceived, that underlies an eruption. Rumour is an important trigger and may take the form of some atrocity attributed to a rival community. Unscrupulous tribal or communal leaders may then fan the flames. A recent example of a rumour underlying a potential conflict was when mobs in several Islamic countries went on the rampage after perceiving insult to Islam in the words of Pope Benedict. Hardly any of those rioting, it transpired, had read the actual words uttered by the pontiff which, in fact, consisted of a somewhat dull historical *exegis* on the relations between Christianity and Islam but, nonetheless, explosive when conveyed second hand to the unlettered. It is usually the case that some intellectual or pseudo-intellectual justification is required for even the most heinous of acts, a lesson one may also usefully learn from the Nazis.

13.2   SUICIDE TERRORISM

Conflicts of the kind outlined above concern individuals drawn from warring communities. An outsider, unless singularly unfortunate or drawn to the conflict by some professional duty such as being engaged in supplying humanitarian aid or reporting events as a journalist, is not usually affected by the situation of conflict. Suicide terrorism – the occupation of the suicide bomber – has changed the rules somewhat by putting into the front line everybody who comes to be caught in the vicinity of the blast. The fear of suicide terrorism now stalks every citizen in many lands, some far removed from the immediate locus of the conflict. The subject has been reviewed by Salib (2003). He traces the historical roots of suicide terrorism. Far from being some new phenomenon it appears, in fact, to have been deployed as an act of warfare from ancient times. In the middle ages the Jewish Sicairis and the Islamic Hashishiyum sects were infamous for such attacks. In the eighteenth century such attacks were made in India, Sumatra and the Phillipines. In the twentieth century the *kamikaze* raids of the Japanese brought renewed terror to conventional warfare. Between 1980 and 2002 an estimated 340 suicide terrorist attacks are estimated to have taken place, including, in September 2001, the raids on the World Trade Center in New York which killed 3000 people. Among the countries receiving these attacks were Lebanon, Kuwait, Sri Lanka, Israel, Palestine, India, Panama, Algeria, Pakistan, Argentina, Croatia, Turkey, Tanzania, Kenya and the USA. To their number can now be added Britain and Spain.

What goes through the mind of such a suicide terrorist? He (and increasingly she and also they, namely, young children) is carefully selected, well trained and is one who is willing and able to undertake this murderous mission, with his own death as the suicidal component, in what has been described as a 'state of almost hypnotic transformation'. As far as the Islamic suicide terrorist is concerned, his own death is a precondition for the success of the mission for he will then be called to Paradise and have immortal honour bestowed on him. These individuals make elaborate preparations for death and for the after life. Wills are written, purification ceremonies are undertaken and taped messages are left to the loved ones left behind. With those of other persuasions different considerations may apply for heaven may not be the destination; the success of their cause or the defeat of the enemy may be sufficient reward.

The leadership of the group organising these acts of terror is crucial, for without the charisma of the leader and his fanatical singlemindedness and belief in the cause, the actual terrorists will not be recruited. There must also be an element of irrationality and brainwashing involved. But of the presence of mental disorder there is little evidence, certainly among the leadership of these groups. One could even argue that to be a leader of a cause dedicated to outrages of this kind one would be required to be exceptionally stable and clear-headed, however misguided he might be. It is, however, possible, that mental instability or disorder of some kind afflicts some of those chosen to undertake these attacks. One recalls the recent case involving the Exeter bomber, a native white Englishman, who suffered from learning difficulties and possibly also from mental illness, one who was recruited and was found to be susceptible to brainwashing and training in the methods of terrorism. The issue arises as to whether these individuals could be deluded. A delusion is defined, as we have seen, as a false belief that is unshakeably held in the face of evidence to the contrary, taking into account the subject's social and cultural background. Take now the case of a suicide bomber who believes Western targets are legitimate for the West has harmed Islam and those regions of the world where Islam is the premier religion. This can hardly be called a false belief for it is certainly arguable that the war in Iraq did harm to that country or that the Arab-Israeli conflict might have harmed those whose faith is Islam. This is a matter of opinion, not a matter of truth or falsehood. Next, if one takes account of these terrorists' social and cultural beliefs one can hardly say these beliefs are unshared by others of a similar background. Indeed, one may go so far as to say the success of political movements behind suicide terrorism is owed to the support that is derived from many ordinary individuals who may, nevertheless, not condone extreme measures but, yet for all that, are in sympathy with the broader aims of the political movements of which the suicide bombers are members. It does not appear to be the case that the run of the mill suicide terrorist is deluded or psychotic. He is, in fact, a religious or pseudo-religious fanatic, the kind of wrongheaded individual of extreme views who has been known through the ages.

13.3   ADOLF HITLER

As we have already noted, there is little evidence to suggest that formal mental illness afflicts most of those engaged in tyranny and terror. Despite this knowledge, it is still common to find historical figures such as Adolf Hitler described as having been 'mad' and even for their actions and the consequences that followed to be attributed to the effects of madness rather than due to forms of perverted human behaviour. Even the word 'evil', imprecise though it may be in its meaning, is preferable to 'madness' or 'lunacy' to describe these actions. Although knowledge about Hitler and the Nazis can now be derived from diverse sources, including the monumental work of Sir Ian Kershaw, we base this account on a somewhat unusual source – the acclaimed biography of Hitler by Joachim Fest, the first major German study of Hitler and the Nazis (1973, 1982). Fest starts off by remarking that 'Hitler's peculiar greatness is essentially linked to the quality of excess'. To attempt to understand

Hitler one needs to seek out his roots and here we encounter another remark of Fest's – 'Hardly any other prominent figure in history so covered his tracks, as far as his personal life was concerned'. He always remained aloof and maintained an air of mystery. He had in early adult life once spent time in a hostel for the homeless. When one of his chums from those days surfaced later, Hitler had him killed. He was not, of course, a German but was Austrian, born in a small town in that country, and it is a remarkable fact of history that from Alexander to Napoleon to Stalin that many revolutionaries and conquerors have been aliens in their adopted lands. Hitler's origins were entirely unpromising, springing from peasant stock with a history of generations of inbreeding although his father did become a minor civil servant. There is doubt, never dispersed, about his precise origins and descent. What is known of his childhood is that while intelligent and quick on the uptake he was lazy and disinclined to work regularly or methodically. He preferred the arts among the subjects offered at school but his work generally was reported as being 'unsatisfactory'. He left school with no qualifications. He had also made no friends there and he went on to fail academically at another school.

He now decided to become an artist and said he disdained regular employment. When not drawing he was mostly idle. He cultivated the 'expectations and egotism of genius'. Most of the time he appeared to exist in a world of fantasy and although unoccupied he appeared to observers to be preoccupied. Already he had resolved that the world must be 'changed thoroughly and in all its parts'. Even in his chosen arts he remained a dilettante, incapable of systematic work. At 18 he set off for Vienna, spending the next six years of his life in that city. He was full of hope but the Academy of Fine Art in that city, which he had set his heart on entering, turned him down and called his sample drawing unsatisfactory. This was a cruel blow. He was advised to take up architecture but his poor school record denied him this chance too. Still he remained a dreamy idler engaged in some elaborate fantasy life. There were already fits of fury and despair that he was subject to, with deep depression alternating with bouts of exaltation. He tried for a second time to enter the Academy and failed again. Thereafter he conceived a lifelong hatred of schools and academies, saying, 'they had misjudged Bismarck and Wagner also'. By this time he had started to live in doss houses and said he had turned against the bourgeois world.

Antisemitism was endemic in Vienna, and everywhere else in Austria, and Hitler imbibed this poison with everyone else. In his case his own frustrations, the inner rage and hatred against those whom he believed had thwarted and kept him down, now found a focus against the Jews. It was perhaps this personal attitude that set his views apart from the routine anti-Jewish sentiments that were so widespread at that time and in that place so as to become commonplace. He had also been in financial difficulties as his parental legacies had run out and he had no hesitation in blaming the Jews for this lamentable state of affairs. He had effectively become politicised.

Times were hard for Hitler in his early twenties before the start of the Great War. He was sleeping rough on park benches although was later to graduate to a hostel for the homeless. He seemed to be kept going by his grotesque fantasies – 'but in imagination I lived in palaces'. He remained virtually friendless. He had a wide range of dislikes, not merely Jews but Slavs, the House of Hapsburg and the Social Democratic Party. However, he had also located a hero, Richard Wagner who was to provide inspiration and succour to so many fascists and anti-semites. Hitler was later to call his Vienna years 'the hardest though most thorough school of my life'. He was to hate and resent the city thereafter.

He was 24 when he left Vienna for Munich. It was the eve of war and he carried with him an assortment of prejudices. It transpired later that Hitler had actually moved to Munich to avoid conscription in Austria. Nonetheless he was tracked down by the authorities and arrested for 'draft dodging'. He was then discovered to be unfit for military service and released. Undaunted, he volunteered to join a Bavarian regiment. He was accepted and so began 'the greatest and most unforgettable time of my earthly existence.'

Throughout the war he served as a courier or despatch rider. His reputation among officers appears to have been good. He received the Iron Cross, recommended by a Jewish officer, but it has never been clear what act of valour underlay this honour. Despite this he did not achieve promotion beyond the rank of private, first class. Yet, he appeared at long last to have found his *metier* in the army and also a 'homeland'. He was one of those who had been redeemed by the experience of war.

But Germany lost that war, Hitler learning of the inevitable end as he lay temporarily blinded in a gas attack. Hitler, now aged 30, shared with his fellows a feeling of misfortune and betrayal. He himself claimed that this was the defining moment in his life when he saw what his destiny was going to be – 'The hammer stroke of Fate which throws one man to the ground suddenly strikes steel in another'. He now began to make political speeches and learned for the first time of the power of his oratory.

These appear to have been the formative influences on Hitler. As we have seen in Chapter 8 on the personality disorders there are criteria available by which Hitler's personality is to be judged. On a study of the evidence relating to him we may discern there is little likelihood that he suffered from any formal mental illness in the early phase of his life. It is possible that towards the end of the war when he was liberally dosed with medication – which could have included the stimulant drugs such as cocaine and the amphetamines – there might have been some features suggestive of psychotic symptoms. The impulsiveness, the erratic behaviour, the rages and the lapsing back into fantasy life are compatible with drug-induced states although it is also clear that these could have been an exaggeration of traits already present. In any event these drug- and stress-induced features were experienced towards the terminal stages of his life. What is prominent throughout his life is behaviour which may be deemed to be out of the ordinary. As we have seen, the oddness had an early onset. Despite what appears to have been the possession of intelligence also above the average Hitler's life had been a palpable failure until the coming of the Great War. He failed at school and was ill fitted for any occupation besides that of a painter of the utmost mediocrity. He was socially isolated and solitary, virtually incapable of forming or sustaining any intimate personal relationships. He was in a constant state of conflict, raging against the world and harbouring the keenest sense of resentment against all manner of individuals and groups. Perhaps it was the chance factor of early existence in Austria, a land renowned for its anti-semitic sentiments, that gave him a ready focus for his hatreds and resentment against the Jews. The war provided him with another focus. Despite his lowly rank in the army he found a purpose, was also wounded and decorated. For once he found himself appreciated. This is not an uncommon experience among neurotics and misfits who find they are able to put away their trivial egotistical concerns when faced with some real purpose and face personal danger, for once of the real kind. A parallel can be drawn with the oft-uttered truism that the British empire was created by misfits, men (and some women) who were maladjusted, misunderstood and at risk of wasting their lives at home but who, when they were given the opportunity, seized it and rose to the challenge of building something higher than had existed before. Hitler portrayed a similar maladjustment. It is undeniable that on the evidence that we now have of his behaviour he would have met the criteria for a personality disorder of a most significant degree.

13.4   JOSEPH STALIN

Similar considerations apply when evaluating the early life and formative years of Joseph Stalin who was born at Gori, in the now troubled state of Georgia, in 1879. His father was a shoemaker who married a girl who was the daughter of a serf. We base this account on the book by Isaac Deutscher (1966). His childhood was marked by numerous infections including small pox and later he was to suffer from blood poisoning. He was left with disabilities from the latter infection which made him unfit for military service. He grew up amid poverty and squalor as his father's business never attained any measure of success. The reason for this was probably paternal drunkenness. Along with the drink came the violence which marked the young Stalin whose 'defences against his father's heartlessness were distrust, alertness, evasion, dissimulation and endurance.'

At the age of nine he was sent to a church school at Gori. His mother's ambition for him was to become a parish priest and command the respect of the community. He remained at this school till the age of 14. He was one of the best pupils in his school, showing a quite extraordinary memory and being adept at his lessons. Already he was exhibiting a streak of self assertiveness and competitiveness especially against the boys from wealthier and more privileged backgrounds. He could also outshine his peers in the playground. It is said it was at this school that he first came to appreciate class differences and class hatred. He was also an outsider, a Georgian under domination by Russians. He thereby became aware of both social and national inequality. His intellectual development was precocious and by the age of 15 he was publishing poetry.

At that age he matriculated from a theological seminary, helped by a scholarship to which he was assisted by the school and a local priest. He remained at this seminary for five years, decisive years for his intellectual development. It was a time of intellectual and political ferment which introduced him to political thought and action. However, by his third year there, the monks in charge noted he was going astray – he was reading too widely. Some of these books he borrowed from the public library. He was punished for these transgressions. He retaliated by joining a secret debating society and a socialist organisation. Later he would explain, 'I became a Marxist because of my social position (my father worked in a shoe factory, my mother was a washer woman) but also because of the harsh intolerance and Jesuitical discipline that crushed me so mercilessly at the seminary.' He had by now joined revolutionary circles and inevitably he was expelled from the seminary.

Despite his intelligence and his obvious intellectual abilities, there was a festering sense of inferiority present in him. He was the son of Georgian peasants and thus not only inferior to the caste ridden officials of Russia but also to the middle class revolutionaries fomenting social upheaval.

He first became a political essayist and writer but otherwise had no settled occupation. He squatted among like-minded young men and earned some money by providing tuition. Finally he got a job at the observatory. The police had still to be kept at bay and he became cautious, taciturn and observant. Sharp wits were required to survive in this environment and he managed to evade arrest on numerous occasions. But he remained a hunted man and had to shed his identity. He had also to leave his employment and existed on charity. He proceeded to revolutionary journalism and became part of the revolutionary movement. He tasted prison and later deportation. He then joined the underground political movement and was drawn to the Bolsheviks, meeting Lenin. At about this time he began to play a more national role, also assuming the name of Stalin (man of steel). He rose effortlessly in the Bolshevik movement despite spending seven years in the decade up to 1917 in prison or banishment. He contributed little to the intellectual debate but was reputed to be a sound, practical organiser. He caught Lenin's eye and in October 1917 was in the first Soviet cabinet. His influence grew in time and by 1922 he had become General Secretary of the Central Committee.

Within a couple of months of this appointment Lenin had suffered the first of his disabling strokes. He was to die in 1924. These events led to pandemonium within the Bolshevik leadership. Stalin's relative state of detachment from the Leninist apparatus assisted him at this juncture. Lenin, in his weakened state before death, had referred to Stalin as a possible successor although relations were to become strained between the two men. There were forces, which Stalin joined, to prevent Trotsky succeeding to the leadership after Lenin's expected death. Stalin was regarded as the tactician of this group and much was made of his faceless personality while in the background lay the fear of some more forceful personality making an impact with the party and the people. Stalin had the common touch and was regarded as being accessible. Remaining rather taciturn by nature, he was a good listener and was rather secretive, revealing little. His private life was also beyond reproach or suspicion. 'He has no vices,' said his secretary. 'He loves neither money nor pleasure, neither sport nor women. Women, apart from his wife, do not exist for him.' His tolerance, by the standards of Bolshevism, was also praised.

Five years after Lenin's death there began the second Russian revolution, with its rapid industrialisation. More than a hundred million peasant farmers were compelled to give up their smallholdings and set up collective farms. Tens of millions were forced to become literate. The cost was immense in human terms. Stalin, the author of these reforms, was compared to such historical figures as Peter the Great and Ivan the Terrible. Those closest to him were surprised by the turn of events as Stalin had hitherto appeared to be a cautious middle of the road figure. Constantly underrated by his opponents, Stalin manipulated and manouevred his position to one of complete ascendancy and by 1929, in his fiftieth year, he was the unchallenged leader of the land. Massed collectivisation and the forced march to industrialisation were disastrous ventures – some 20 million are believed to have perished – and the surprise was that the measured and calculating Stalin could have persisted with it. His popularity fell and there was now a rising tide of discontent which made him anxious for his position. His wife, protesting against excesses, was publicly denounced by Stalin and proceeded to take her own life. Stalin considered resigning his position, but carried on and in the 1930s he destroyed his opponents in a series of purge trials. He turned against those who had cultivated links with Trotsky who was in exile. Stalin became isolated and began to fear for his personal safety. There were fears of uprisings. From about this time to his death in 1953 he governed the Soviet Union in a state of tyranny. The lot of the ordinary citizen had barely improved since Tsarist times and millions had died in the cause of collectivisation and forced labour. As was said, Stalin aimed to drive barbarism out of Russia by barbaric methods. Opposition, even rumoured opposition, was ruthlessly crushed and opponents were put to death. Stalin was often described as being paranoid and fearing plots around every corner.

As this account shows, there was remarkably little by way of maladjustment in Stalin until some years after he had assumed the Soviet leadership on the death of Lenin. There is in him no question of any personality disorder that is discernible in him in terms of the clinical criteria usually employed. His character, as seen, was strong enough to overcome the disadvantages of poverty and lack of privilege. He lacked any observable vices. It was power that appears to have unseated, if not his reason, then his judgement and moral balance. Everything became geared to his ideology and his vision for Russia. Even the paranoid behaviour of his last years was due to his political beliefs and actions which made him enemies everywhere, enemies against whom he could act with exemplary ruthlessness. There is little evidence that he suffered from any clinically diagnosable paranoid psychiatric disorder. Indeed, his ailment is what tyrants commonly suffer from; the side effects of the hunger for power and the thirst for revenge. A history of this kind is altogether more common than any story of mental illness in the lives of the vast majority of leaders.

APPENDIX 1

THE PSYCHIATRIC EXAMINATION IN CASES OF VIOLENT BEHAVIOUR

A full psychiatric examination is required in all cases involving actual, attempted or potential violence. This follows the standard pattern and involves:

1. The history.

2. The mental state examination.

As a medical specialist, the psychiatrist, when conducting an examination, sets out to elicit symptoms and signs which are then evaluated in order to produce a diagnosis (if applicable) following which, he hopes, treatment will be feasible. The state of development of psychiatry is such that clear-cut approaches to this task are not always possible. Symptoms in the rest of medicine are what the patient complains of and signs are what the doctor elicits, usually through some means of physical examination. In psychiatric practice it is not always possible to separate symptoms and signs and some professionals refer to all clinical features as symptoms. These symptoms may be described by the patient or by another party who could be a friend or relation of the patient. It used to be said that a history given by the patient, especially one suffering from a psychotic disorder, should be deemed to be part of that patient's mental state.

A1.1 THE HISTORY

Nevertheless, it is possible to divide with some logic, even in psychiatry, as between history taking and the mental state examination. Many patients are referred by the GP and in most instances in this rushed age what the GP's referral contains is a summary, often brief, of what the patient has said to the doctor. Some patients are reluctantly present at a psychiatric examination, attending there under greater or lesser duress, often, when involved with the criminal law or in family and childcare cases, only to comply with sentences imposed by the court and orders and directions given by the court and allowance must be made for the lack of reliability in the history which may follow protests in those circumstances. The history taken follows the pattern established in all medicine – the onset of symptoms, their nature and the duration of symptoms (by asking the patient when he last felt well) – suitably modified in cases involving substance misuse by attending to the details of misuse. The information elicited is recorded with the patient's view of how the symptoms might have originated, that is, any stressful situation or other precipitating factor that he feels could have been causative.

It is logical to enquire at this stage into the presence of any family history of similar or other psychiatric problems or, indeed, a history of physical illness. In the present state of knowledge it is not always possible to determine in the individual case involving substance abuse whether genetics or the environment could have played the decisive part in the onset of misuse. There is reasonably good evidence in cases involving alcohol misuse that there could be genetic factors playing a part. But in many cases it is the family environment in which the patient has been brought up that often appears to have played a more important role. The cross-relationship between substance misuse and a predisposition to mental disorder must also be noted. The phenomenon of 'depressive equivalents' has been mentioned in the text previously. In this state, a patient who could be predisposed to depressive illness may, instead of developing depressive illness, be led to the misuse of alcohol or, perhaps, even the misuse of illicit substances. The opposite may also be true, a depressive illness developing instead of dependence on a variety of substances. These matters are not always reliably investigated by speaking to a patient or even by looking into his medical records (where what is entered might only have been information supplied by him on a previous occasion). In cases where a clear genetic basis to some disorder is suspected, there may be no alternative to interviewing family members and, with their consent, examining the relevant medical records.

The next logical step is to consider the personal history of the patient. For what it is worth, he should be asked about his childhood. It has been said by experts in the field of childhood memory development that no valid or systematic memory is available to a child until it reaches the age of about seven. This must put into some doubt any claims to a reliably recounted history of early childhood abuse or unhappy experiences before that age; often what is believed to be early childhood memory is a result of later hearsay. Questions routinely asked about family life, the atmosphere therein, relationships between family members, the stability of the family and the misuse of substances involving family members also suffer from this potential source of unreliability. Educational and employment history are more reliably established, or at any rate capable of being independently verified. The school history is not only valuable for information to be gained about academic accomplishment (which has a bearing on the evaluation of intelligence possessed by the patient which is a feature in every psychiatric examination) but also for evidence of behavioural and conduct disorders which have their onset in childhood and adolescence. As has been repeatedly noted, the diagnosis of personality disorder – to be undertaken at deemed psychological maturity of an individual – requires also investigation of the presence of childhood misconduct in that individual. In those individuals who are thus afflicted not all childhood naughtiness is seemingly outgrown. The misuse of substances might well have had their onset in the course of school days and the educational record, especially in cases of behavioural and conduct disorders involving the individual as a child, could make reference to problems involving substance misuse.

The employment record is equally valuable for any lack of correspondence between academic attainment and intellectual promise and the employment that has actually come to be secured may indicate some mental problems as well, usually in terms of personality, sometimes due to formal illness, which is deserving of further enquiry. Furthermore, the employment record itself, if procurable, often gives an independent and objective account of the individual's capacity for work and also his personality. It is especially valuable as a source of information concerning suspected or proven substance misuse which could have involved the occupational health service and also external medical evaluation. Significant substance misuse often leads to an adverse impact being made on an employee's functioning at his work place, matters which may well not reach a GP's ear. Particular attention should be paid to any warnings received, records of meetings with superiors and line managers for unexplained or unauthorised absence or impaired performance, any sanctions imposed and, of course, the steps that might have been taken leading up to the individual's dismissal from employment. The employment record is a crucial document to study especially in cases involving employment where it is alleged that the functioning of the individual concerned could have been impaired by substance misuse. It is a truism to say that the effects of substance misuse could be concealed in every situation except the modern work place.

In family and child practice the sexual and marital history of the patient is of obvious relevance. Sadly, reliability is not always achieved when it comes to evaluating the quality of the relationships formed but the bare enumeration of the number and duration of relationships is capable of independent verification. Any current relationship is noted, as are more mundane matters such as the nature of the accommodation the individual has and the receipt of social benefits.

An important sub-category of the personal history usually taken from the patient involves enquiry into the consumption of alcohol and illicit substances. It is of obvious importance in cases involving substance misuse. These details are usually recorded from personal report, objective or independent verification from any available witnesses and a limited range of laboratory investigations. It cannot be emphasised too often that a proper evaluation of alcohol and illicit drug use requires a comprehensive assessment of all areas of personal and psychological functioning for, especially in family and child practice and employment practice, what one is looking for is some disturbance in behaviour which is likely to adversely affect the patient's responsibilities as spouse, partner, parent or employee. Absolute levels of consumption of these substances may have general forensic relevance (eg convictions for driving with an excess of alcohol, possession or distribution of illicit substances) but in itself it is not necessarily of direct significance to the issues arising in criminal or family and child proceedings. Similar considerations apply in cases involving employment where the functioning of the individual is usually more important than the fact of substance misuse or its extent. However, an increasing number of employers now insist that their employees desist from all illicit substance misuse and also that they consume alcohol only in moderation. The fact of misuse may assume importance in these circumstances. The details of substance misuse must be set out. The age and circumstances of first use must be noted and recorded. The evolution of the misuse must be considered, setting out the periods in the individual's life where misuse waxed and waned. The source of his supply and the costs involved must be enquired for. Any periods of relative or complete abstinence must be noted, as must be any report of withdrawal symptoms. Any medical help sought must be enquired for and recorded. The details of current use must be noted. The effects on the individual's general medical health, psychiatric health, interpersonal relationships, employment record and any financial difficulties resulting from substance misuse must also be noted. There will be an overlap between this area of enquiry and matters touching on employment, family relationships, offending behaviour and the medical and psychiatric history.

A forensic history is of similar importance. A recent history of convictions and cautions gives objective support to what could otherwise, in many domestic instances, be emotionally charged accusations of violent and aggressive behaviour. Ideally, one should also have available the facts of any incident leading to conviction, although much useful information may be found in previous forensic psychiatric and pre-sentence reports. Particular attention must be paid to substance abuse-related offending which may include road traffic offences, public order offences, offending in relation to possession and distribution of illicit substances, convictions for soliciting, orders for anti-social behaviour (ASBO) and, of course, any violence directed against the person and property. It is also important to study the details of cautions, warnings and reprimands issued as well as the convictions received as the former deal with most minor cases of possession of illicit drugs.

Following an evaluation of personal history, the next step is to consider the past medical history of the patient. This would appear to be an obvious step, for many disorders tend to recur. The most useful source of this information is the full medical record of the patient. Often the GP records are retrieved more easily than the hospital records. The former are less complete when hospital intervention has taken place but copies of all correspondence routinely sent from hospitals – letters, discharge summaries including results of investigations – should be available as part of the GP record. Sometimes they are not and it remains a matter for scandal that in an age which purports to be one dedicated to the proper transmission of vital information that so many patients do not have readily available access to a comprehensive and reliable record of their medical history to present to any examining doctor. The time has probably come – and the necessary technology is available – for information concerning patients to be given to them, to be held responsibly and to be produced to authorised professionals. It strikes one as being a more useful investment of public funds than attempts to confirm mere identity.

Be that as it may, the past medical history is divided conventionally into physical illness and mental disorder, which is not strictly logical but convenient. The details of physical illness suffered in the past must also include details of therapeutic drugs used previously and those which may continue to be taken by the patient, for many drugs do have adverse side effects which may themselves precipitate or aggravate psychiatric disorder. Complications due to possible substance misuse eg pathology involving the liver in cases of alcohol misuse, the detection of HIV/Aids and hepatitis C are points on interest and there could have been previous medical interventions to deal with the medical *sequelae* of substance misuse. The importance of past history of mental disorder is self-evident. The patient may not have reliable information to give in respect of past psychiatric disorders or interventions – it is striking how many patients lack such essential information as the diagnosis or treatment previously given, length of hospital stay or whether admission had been voluntary or under the compulsory provisions of the MHA. A study of the past medical record is essential, although their availability is not always assured. In cases of substance misuse any details of intervention made by the GP or on referral to the local drugs and alcohol team and the results obtained there must be studied. As important is the record of non-co-operation with treatment on the part of the patient.

From what has been said already – and repeatedly stressed through the course of this book – the personality of the patient, that is, the element on which any illness or disorder comes to be grafted, is important to evaluate. There is very clear evidence that defects in the personality, whether or not they amount to any formal personality disorder, provide a significant predisposition to substance misuse. Substance misuse itself may lead to disturbance found in the personality later. The study of ante- or pre-morbid personality is a well-recognised feature of the psychiatric examination. However, as with his reputation, what is the personality of an individual is a matter to be determined by other persons. Individuals are notoriously unreliable in the self-assessment of personality. Sadly, in family and child practice, the significant other person in an individual's life – spouse or partner, especially when estranged – can himself or herself come to provide information which materially distorts the picture that more independent or objective witnesses may draw of an individual. There may be a similar unreliability creeping into assessments made in cases where offending is in issue where the family's recollections of the individual may be far removed from reality as they attempt to emphasise his normality before substances enveloped him. Despite the protestations of psychologists, there are few reliable tests of personality assessment for use in ordinary clinical practice. The doctor is left with evaluating the evidence as a whole and it is in this respect that independently made records such as employment history or the documentation of the criminal record may give a more reliable picture. One must also always bear in mind the huge variations that are possible in the attributes of a personality, and what is the normal range for any attribute is scarcely to be ascertained with any convenience. The distinctions invariably to be made with any behaviour of psychiatric relevance – what is abnormal, what is pathological – are to be borne in mind also when assessing personality. It should also be remembered constantly that one could be grossly abnormal in one's behaviour in terms of the norms of any society but that fact alone does not preclude acceptable participation as a citizen, employee, spouse, partner or parent. And the world would be a duller and more primitive place if not for the abnormal personalities who have existed in every age.

A1.2   THE MENTAL STATE EXAMINATION

This is the equivalent of the physical examination in general medicine and surgery. It is, of course, a vital part of any examination of a patient but it is possible to overstate its importance. By that one means a history and examination both must be undertaken and many experienced psychiatrists will argue that the history – with its scope for eliciting objective, independent information – is the more important component. In fact, in family and child practice, with the possibility of a study of the papers which are routinely disclosed to the psychiatric expert along with the available medical record, it should be possible in the average case to predict about 90 per cent of the contents of the report that waits to be written on a study of these documents alone. If sufficient knowledge has not been obtained in this way, one of two situations exist. Firstly, the papers are incomplete, in particular the medical records might not have been included within them. Secondly, sufficiently careful reading of the papers has not been undertaken. While psychotic conditions and other obviously revealing disorders such as a depressive illness may be detected by an examination of the mental state alone, other conditions of particular relevance to family and child practice and in cases involving an individual's employment and often in criminal practice, especially the personality disorders, may be difficult to identify without access to the kind of information which makes up the history, whether such information is to be found in the papers in cases where litigation is afoot or is derived from persons independent of the patient such as friends and relations, although care must be taken to see that those acquainted with the patient do not exaggerate – by maximising or minimising pathology – so as to make their own case.

Notwithstanding this, a current mental state examination is essential if a fully informed diagnostic formulation is to be arrived at. It sometimes happens that in family and child practice a spouse, partner or parent refuses to undergo a psychiatric examination as directed and the expert may be left to work on the available papers alone, sometimes by a further direction of the court, more usually on the instructions of the solicitor. Although, in view of what has been said above, it is perfectly feasible to produce a report in those circumstances to assist the court, the expert must ensure that he conveys to the court the information that the peculiar insights that may be possible on examination – the 'feel' of a patient, so to speak – is only possible on personal contact with a patient.

For our present purposes we shall merely summarise the heads of the mental state examination and briefly note the significance of any findings.

A1.3   Appearance and behaviour

It used to be said to medical students that a skilled and experienced doctor could make a diagnosis even while a patient was walking through the door of the consulting room. This art was carried to its peak in the works of Sir Arthur Conan Doyle who based his fictional creature, Sherlock Holmes, on a real individual, his teacher at Edinburgh Medical School, Dr Joseph Bell. Conan Doyle said of his mentor that he would sit in his room 'with a face like a Red Indian, and diagnose the people as they came in, before they even opened their mouths. He would tell them their symptoms and even give them details of their past life, and hardly ever would he make a mistake.' The maestro Bell himself explained the basis to his apparently wondrous facility: 'The precise and intelligent recognition and appreciation of minor differences is the real essential factor in all successful diagnosis.'

Things are a little more complex in psychiatric practice. Eccentricity of manner and exotic dress may indicate psychiatric disorder and is especially common to see with exuberant manic patients. Self neglect, on the other hand, may not necessarily indicate pathology; lack of means could be the reason. However, alcohol and illicit drug misuse may also lead to self neglect on the part of the patient as can schizophrenia or some forms of personality disorder. Overactivity is characteristic of mania although some depressed patients appear agitated. Most of the stimulant drugs such as cocaine and amphetamine may also give rise to overactivity and agitation on the part of the user. The paranoid patient may be suspicious and the occasional sufferer from paranoid psychosis or paranoid personality disorder may insist on tape recording his encounter with the doctor and may also be given to misinterpreting even the most trivial of occurrences e g the doctor speaking on the telephone or into a dictaphone. Persecutory ideas are common adverse effects with many stimulant drugs. Yawning is not merely a sign of boredom but could indicate oversedation and may be one of the withdrawal symptoms seen in opiate dependence.

A1.4   Physiological symptoms

These are usually the most straightforward features to elicit in the examination of the mental state. Sleep in mental disorder may be disturbed in a variety of ways, and dreams and nightmares may indicate an underlying anxiety state. No intricate exploration of dream phenomena is undertaken in mainstream psychiatry; that is the historical task of psychoanalysis and even there the analysis of the content of dreams is now deemed of doubtful value. Appetite, as will later be discussed, may be altered in many psychiatric conditions as may bowel habits, menstrual regularity and libido. Many of these physiological symptoms may come to be deranged with substance misuse including the states of withdrawal found on the cessation of use.

A1.5   Mood

Under this head depression, anxiety and irritability are investigated. These mood states are commonly found within the affective disorders. Schizophrenia may be associated with subtler changes involving incongruity or flattening of affect. Indifference – *la belle indifference* – used to be believed to be a classical feature of hysterical or dissociative states (although the current belief is to question the significance of these states of indifference). The examination of suicidal thoughts also comes within an investigation of mood. As is well established and described, there are gradations in suicidal ideation passing from fleeting ideas that life may not be worth living through active suicidal ideas to elaborately crafted plans to take one's life. Anxiety states may include features of generalised anxiety with or without the presence of phobic states and a particular feature of anxiety states is the presence also of the symptoms of depersonalisation and derealisation where the patient feels he has changed or the world has changed. Mood changes of a variety of forms are the commonest features seen with substance misuse and upon discontinuing this misuse.

A1.6   Speech

This is studied from the point of view of both form and content. Form refers not only to the rate of speech – considerably slowed as with all other functions in depressive illness and speeded up in mania – but also the quantity and quality. There is poverty of speech noted in those with compromised intellectual functions. The pattern of speech is also considered when logic may be lacking in speech, a state of affairs which is believed to reflect thought disorder, characteristically seen in schizophrenia. The terms speech and thought are often used interchangeably although speech should be reserved for actual talk while thought is to be inferred from the content of talk which gives a window into the mind. In cases of substance misuse that lead to the emergence of psychotic features, speech may be disordered as it is with ordinary psychotic conditions. The slurred speech of the drunk is, of course, well known but a misuser of cocaine and the amphetamines may also show the rapidity and disorganisation of speech that is usually associated with the manic patient.

A1.7   Thought content

These may include the variety of delusions associated with psychotic conditions such as schizophrenia and mania, and rarely in cases of severe depressive illness. There are rarer phenomena such as thought insertion, thought withdrawal and thought broadcasting which refer to abnormal processes involving thinking that reach delusional proportions. An extreme variant of this is passivity where the patient feels his body has been taken over and is controlled by some extraneous or alien force. These are characteristically features of an acute schizophrenic illness. Obsessional thoughts and compulsive behaviour, although normally features of a non-psychotic illness, may also be dealt with under the investigation of the processes of thinking. Misuse of substances – including the stimulant drugs, LSD and Ecstasy – may lead to the presence of grossly disturbed and abnormal thoughts.

A1.8   Abnormal perceptions

These include illusions and hallucinations. Occasionally there is confusion between the two phenomena. The former are common and usually harmless. One is not uncommonly startled by the shadow of an object, say a tree in moonlight, and comes to believe it could be a person, usually one carrying a malevolent design. Hearing a chiming church bell calling out, 'Turn again, Whittington' is an example from legend. The significance of auditory hallucinations can only be evaluated within the context of the entire clinical picture. It is a common symptom of acute schizophrenia, although normal individuals experiencing stress or grief or unwanted solitude can also have these perceptions. Visual hallucinations are invariably significant and suggest organic brain disorder. They are notoriously experienced in states of withdrawal from alcohol and also with illicit drug use. This and other hallucinations may also be a presenting feature of space occupying lesions of the brain such as tumours. Substance misuse involving the hallucinogenic drugs is notorious for producing disorders and distortions of perceptions as well as of time and stimulant drug use, especially that involving cocaine, is known to produce somatic sensations.

A1.9   Cognitive functions

It is traditional to make a clinical examination of the higher brain functions although full psychological testing is recommended for all formal purposes such as litigation and also in complications arising as a result of substance misuse, in particular the Wernicke-Korsakoff syndrome seen in states of alcohol withdrawal. The specialist investigation of psychological functions are labour-intensive and time-consuming although resources are normally available for psychological testing in family and child cases. Consciousness is not usually a problem in the parties involved in legal proceedings although it is the first cognitive state to be examined usually. There is much confusion regarding the state of confusion itself and disorientation. Confusion, although colloquially applied to any state where an individual does not know what is going on, technically means a state of disturbed consciousness. Disorientation, on the other hand, concerns a lack of knowledge which leads to impaired appreciation of such details as time (not knowing day, date, month etc), place (where one is), or person (who people are). As a rule, demented patients are disorientated, not confused, though these patients, like anyone else, may also become confused when afflicted, say, by an infection. Confusional states are common in cases of substance misuse and in states of withdrawal from their use. Attention and concentration are impaired most commonly in states of depression and anxiety although almost any condition, not to mention their treatment, can lead to this phenomenon. These functions are also commonly affected with substance misuse. Their importance lies in that they may give rise as a consequence to poor short-term memory which is not to be attributed to 'organic' factors but is related to the poor registration of memories which follows poor attention and concentration. There are more specialised tests for higher function such as those for dysphasia (difficulties in receiving or expressing spoken speech) or dysgraphia (difficulties in receiving or expressing the written word) but these are matters for specialist neuropsychological testing. Short-term and long-term memory may also be clinically tested. The focus is usually on the former which, as is well known, is preferentially affected in most disorders. Remote memory is preserved for a long time even in fairly severely demented patients who can, for instance, converse knowledgeably about Mr Churchill as prime minister but who may have no idea who the current incumbent might be. The formal detailed testing of memory function is also a matter for expert psychological testing. As was said earlier, it is usual also to make some assessment of intelligence possessed by the patient. In fact, the purpose of seeking information about schooling and educational attainment is at least, in part, directed to the aim of seeing whether later occupational achievement has matched intellectual promise or whether there has been a shortfall possibly related to mental disorder. Questions on general knowledge of current affairs, intellectual interests admitted to by the patient and the content of the patient's talk in interchanges with the examiner may also indicate the level of intellectual functioning of the patient. Needless to say, formal detailed assessment of intelligence also resides in the province of the specialist psychologist.

A1.10   Insight

It is usual to end any examination of the mental state with an assessment of the insight possessed by the patient. This term refers to the understanding in general terms the patient has achieved in regard to the nature of the disorder he has suffered and its cause. At its most basic level the patient is able to recognise he is ill although he does not acknowledge mental disorder. One level up, he accepts he is ill and also that the disorder is of nervous or mental origins. When insight is completely lacking, disorder is denied *in toto*. Psychotic conditions are usually associated with some impairment of insight while those patients with non-psychotic disorders usually retain insight. However, there are exceptions. Hysterical patients are notoriously lacking in insight, sometimes totally, even while hysterical (dissociative/conversion) states are classified usually as non-psychotic conditions. As has already been indicated, cultural beliefs may decisively influence whether mental or nervous disorder is acknowledged by the patient. Insight of a different kind has to be sought in the patient involved in substance misuse. Here one is seeking acceptance of a problem by an individual who is prepared to acknowledge, say, that his consumption of alcohol has reached hazardous or harmful levels. Recommended safe values for alcohol consumption may be employed to test this awareness. Not uncommonly, social and cultural factors may play a part in the individual accepting there is any problematical use of a substance. So widespread is the use of cannabis – and substances such as khat within certain migrant groups – that an individual, comparing himself to the norm for such habits, may not accept that any harm could befall him. It cannot be asserted in those circumstances that he is lacking in insight which, like most matters in psychiatry, is to be evaluated against a background of social and cultural belief.

A1.11   Rating scales

As we saw in Chapter 2, it is increasingly the practice to employ rating scales to assess the risk of violence. One of the better known among these devices is the HCR-20 scale referred to there (Webster, 2002). The rating scale puts into systematic form what a clinical psychiatric assessment, properly undertaken, would normally uncover. As noted, the rating scale has three subdivisions.

Ten items refer to historical data. These are mostly static in nature and unlikely to fluctuate with time.

1.   Previous violence is the actual, attempted or threatened harm to a person. This item is based on the principle that past violence is generally the best predictor of future violence.

2.   Young age at the time of the first violence reflects the finding that that the younger an individual is at the time of the first violent incident concerning him, the greater the likelihood of future violent conduct.

3.   Relationship instability applies to intimate or non-platonic relationships and excludes relationships with family and friends. Instability is defined as either many short-term relationships, absence of any relationships or the presence of conflict within long-term relationships. It has been shown that individuals who are violent within relationships have a tendency to be violent generally.

4.   Employment problems. There have been shown to be links between income, conduct on parole, unemployment and criminal recidivism.

5.   Substance use problems. There is a strong relationship between substance misuse and violence.

6.   Major mental illness refers to disorders involving disturbances of thought and affect which are associated with violent behaviour.

7.   Psychopathy. This is a high risk factor for violent behaviour.

8.   Early maladjustment. This refers to maladjustment at home, at school or in the community before the age of 17.

9.   Personality disorder. As shown previously, there is an association between personality disorder and violent behaviour.

10.   Prior supervision failure.

Five items refer to clinical data. These refer to current mental, emotional and psychiatric status and include risk markers that are dynamic and therefore likely to change.

1.   Lack of insight refers to the degree that the individual fails to acknowledge and comprehend his mental illness and its effect on others.

2.   Negative attitudes refer to anti-social attitudes that have some potential to lead to eventual violence.

3.   Active symptoms of major mental illness.

4.   Impulsivity refers to behavioural and affective instability which are related to how the individual could react to real or imagined slights, insults or disappointments.

5.   Unresponsive to treatment.

Five items refer also to risk management. These are concerned with forecasting the future social, living and treatment circumstances as well as anticipating the individual's reactions to those conditions.

1.   'Plans lack feasibility' considers the chances of success for the plans made by the individual.

2.   'Exposure to destabilisers' refers to situations in which the individual is exposed to hazardous conditions which could trigger episodes of violence.

3.   'Lack of personal support' refers to the presence of emotional, financial and practical support available from family and friends.

4.   Non-compliance with therapy.

5.   Stress in relation to the particular vulnerabilities of the individual and the likely exposure to stress in the future.

APPENDIX 2

DOMESTIC VIOLENCE: A NATIONAL REPORT (MARCH 2005)

MINISTERIAL FOREWORD

Over the last thirty years domestic violence in the UK has gone from being a largely unspoken subject to one which is being tackled and confronted by Government and Statutory Bodies and the voluntary sector. In 1971 Refuge opened the first safe house for women and children experiencing domestic violence. Today there are over 400 refuges nationally and domestic violence receives much greater attention.

This month, March has been designated National Domestic Violence Month, which reflects the seriousness of this horrific crime.

This report provides an overview of our achievements to date, whilst understanding that for this positive momentum of change to continue, we must set new objectives. This is reflected and underpinned in our national working plan with recommendations and mechanisms put in place for tackling domestic violence through early identification, prevention and improved response.

We know that all agencies that come into contact with victims, their children and perpetrators must be able to give an appropriate response, with safety of the victim paramount.

We know that domestic violence is a serious public health issue and that the statistics are shocking. For women aged 19-44, domestic violence is the leading cause of morbidity, greater than cancer, war, and motor vehicle accidents. 89% of the victims who suffer sustained domestic violence are female, however we also know that domestic violence can affect the lesbian, gay, bisexual and transgender community and male victims. We know that domestic violence can be perpetrated by family and extended family members, through forced marriage, female genital mutilation, and so-called 'honour crimes'. More worryingly, a recent survey by the National Society for the Prevention of Cruelty to Children (NSPCC) revealed that far too many of our young people are already being subjected to relationship abuse in their teenage years. This illustrates that we still have much to do if we are to create a culture change that makes domestic violence socially unacceptable for the next generation.

In addition, there are compelling economic reasons why we have to tackle this problem head on; the cost of domestic violence is staggering, with combined tangible and intangible costs of £23 billion in the UK annually.

Government action on domestic violence is led by an Inter-Ministerial Group on Domestic Violence, set up in 2003.

This Group is chaired by Home Office Minister Baroness Scotland, QC. It includes Ministers from key Departments, including Constitutional Affairs, the Solicitor General, Health, Education, DTI, Office of the Deputy Prime Minister, and Work and Pensions. Wales and Northern Ireland are also represented. This is to provide a joined-up and robust programme of work.

The Government's strategic approach to tackling domestic violence was set out in the consultation paper *Safety & Justice.* This approach has led to the Domestic Violence, Crime & Victims Act 2004, the biggest piece of legislation on domestic violence in over 30 years.

This report represents the road we have travelled so far and the National Domestic Violence Delivery Plan signposts the direction we need to travel in the future. This report should act as an encouragement to those statutory and voluntary organisations working in the field of domestic violence and demonstrate that your work has been recognised and appreciated. The Government has now become a full member of that partnership.

DELIVERING SERVICES FOR SURVIVORS OF DOMESTIC VIOLENCE: THE GOVERNMENT'S PROGRESS AND FURTHER ACTION

Part 1 – Introduction

Purpose

1. This document is aimed at all those working in the field of domestic violence, both the voluntary and statutory sectors. It is also, of course, aimed at domestic violence victims themselves. It has two key objectives:
    *   to set out briefly the significant progress that has been made in implementing the proposals outlined in *Safety and Justice*: The Government's Proposals on Domestic Violence' and;

- to highlight new commitments which form the 'next steps' in delivering services and support to victims of domestic violence. This includes an outline of a working document called the National Domestic Violence Delivery Plan (ANNEX A).

2. We want to ensure that victims of domestic violence are aware of all the options that are open to them in order that they can make informed decisions about the route they wish to take to end the abuse and rebuild their lives. These options include seeking the intervention of the courts. However, we recognise that not all victims will wish to pursue a legal remedy. For all victims, whether or not they seek the protection of the courts, it is vital that they are aware of, and have access to, all the voluntary and statutory support that is available.

Background and context

3. On 18 June 2003, the Home Secretary published the consultation paper *Safety and Justice: the Government's Proposals on Domestic Violence. Safety and Justice* sets out the Government's strategy for tackling domestic violence through three strands: prevention, protection and justice and support. It included proposals for legislative and non-legislative changes to the way domestic violence is dealt with in England and Wales. 470 responses were received to the document from a wide range of stakeholders, including survivors, voluntary and community sector groups working in the field, statutory agencies and concerned members of the public. In conjunction with voluntary and community sector groups, a series of workshops with survivors from a diverse range of communities were run.

4. In December 2003, the Government published 'Summary of Responses to *Safety and Justice*: the Government's Proposals on Domestic Violence'. It accompanied publication and introduction into Parliament of the Domestic Violence, Crime and Victims Bill; and set out a number of non-legislative measures which the Government would be pursuing in the short to medium term.

5. The Inter-Ministerial Group on Domestic Violence – which brings together Departments central to tackling domestic violence and supporting survivors and children, with colleagues from the Devolved Administrations – has been responsible for driving forward the Government's work on domestic violence within this strategic framework.

6. This document highlights briefly the progress made in tackling domestic violence since the publication of *Safety and Justice* and,

more importantly, sets out an ambitious cross-government programme to deliver better services and support for victims of this terrible crime.

Part 2 – Progress

Safety and justice

7. Nearly two years on from the *'Safety and Justice'* consultation paper, and culminating in the passing of the Domestic Violence, Crime and Victims Act 2004, much has already been achieved to deliver on many key commitments, not just in legislative terms but also in delivery on the ground. We have and will continue to learn from the feedback from that consultation exercise, and from other research and work, to develop our plans still further.

8. Reported below is an overview of progress made to date, in developing the proposals outlined in *Safety and Justice.*

9. As well as taking forward action points outlined in *Safety and Justice* we have also addressed two further key issues.

A core definition of domestic violence

10. To support delivery across Government and its agencies through a common understanding of domestic violence, we now have a common definition. This follows the definition already used by the Association of Chief Police Officers, and is:

> 'Any incident of threatening behaviour, violence or abuse (psychological, physical, sexual, financial or emotional) between adults who are or have been intimate partners or family members, regardless of gender or sexuality.'

This definition is wider than the previous Home Office definition and incorporates violence between family members over 18 as well as between adults who are, or were, intimate partners. This ensures that those issues of chief concern to BME communities, such as forced marriage, so-called 'honour crimes' and female genital mutilation, are properly reflected and reflects concerns voiced by many in response to *Safety and Justice.*

An adult is defined as any person aged 18 years or over. Family members are defined as mother, father, son, daughter, brother, sister, and grandparents, whether directly related, in laws or stepfamily.

Actions to prevent domestic violence

- Published information sharing guidance for practitioners http://www.homeoffice.gov.uk/rds/pdfs04/dpr30.pdf so they are aware of what they can and should do if they suspect or are told about domestic violence.

- Completed piloting and evaluation of the Bristol pilot of routing enquiry by midwives; and appointed the first National Domestic Violence Coordinator within the heath service.

- Ran the first national awareness campaign which sought to promote the new 24 hour freephone national helpline number as well as raising general awareness.

- Funded and distributed to all secondary schools a new series of the teenage soap series 'Watch Over Me' aimed at educating young people about domestic violence.

- Funded the first phoneline for perpetrators who want to address their behaviour. This was launched by RESPECT in September 2004.

- Rolled out accredited perpetrator programmes within the Probation Service – these occur following use of the Spousal Assault Risk Assessment (SARA) tool and ensure that the safety of the victim is then managed within inter-agency public protection arrangements.

- Funded a national phoneline for Lesbian, Gay, Bisexual and Transgender communities, launched by Broken Rainbow.

- Published good practice guidance on how to implement strategies to encourage and enable disclosure of domestic violence in a range of health settings.

Actions to protect victims and bring offenders to justice

- Domestic Violence, Crime and Victims Act 2004 received Royal Assent in November 2004.

- Association of Chief Police Officers (ACPO) and the National Centre for Policing Excellence (CENTREX) have published comprehensive guidelines for investigating domestic violence which take on board all relevant recommendations from the HMCPSI/HMIC report.

- CPS updated Policy and Guidance documents in February 2005 to reflect the new CPS initiatives and the substantial legislative changes since the issue of the last version in November 2001. The CPS also produced with CENTREX a joint national training programme for police and CPS staff.

- In March 2004 the Government met a Manifesto commitment by publishing an evaluation of specialist domestic violence courts. There are now seven specialist courts running and more are planned.

- In 2004 the Judicial Studies Board launched a new domestic violence training programme for magistrates.

- In July 2004 the Sentencing Advisory Panel published a consultation paper on sentencing in domestic violence cases. Consultation ended on 12 October 2004. Draft guidelines are likely to be published for consultation in the autumn of 2005.

- Published a series of good practice guides and overall findings from the Crime Reduction Programme Violence Against Women initiative, including how advocates can support victims to move towards living violence-free lives.

Actions to support victims and their children

- National 24-hour freephone helpline – run in partnership by Women's Aid and Refuge – is now fully operational and supported by the online database system Ukrefugesonline.

- £32 million has been provided for improvements to existing and new refuge places through ODPM's Homelessness & Housing Support Directorate and the Housing Corporation.

- The voluntary sector has continued to provide key services to victims of domestic violence and their children, and has begun work on issues of quality and standards of service.

- The Children Act 2004 was passed giving effect to key reforms to children's services envisaged by 'Every Child Matters'.

- Published good practice guidance in 2004 on how to support children who have witnessed domestic violence: 'Tackling Domestic Violence: providing support for children who have witnessed domestic violence'.

- In January 2005 new forms were introduced to enable allegations of domestic violence to be made right at the start of court applications for contact and residence involving children.

- From January 2005 the law was clarified to ensure that the courts must consider the harm a child might suffer as a result of witnessing violence on another person.

The Forced Marriage Unit

11. The Forced Marriage Unit was launched on 26 January 2005, and is another example of joined-up interdepartmental working between the Foreign and Commonwealth Office (FCO) and the Home Office. The unit has funded two Forced Marriage Conferences, in April 2004 and more recently a successful national conference on 16 February, with delegates from several countries attending. The unit oversaw and funded the first UK-wide working group on Forced Marriage and the Womens' National Commission (WNC) have been invited to sit on the steering group. We have also funded national awareness raising materials, a 'Step-by-step' guide for Black Minority Ethnic (BME) victims of domestic violence that went to consultation in November 2004 and will be published in the summer 2005; a BME website that will be launched in April 2005 that will include focus groups across the UK from many BME specialist organisations. Further funding was allocated to seven community events and awareness raising sessions around the revised Female Genital Mutilation (FGM) Act.

Measuring success: performance indicators

12. We referred in *Safety and Justice* to the difficulty of using one headline target to measure our success in tackling domestic violence. At the heart of this is the difficulty of gaining an accurate picture of the true levels of domestic violence occurring within our society.

13. Accordingly, we have identified a number of 'proxy' indicators against which we intend to measure the medium to long-term success of our strategy. More details are included at Annex B, but in brief the indicators cover key agencies and are as follows:
    (i) number of domestic homicides;
    (ii) prevalence rates as measured by the British Crime Survey Inter-Personal Violence module;
    (iii) attitudes towards the acceptability of domestic violence;
    (iv) domestic violence arrests;
    (v) domestic violence offenders successfully prosecuted in the courts;
    (vi) number of non-molestation, occupation and restraining orders made;
    (vii) quantity and quality of domestic violence services commissioned by Local Authorities;
    (viii) survivor satisfaction with the support they receive; and

(ix) increased reporting of risk of harm to children as a result of domestic violence.

14. The police will also continue to collect information on rates of repeat victimisation, although we recognise that these data can only show the rate of repeat reporting to the police, rather than true underlying rates of repeat victimisation.

Part 3 – From developing policy to delivering services and support for victims

15. While real progress has been made in tackling domestic violence, we recognise that there is still much more to be done. We are committed to our three core objectives of Prevention, Protection and Justice and Support for domestic violence victims. A range of further measures are in hand to build on the progress made and which will ensure further improvements in delivery of services for victims. We have detailed below 15 commitments across the statutory and voluntary sector grouped under the headings in *Safety and Justice*: *Prevention and Support and Protection and Justice*. Many of the commitments are inter-linked and in some cases, such as Independent Support and Advice for Victims and the Development of Specialist Domestic Violence Courts, they are inter-dependent.

Prevention and support (early identification and early intervention)

Commitment 1: independent support and advice for victims

16. We want to address two key challenges that were highlighted in the *Safety and Justice* consultation and in subsequent work undertaken by the Department for Constitutional Affairs (DCA) Consumer Focus Strategy:
   (a) Professionals in the statutory sector may be reluctant to seek disclosures, regardless of training and guidance, if there are no services on to which to refer victims and
   (b) Each professional will be expert only in his or her own field. They will each be able to help the victim, but only to a limited extent. This often leaves victims having to approach a range of agencies to tell and re-tell their stories.

17. Victims and frontline organisations have made clear through consultation their belief that the most effective solution to these problems is the availability of dedicated advice and assistance from an independent source, available to those both inside and outside the criminal justice system. This independent source would give personal advice and support direct to victims to help them make decisions

about their future and also help them access the range of services they need. This view is supported by evidence of outcomes where such services already exist.

18. A range of names have been suggested for these independent advisors, for instance – advocate, navigator, DV victim support worker. For ease, in this paper we are using 'independent domestic violence advisors' or IDVAs. While we are very willing to consider alternatives, we do think that a generic name is essential, so that all victims and those who support them can be clear about who should be contacted and what their role will be.

EVIDENCE OF OUTCOME AND COST-EFFECTIVENESS OF IDVAs

19. IDVAs are not a new idea, there is strong evidence from existing projects that they are effective in terms of outcomes for the victim and in terms of cost efficiency. Evidence comes from projects established and originally funded under the Home Office Crime Reduction Programme Violence Against Women Initiatives (CRP VAWI) – the evaluation of the 27 projects was published in February 2005 along with two good practice guides which provide advice on how practitioners can provide effective and timely support to victims and also those from Black and other minority ethnic communities. The value and significance of IDVAs were reiterated by the evaluation of Specialist Courts which identified the role as being critical to the courts' success – see Commitment 3.

20. The evidence shows that support from IDVAs:
    • reduces repeat victimisation;
    • reduces attrition rates in the criminal justice system;
    • increases victim satisfaction and confidence; and
    • is cost effective.

WHAT IS MEANT BY INDEPENDENT ADVOCACY, OR IDVAs?

21. There are a number of elements present within an independent advice service. These are set out below:
    (a) Independence: the role of the advisor is to advise and support victims to help ensure their safety. To do this effectively, the advisor must be independent of any single organisation. The key outcome of their work must be survivor safety rather than better results for a particular agency (such as increased arrests, prosecutions, etc).
    (b) Professionalism: the service involves supporting a survivor with a named caseworker. This requires training and is not naturally suited to be carried out by volunteers.
    (c) Safety Options: advisors need to understand the full range of remedies and resources available in the civil and criminal justice

systems, as well as the physical safety options available to a survivor through other statutory and voluntary sector services, and to be able to assess their suitability in each case.

(d) Crisis Intervention: advisors work from the point of crisis with a survivor and offer intensive support to help assure their short and long term safety.

(e) Risk: advisors must understand the assessment of risk as it relates to domestic violence victims and how to manage it. The focus of an advisor's work is with high-risk victims where their safety can only be assured through this approach.

(f) Partnership: advisors need to liaise effectively with statutory and voluntary agencies. The service provided by the advisor should ensure that agencies are able to fulfil their obligations to the survivor on a collaborative basis.

(g) Measurable Outcomes: Advice Services have clear outcomes in terms of reduced repeat victimisation, fewer withdrawals of witness statements and increased reporting of children at risk of harm from domestic violence.

22. £1 million will be available in 2005/06 to underpin the quality of IDVA services by supporting the rollout of the Coordinated Response and Advocacy Resource Group (CRARG) accredited training programme for IDVAs and will be supported by the development of occupational standards, as well as the development of more specialist domestic violence courts, linked to IDVA enhancement and expansion (see below).

Commitment 2: our health services

23. The Department of Health has funded a pilot scheme in Bristol to evaluate a programme of routine enquiry. Health professionals routinely ask patients whether they are experiencing domestic violence and provide appropriate information or referral, depending on the response. The pilot included the production of a video and training materials based on the findings of the evaluation, and which have been rolled-out by the Bristol research team. The Department of Health has facilitated three regional training days to support the dissemination of material.

24. A good practice guide, which provides advice on how to encourage and deal appropriately with disclosure in a range of health settings was published in 2004 along with a research report. The findings are from some of the evaluations funded under the remit of the Crime Reduction Programme Violence Against Women Initiative.

25. The Children and Young People and Maternity Services National Service Framework states that all pregnant women are offered a supportive environment and the opportunity to disclose domestic

violence. This is backed up by the Government's commitment in *Supporting Local Delivery*. An Advisory Group has been established to consider what the key elements of a supportive environment should be. The work of the Group is time limited.

26. The Department of Health is also funding a review of 'Domestic Violence: A Resource Manual for Health Care Professionals' which was first issued in March 2000. As with the 2000 manual, this revised version has been developed to help all those health care professionals who encounter victims of domestic violence, to equip them with the skills, knowledge and confidence to be able to address the issue in an appropriate manner. The revised manual is more of a toolkit, incorporating good practice models which we hope will promote networking and information sharing among professionals.

27. In 2005, the proper recording of injuries and/or mental health problems sustained as a result of domestic violence will be underpinned by the new Electronic Patient Records (EPR) system. EPR will contain specific diagnostic codes for domestic violence which will be primary codes in domestic violence incidents – so that, for example, a wrist injury sustained during a domestic violence attack will be recorded as domestic violence first, and wrist injury second.

28. This is important both for the recording of individual injuries (not least so that this documentation can be used as evidence in, for example, court or immigration proceedings) and for anonymised data collection which can give us a better picture of the true extent of domestic violence and use of health services by survivors.

Commitment 3: earlier intervention with offenders

CRARG is a new charity funded by a number of domestic violence advice projects in England and Wales to support the development of services.

29. Although there are estimated to be some 500,000 domestic violence related calls to the police, only around 7,000 incidents result in a prosecution. This means that only a relatively small percentage of perpetrators are managed through Criminal Justice Systems. We know that there are many dangerous abusers who are not currently being managed and we need to find ways not only to increase the numbers of offenders who are brought to justice (and so subject to these offender management systems) but also to identify perpetrators outside the Criminal Justice System who would benefit from more active management or support to stop offending.

30. Many more perpetrators come into contact with the courts system as a whole than come into contact with the Criminal Justice System.

- In 2003 over 30,000 non-molestation and occupation orders were granted to protect victims of domestic violence and a further 4,500 undertakings were given to the courts.
- Around 25% of court applications for contact with a child following divorce or separation involve allegations of domestic violence between the parents.

31. There are currently no mechanisms for referral from these courts to perpetrator programmes. In the Government's Green Paper 'Parental Separation: Children's Needs and Parents' Responsibilities' we consulted on including referral to a perpetrator programme as an option for the family courts when considering a contact application. Following on from the consultation, the power to require attendance at programmes, such as a perpetrator programme, was included in the Draft Children (Contact) Adoption Bill published on 2 February 2005. Perpetrator programmes do not, however, mean that perpetrators will be able to escape prosecution for criminal offences where a prosecution is warranted.

32. In the meantime, we want to get more evidence on the likely effectiveness of programmes to address the behaviour of perpetrators who have appeared in the civil/family courts, but who have not yet been the subject of a criminal prosecution.

Commitment 4: awareness raising

33. During 2004 the Government funded a national campaign to promote the new national helpline and to raise public awareness generally of domestic violence.

34. Advertisements – which were designed with input from Women's Aid and Refuge, appeared in magazines, in washrooms and on the back of till receipts as well as on the radio. Following evaluation, the most successful elements of this campaign will be considered for future campaigns.

Commitment 5: supporting police improvement

35. Under the leadership of the Association of Chief Police Officers, guidance on policing domestic violence has been produced by CENTREX, the organisation responsible for police training. It is one of the first guides to operational policing issued under the auspices of the National Centre for Policing Excellence. One of its cornerstones is proactive policing throughout a domestic violence case. A crucial element of this is making full use of available powers of arrest, with the police taking the decision rather than placing the burden on the victim. The Domestic Violence, Crime and Victims Act 2004 makes common assault an arrestable offence. This will give

police clear and unambiguous powers in many common domestic violence situations where in the past frontline officers have not been clear whether or not they have a power of arrest.

36. Police will still have the discretion to arrest or not, but the clear expectation is that they will do so. This expectation is already backed up by a HO Circular and will be reinforced by a new Circular which will be issued in advance of the implementation of the new Act measures during 2005.

37. In addition, this positive arrest policy is reinforced by the inclusion in the Policing Performance Assessment Framework (the key framework against which police performance is measured, and force by force performance compared) of a measure focusing on the percentage of cases where police are making an arrest where they have the power to do so.

38. The guidance on Policing Domestic Violence is backed by a seven part training package developed by CENTREX for Police. While domestic violence training is optional for existing Police personnel, all new probationer police officers are now taught two of the modules on understanding and investigating domestic violence. The other modules are more targeted at, for instance, communication centre staff or staff in specialist units.

Commitment 6: children's services

39. Children who have experienced, witnessed or lived with domestic violence are at risk. They are at greater risk of exposure to poverty and homelessness, and detrimental effects on their short-term welfare and long-term life chances. As such, these children will benefit from the wide-ranging Government reforms of children's services envisaged in *Every Child Matters* and legislated for in the Children Act 2004. The overall aim of the Act is to encourage integrated planning, commissioning and delivery of services as well as to improve, multi-disciplinary working, remove duplication, increase accountability and improve the co-ordination of individual and joint inspections in local authorities. The legislation is enabling rather than prescriptive and provides local authorities with a considerable amount of flexibility in the way they implement its provisions. It is important that domestic violence is not treated as a separate area but mainstreamed and integrated throughout the children's agenda. The Government will take the following actions to ensure that this happens:
    • Guidance to underpin the new duty to 'safeguard children and promote the welfare of children' introduced in the Children's

Act will promote the role of all the agencies subject to this duty. This will help them respond to children and families affected by domestic violence;

- A Common Core of Skills and Knowledge is being developed for those working with children, young people and their families. It will set out six areas of expertise that everyone working with children, young people and families should be able to demonstrate. It will provide a basic description of essential skills and knowledge for practitioners which can be adapted and enhanced for use in different services and differentiated as appropriate to recognise that in some roles very detailed knowledge may be required, particularly in areas such as safeguarding;
- Putting in place effective inter-agency arrangements to work with children and families affected by domestic violence will be an important role of the new Local Safeguarding Children Boards; and
- Domestic violence will be reflected in the framework according to which new children's structures will be inspected.

40. We believe that these steps will ensure that domestic violence is on the agenda of every mainstream agency whose task it is to safeguard and promote the welfare of children.

41. Guidance has been made available in the form of the inter-agency guidance *Working Together to Safeguard Children* (which can be accessed via www.teachernet.gov.uk) and the guidance *What to do if you're worried a child is being abused*. Training materials to support the latter guidance are currently being developed and will address the specific issues raised in domestic violence situations. A 'Bullying and Domestic Violence' toolkit was launched in March 2005, providing guidance on children affected by domestic violence and the links to anti-social behaviour.

42. A good practice guide on how to provide timely and appropriate support for children who have witnessed domestic violence was published in 2004. The findings are from the evaluation of a number of projects funded under the remit of the Crime Reduction Programme Violence Against Women Initiative.

Commitment 7: immigration services

43. In November 2004 several changes were announced to the way the Home Office's Immigration and Nationality Directorate (IND) handles cases that fall within the domestic violence provisions of the Immigration Rules.

44. In 2002, the rules were amended to widen the category of evidence which victims of domestic violence may use as proof of domestic violence. Applications from victims of domestic violence are now prioritised and, where the applicant is destitute, the usual fees are waived. Victims of domestic violence who are still subject to immigration control cannot access public funds until their application has been decided. However, victims can get access to housing-related support through the Supporting People arrangements, and the Home Office has made a further grant of £80,000, in addition to the £40,000 earlier in 2004-05, to Women's Aid to bolster its Last Resort Fund. Members of Women's Aid can apply for funding from the Last Resort Fund to cover the living expenses of women who are making an application for indefinite leave to remain because of domestic violence. This helps to meet the housing costs of a small number of cases in refuges whilst the application is in process, for up to a period of eight weeks. However this is only a temporary solution and in the coming months IND and other Government Department will be looking for long term solutions for those victims with no recourse to public funds.

45. Many cases are delayed because forms have not been properly filled in or applicants have been unable to produce evidence of domestic violence as set out in the immigration rules. Following close discussions with Southall Black Sisters and Women's Aid, IND will be:
    • giving case-workers additional guidance on making decisions on domestic violence cases;
    • widening the interpretation of the term 'refuge' to include recognised and specialist support services, and, with that, the organisations that can give evidence on behalf of a victim to the IND;
    • producing a proforma for service providers supporting victims, with guidance on submitting applications and supporting evidence correctly;
    • producing an information leaflet on how to apply for indefinite leave to remain as a victim of domestic violence;
    • producing, through Southall Black Sisters (SBS) a step-by-step guide to help black and minority ethnic (BME) victims 'navigate' the system, including making immigration applications, the services that are available and how to access them. This was launched for consultation on 15 November 2004, and will be published by summer 2005. It will be produced in a range of languages in an easy to understand format; and
    • circulating guidance to local authorities on funding women with insecure immigration status in fear of violence.

46. IND will incorporate the broader interpretation of the term refuge into their guidance this Spring, with the information leaflet being

added to the IND website and printed in a number of different languages at around the same time. The pro-forma for service providers has been drafted and sent to Women's Aid and Southall Black Sisters for final comments. IND will then publish and distribute by the summer.

Commitment 8: supporting the voluntary sector in the setting of standards

47. The last decade has seen an increasing professionalisation in many parts of the Voluntary and Community Sector (VCS), both in the management of organisations and the delivery of services by staff and volunteers. The majority of innovative practice has also originated in this sector. Funders increasingly demand certain standards of service, monitoring and evaluation, and financial management, while formal qualifications give staff transferable skills in a mobile job market. The domestic violence sector is no exception. Over the last few years, prompted particularly by the Supporting People programme launched in April 2003, the sector's umbrella organisations have begun drawing up standards of service and training.

48. Women's Aid, consulted widely with their members during the development of the Supporting People quality assessment framework on a broad set of standards to govern quality of service in the voluntary sector beyond those offered through Supporting People. At that time, material was drawn together covering standards in:
     *   refuge provision;
     *   children's services; and
     *   outreach/floating support services.

49. Women's Aid have also made progress in developing training packages which support the delivery of key services by their members. Their ambition – and that of their members, including Refuge – is now to turn those standards and emerging training packages into a more sophisticated system of standard-setting, training and qualification which will enable the quality of services to rise; and the commissioners of services to have confidence in their quality and credentials.

50. The Government shares that ambition. ODPM will be working with Women's Aid, using *Change Up* funding to strengthen front line services provided by refuges and to enable the domestic violence sector to engage more effectively with new regional approaches to investment. This work will be closely linked to the work of the Coordinated Response and Advocacy Resource Group (CRARG) and will inform the emerging occupational standards.

Protection and justice

Commitment 9: expanding network of specialist domestic violence courts

51. When referring to a specialist Domestic Violence court, we are not referring to a court building or jurisdiction, but to a specialised way of dealing with domestic violence cases in the magistrates' courts. There are two types of specialist domestic violence courts currently operating:
    * Clustering – all cases are grouped into one court session to deal with pre-trial hearings, bail variation, pleas, pre-trial reviews, pre-sentence reports, and sentencing. Some cluster courts also hear trials in a specific Domestic Violence session.
    * Fast-tracking – specific pre-trial review sessions are allocated for Domestic Violence with 1 in 4 court slots allocated to DV for all further hearings/trials.

52. A specialist or fast-track court procedure for dealing with DV cases will deal solely with criminal, adult proceedings. Independent Domestic Violence Advisor services (see Commitment 1) are an essential element of the multi-agency approach which culminates in a specialist court.

53. The evaluation of specialist domestic violence courts showed that there were significant benefits to be gained, for the courts as well as for the victims of domestic violence, from such courts. Significant findings from the research were that specialist domestic violence courts:
    * Enhance the effectiveness of court and support services for victims;
    * Make advocacy and information-sharing easier;
    * Improve victim participation and satisfaction; and
    * Increase public confidence in the CJS.

54. We want to ensure that the courts themselves, both criminal and civil, recognise the difficulties and special concerns faced by victims of domestic violence when using the system. We also want to develop courts that put domestic violence victims at the heart of the process. To that end we will continue to develop specialist DV courts and aim to have 25 such courts set up by April 2006.

Commitment 10: pilot an integrated domestic violence court

55. At present a spouse or partner who wishes to make applications arising from domestic violence allegations may have to attend two different courts in two separate jurisdictions, criminal and civil, to present similar or the same facts. This is widely seen as unsatisfactory. An appeal (Lomas and Parle) heard in the Court of Appeal in a constitution which included the President of the Family

Division, Dame Elizabeth Butler-Sloss, brought home vividly the inconvenience, waste of court time, and considerable public expense on concurrent hearings conducted by different courts with different sets of solicitors and different barristers.

56.   The Government proposes, therefore, to support the development of an Integrated Domestic Violence Court (IDVC). The IDVC would hear both the criminal and civil aspects of the same case. Cases would be heard sequentially with the criminal case, where possible, heard first. An IDVC would provide an improved service to families in crisis, by coordinating criminal and civil proceedings where the underlying issue is domestic violence.

57.   A National Implementation Project Board for Integrated Domestic Violence Courts was set up last July (2004) to develop a model for an IDVC. It is hoped that a pilot IDVC will be up and running at Croydon before the end of 2005.

Commitment 11: increasing access to justice

58.   We want victims of domestic violence to have access to high quality legal advice that offers them the information and guidance they need to reach the right decisions about their safety and their future.

59.   Victims using legal services need assurances of the quality and experience of their provider. The Law Society and the Solicitors Family Law Association, recently renamed Resolution, currently have specialist panel membership or accreditation schemes for family solicitors. The Bar have the Family Law Bar Association (FLBA) but this does not have an accreditation scheme. Professionals have specific guidance on domestic violence in the 'Family Law Protocol', a best practice guide for all family lawyers. Although the panels and accreditation scheme are readily recognised on an inter-professional and intra-professional basis, they are not always readily recognised or understood by the consumer.

60.   This is a key area for improvement identified in the recent Green Paper 'Parental Separation Children's Needs and Parents' Responsibilities' and is as pertinent in the area of domestic violence specialist practice as it is in family work generally. It is proposed that a National Accreditation Scheme should be instituted that would be easily recognisable for consumers and would encompass, for the profession, a clear 'career path' and qualification. The Legal Services Commission (LSC) is currently researching how best to take this proposal forward. The Commission would like to work with the legal and specialist professional bodies so that the work that has been accomplished in building the present level of panel and accreditation schemes within the profession is encompassed within any plans for

national accreditation resulting in a single, nationally recognisable accreditation. Any national accreditation will seek to address the need for solicitors to recognise the issues surrounding domestic violence, beyond strictly legal remedies. This should include a knowledge and understanding of appropriate local services, and the ability to signpost clients to them.

61. As part of the Family Advice and Information Service Project, the LSC will also work with practitioners and their representative bodies to look at ways in which a training programme for unqualified but experienced legal executives who work in solicitors' offices (and who often end up doing much of the domestic violence work) could be established. We want to ensure that an appropriate level of skills based training is offered, particularly in sensitive areas of practice such as domestic violence, and we are working with partners to establish how it might best be provided. This also reflects the enhanced need for effective and sensitive communication between solicitors and their clients as a result of the introduction of revised forms for applications under section 8 of the Children Act 1989 (contact, residence, specific issues and prohibitive steps) in January 2005. These forms will encourage allegations of domestic violence to be raised and considered right at the start of proceedings.

OTHER AVENUES FOR ADVICE

62. Research has indicated that 80% of people dealing with family problems approach a solicitor first. However, there is no reason why other sources could not be used, if not for the actual legal process, at least by a victim establishing their options. Many victims of domestic violence in particular may be reluctant to go directly to a solicitor because of, perhaps, fear about the cost or doubts about whether the law can help. That is why we want to develop other avenues for victims to make the first step in seeking legal advice so that they can better understand what the law can do to help and how to access that help. The LSC is developing a range of proposals to expand victims' ability to receive advice. These include:

   • Leaflets. Many services provide web-based information relating to domestic violence and associated issues, the majority of which are downloadable as fact sheets at no cost. The LSC provides this service via its Community Legal Service Direct website, and these leaflets can also be ordered from the Community Legal Service Direct telephone helpline. A leaflet dealing with options relating to domestic violence was added in September 2004.

   • 'One Stop Shop'. Research has shown that the more often people seeking help are referred on, the less likely it is that the referral will be successful. This is exacerbated for those experiencing domestic violence, who are usually already fearful, distressed and disempowered. The presence of domestic violence often indicates a cluster of associated or potential problems, including housing, debt, divorce and children matters. Closing the gaps through which victims might fall leads to more accessing the advice and support they need. Being able to access advice for all their problems in one place enables their various needs to be addressed in a comprehensive and holistic manner, reducing the risk of drop out. The LSC will be running a pilot to build on existing models of good practice of a single gateway to services for those experiencing domestic violence.

- Consideration is also being given to piloting a Family Legal Helpline and an email enquiry facility.

Commitment 12: implementing the provisions in the Domestic Violence, Crime and Victims Act 2004

63. The Domestic Violence, Crimes and Victims Act received Royal Assent on 15 November 2004. The key measures in the Act which will offer victims of domestic violence more protection and support are:

- **making breach of a non-molestation order a criminal offence,** punishable by up to five years' imprisonment. This makes it an offence for which a police officer can arrest without a warrant. Courts will also be compelled, when deciding whether they should issue an occupation order, whether they should also issue a non-molestation order. This will mean civil orders can offer better protection to victims;

- amending the Family Law Act 1996 so that courts making occupation orders no longer have regard to the fact that cohabitants have not given each other the **commitment involved in marriage**, and instead look at the level of **commitment involved in the relationship;**

- giving **cohabiting same-sex couples** the same access to non-molestation and occupation orders as opposite-sex couples;

- making **couples who have never cohabited or been married** eligible for non-molestation orders;

- **introducing domestic violence homicide reviews,** which will be an opportunity for those people and agencies which may have known about or suspected the attacks – like the police, health or social services – to look at the background and their involvement in each case, and learn lessons for the future. It also gives the Secretary of State the power to direct that an agency sets up or takes part in a review in a particular case;

- **making common assault an arrestable offence** by adding it to the list of offences for which a police officer may arrest without a warrant;

- **extending the availability of restraining orders to all violent offences**. This includes cases where there has been an acquittal in a criminal court but where there is sufficient evidence to warrant a restraining order;
- giving any person mentioned in a restraining order **a right to make representations in court** if an application is made to vary or terminate the order.

64. Now that the Bill has received Royal Assent appropriate training and guidance will be promulgated. The first tranche of orders have now been commenced:
- Section 5-8 Causing or allowing the death of a child or vulnerable adult;
- Section 11 Common assault as an alternative verdict;
- Section 22-26 Changes to the insanity legislation;
- Section 28-29 Fine enforcement – disclosure orders and procedure on breach of community penalty; and
- Section 31 intermittent custody.

The other measures in the Act will be rolled out over the next year.

Commitment 13: ensuring the courts deal appropriately with child contact cases where domestic violence is an issue

65. About 25% of applications for contact or residency following parental separation include allegations of domestic violence. The guidelines published for the courts by the Children Act Sub-Committee (CASC) made clear that contact should only be awarded between a non-resident parent and a child if the safety of the child and resident parent could be assured before, during and after contact. In order to ensure that the courts have all the relevant information before deciding issues of contact and residency, new forms were introduced on 31 January this year. Disclosure of domestic violence at the point these forms are completed will depend, to a certain extent, on the skill of the solicitor in talking their client through the form. This is an area we intend to address by appropriate training and accreditation, as outlined above. This will ensure that allegations of domestic violence will be raised right at the beginning of proceedings so that the judge can make decisions about contact in the light of all the facts.
A duty is imposed on chief police officers, local probation boards, local authorities, strategic health authorities, primary care trusts, local health boards, NHS trusts and equivalent bodies for Northern Ireland to have regard to the guidance issued on holding such reviews.

66. On 31 January 2005 we also implemented section 120 of the Adoption and Children Act 2002, which clarifies the Children

Act 1989. In considering the harm a child might suffer, the courts have to consider not just direct violence on the child but 'impairment suffered from seeing or hearing the ill-treatment of another'.

67.   We are committed to evaluating the effectiveness of the new forms and clarified definition of harm in how the courts deal with applications for contact where the issue of domestic violence is raised.

Commitment 14 CAFCASS: improving delivery for survivors of domestic violence

68.   In all matters relating to the family courts, Children and Family Court Advisory and Support Service (CAFCASS) has an essential role to play in advising the courts and supporting the parties to the case. In relation to domestic violence, CAFCASS has been consulting on its draft Domestic Violence Policy, Procedures and Toolkit – consultation closed on 25 March 2005. The agenda for change would include the following:
   •   ensuring staffing resources are available by courts reducing the demand for reports, and using capacity for other purposes, including supporting families which have survived domestic violence;
   •   ensuring survivors' needs are assessed, and they are aware of how to access local Domestic Violence Support agencies;
   •   developing links with other agencies about appropriate support (e.g. housing to re-accommodate; family therapists; counselling services for children; police through domestic violence fora to provide future protection and contact centres);
   •   identifying CAFCASS practitioner learning needs, and providing training.

69.   In order to improve CAFCASS' handling of domestic violence cases it has developed two new training packages:
   •   a new three day training package to be undertaken by all new CAFCASS Officers. The module was piloted in the summer 2004 and was available to all new starters from November 2004. The aim of the training is to develop Family Court Advisors' (FCAs) understanding of the dynamics and impact of domestic violence, and to improve their ability to work with families where there is domestic violence in order to safeguard and promote children's welfare. One of the key learning outcomes is to enable FCAs to assess the risk of domestic violence, make decisions about specialist assessments and recommend interventions, including contact arrangements which promote and safeguard children's interests.
   •   A new one day training package for practitioners moving either from private law practice to public law or vice versa. The aims

of the training are the same as the 3-day package, but assume a greater contextualised knowledge of domestic violence than is the case with new entrants.

Commitment 15: supporting improvement in the CPS

70. The Domestic Violence Policy and Guidance documents were revised and published in February 2005 and copies issued to all CPS Areas. The new national joint CPS and CENTREX training programme was launched in February 2005. A specific module for prosecutors has been devised to ensure that the police and the CPS will receive the same training. This promotes consistency from investigation through to prosecution. CPS Domestic Violence Coordinators have been trained on the new policy in March 2005. Guidance is being produced to help all Areas devise individual domestic violence training plans by June 2005 as part of the overall CPS Training Plans 2005– 2008. All prosecutors and caseworkers are to be trained by 2008. Specialised prosecutors working in existing or planned specialist Domestic Violence courts will receive extended training. Domestic violence training is also being delivered to the lawyers seconded to CPS Direct.

71. A more unified approach for CPS Domestic Violence Coordinators in each area is planned, with key tasks agreed across all areas.

72. The two-year national domestic violence project has published a report on the evaluation of specialist courts, and on the use of expert witnesses in domestic violence cases, has established two pilot sites in Gwent and Croydon and has published an interim report on the findings from both. The final report will be launched in June 2005 and the good practice findings and recommendations will be disseminated at a national conference and rolled out across all areas.

73. A new National Domestic Violence Virtual Implementation Team with staff from Policy Directorate, Equality & Diversity Domestic Violence Project and Business Development Directorate will develop plans for implementation of policy, guidance, training and good practice from 2005-2008. A section of the overall CPS Business Plans 2005-06 include action on domestic violence. A new Hate Crime Indicator will inform the Policing Performance Assessment Framework (PPAF) in relation to the number of offenders successfully prosecuted in the courts (see Appendix B). An audit of all areas' of domestic violence work will be carried out by June 2005, alongside the development of three year Training Plans. A domestic violence section of local Area Business Plan 2006 – 08 will include more detailed implementation plans with good practice recommendations from Domestic Violence Project, community engagement, links to CCMP and other key projects.

CHARGING, CONDITIONAL CHARGING & BAIL CONDITIONS

74. CPS prosecutors will provide early consultations and charging decisions (in all but minor cases), 24 hours a day, seven days a week through the charging initiative when it is fully operational. Statutory Charging Scheme arrangements are now operating in the Government's 13 priority Areas and Cleveland. 28 have shadow arrangements, and will migrate to the statutory scheme between April 2005 and April 2006. The police and CPS have now agreed that all domestic violence cases should be referred automatically to a Crown Prosecutor for a charging decision unless there is manifestly no evidence on which a prosecution could be built. This sends a clear message to both police and prosecutors that domestic violence must be taken seriously. Prosecutors will also provide early consultation to the police and ensure that victims' and witnesses' needs have been evaluation from the outset, all of which aim to improve CJS handling of domestic violence.

75. CPS Direct provides out of hours charging cover to the police as part of the statutory charging arrangements to provide a 24-hour charging service. As all domestic violence cases will now be referred to a charging lawyer where and when the scheme is operational, it is important that these prosecutors are aware of the particular dynamics and evidential requirements in domestic violence cases. As well as improving the CPS's response to domestic violence, this should help spread good practice in the wider CJS given the gatekeeper role that the CPS now has. The revised Policy and Guidance documents and the new CPS training programme and easy to use recording sheets especially designed for duty prosecutors; aim to improve the level of charging in domestic violence cases.

76. Many voluntary and community organisations working with victims are concerned that cautions are used too frequently in domestic violence cases. There is a general agreement that cautions, formal warning, undertakings and offences taken into consideration are not appropriate responses to domestic violence. The first incident brought before the police is unlikely to be the first offence and while cautions do require the offender to admit guilt and receive a criminal record, in most cases they do not provide an effective means of protecting the victim for the future, or holding the offender to account. Cautions are not encouraged in the ACPO/NCPE domestic violence Guidelines, the new guidance to prosecutors will say that cautions are not generally appropriate in domestic violence cases, and the need to use them sparingly will also be reinforced in the new HO Circular required by the Domestic Violence, Crime and Victims Act 2004.

77.   The introduction of conditional cautions does allow police to make additional requirements of the perpetrator. Whilst a caution of this kind will still not be the most effective response to domestic violence, in exceptional circumstances, a conditional caution could be offered to the perpetrator. Again, we would envisage them being used sparingly in domestic violence cases. Conditions are likely to include not approaching the victim (where the two live apart) or a condition of non-violence where they are still living together. Where high-quality perpetrator programmes exist which take non-convicted perpetrators, participation on such a programme may also be an option and we want to explore this further. The offer of any caution – conditional or otherwise – should be only be considered in the context of the safety of the victim and any children.

78.   We intend to issue a new Home Office circular on the importance of treating domestic violence cases seriously, and the factors to be considered before deciding not to proceed with a prosecution. The revised Domestic Violence Guidance to CPS staff provides advice on how to proceed if victims withdraw, including the use of evidence other than the victim's, when and if summonses may be required and which factors should be considered, advice on warrants and reasons to discontinue. In this Circular, police and prosecutors will be reminded of the need for effective gathering of evidence such as photographs of injuries, 999 tapes, CCTV evidence and statements from other witnesses both to strengthen the case and to enable a case to progress, even if victims withdraw their support for the prosecution. Finally, it will remind judges and magistrates of the options open to them around bail and the conditions they might consider imposing if they decide to grant bail.

79.   Appropriate use of bail conditions by police, prosecutors, judges and magistrates is also important. Granting bail in inappropriate cases, not using conditions or, where they are imposed, not enforcing them, puts victims and children at risk. It is also important that there is effective exchange of information between the criminal and civil jurisdictions so that bail conditions do not contradict, for instance, contact orders made in the family courts. Our proposals on integrated courts (see Commitment 10) and the development of specialist courts are starting to address this issue.

Regional and local delivery

Partnership working in the criminal justice system

80.   Partnership working between CJS agencies is key to providing better services to victims and witnesses, bringing more offences to justice

and increasing public confidence in the CJS – all of which form part of the vision for Criminal Justice in 2008 and are key in dealing with domestic violence cases.

81.   Innovative approaches to joint working include at a *national level*, the creation of the National Criminal Justice Board to provide strengthened leadership on criminal justice and ensure delivery of Government targets and priorities. Ministers from the three CJS departments sit on the National Board together with heads of the main agencies such as the Crown Prosecution Service, Courts and Correctional Services. The Association of Police Authorities and the Association of Chief Police Officers as well as the judiciary are also represented. In addition, the Office for Criminal Justice Reform has been established, offering a cross-departmental team that supports all CJS agencies in working together to provide an improved service to the public.

82.   Effective joint working is also necessary at a *local level* if victims and witnesses are to get a good service and more offenders are to be brought to justice. So Local Criminal Justice Boards were established in April 2003 based on the police force structure. They bring together the Chief Officers of police, prison and probation, the Crown Prosecution Service, the Courts and Youth Offending Teams.

83.   Together the agencies have a collective responsibility to deliver Government targets and priorities in their local area. The Local Criminal Justice Boards report to the National Board which has a rigorous performance management framework to ensure it receives regular performance reports, monitors delivery of CJS targets and holds Local Boards to account both by supporting good performance and challenging poor performance. Working together, across traditional boundaries has resulted in new ways of working including:

•   The targeting of prolific offenders where the police, probation, youth offending teams and others work together to identify the main offenders in their local area and agree priority actions for dealing with them;

•   A charging scheme with the Police and CPS working together on a 24/7 basis to ensure that suspects are charged with the right offence, resulting in more early guilty pleas and better prepared cases;

•   The creation of new Witness Care Units, jointly staffed by the police and CPS, assessing the needs of each individual witness and providing a single point of contact for witnesses from charge through to sentence of the offender;

•   A new shared focus on enforcing outstanding fail to attend warrants via *Operation Turn Up,* dealing robustly with defendants who skip bail;

- Greater emphasis on raising the sanction detection rate from 19% to 25% by, for example, deploying new technology, including enhanced DNA testing and Automatic Number Plate Recognition systems, across the country to target criminals more effectively;
- An Effective Trial Management Programme to reduce the number of ineffective trials involving case progression officers in the Police, CPS and Courts working closely with each other to actively prepare and progress cases in and out of court.

All of this has been underpinned by major investment in Criminal Justice IT so that CJS staff can share information and do so securely.

84. Domestic violence is a volume crime and a key component of the tackling violent crime programme. At local level it has to be considered as part of local crime audits and crime reduction strategies. In some areas domestic violence will form a major part of Crime and Disorder Reduction Partnerships (CDRPs) programme of work.

85. But tackling domestic violence effectively needs close inter agency working and requires a number of strategic partnerships and networks to develop joined up responses to provide both safety and justice. There are new challenges, for Local Criminal Justice Boards (LCJBs), CDRPs and Local strategic Partnerships (LSPs), to marshal the resources of criminal Justice agencies, Health, social services, education departments and others, to work with the key stakeholders in the voluntary sector to provide comprehensive services.

86. The Government Offices in England and the National Welsh Assembly have an important role in supporting the delivery and performance managing a range of Home Office programmes and initiatives. They will have a key role to play in developing regional domestic violence plans and ensuring that local partnerships are given support, information and advice on delivering domestic violence services.

87. This paper has illustrated that there are many strands of work being developed across a range of Government departments and systems, all of which are designed to make a significant impact on reducing the incidence of domestic violence. The core task for government in the coming year is to find the most effective mechanisms by which to deliver the national plan (Annex B) and offer real protection and justice to victims of domestic violence.

Annex A

National domestic violence reduction delivery plan

To underpin the commitments and proposals outlined in this update paper, the Home Office, in partnership with the Prime Ministers Delivery Unit, has been working on developing a National Domestic Violence Delivery Plan for 2005/06.

This Plan focuses attention on five identified outcomes which the Government is committed to achieve. These are to:

1.   reduce the prevalence of domestic violence, particularly in high incidence areas and/or communities;

2.   increase the rate that domestic violence is reported, particularly in high incidence areas and/or communities;

3.   increase the rate of reporting domestic violence offences that are brought to justice, particularly in high incidence areas and/or communities as well as in areas with high attrition rates;

4.   ensure victims of domestic violence are adequately protected and supported nationwide;

5.   reduce the number of domestic violence related homicides.

The achievement of these outcomes is dependent on the delivery of seven key work objectives which marshal the improvements outlined in the paper into a coherent plan. Under each of these objectives are several work streams which will be performance managed and monitored regularly and progress reports provided for Ministers and other key stakeholders.

Objective one:

To increase the early identification of, and intervention with, victims of domestic violence earlier by utilising all points of contact with statutory services.

Research indicates that victims of domestic violence will suffer many attacks before seeking help and that these attacks tend to grow in frequency and intensity. Yet we know that victims do not live in a vacuum and their suffering is often visible to a number of statutory and non statutory individuals and services.

The Government wants to encourage earlier reporting by making domestic violence part of routine inquiry and comprehensive assessment processes in a number of primary health and social care settings. This will require a greater co-operation between agencies and a greater willingness to share sensitive information in order to protect victims. A work stream is being developed to encourage and enable different disciplines to work together.

This is particularly important when identifying not just victims of domestic violence, but when to recognise those victims who are at highest risk of serious injury or homicide.

Multi agency collaboration is essential when trying to prevent domestic violence murders.

Objective two:

To build capacity within the domestic violence sector to provide effective advice and support to victims of domestic violence.

There is a wide variation in the provision and quality of services being offered to victims of domestic violence across the country and the Government and members of the voluntary sector, are committed to introduce new quality assurance measures into the training of staff and by producing occupational standards for staff and services.

Services will also need to be accessible to a wide range of black and minority ethnic communities which will require local partnerships to ensure equality of access to their local partnerships.

Objective three:

Increase the use of existing and new powers and methods by statutory services to protect identified victims of domestic violence.

The Government's legislative proposals contain a commitment to put victims at the centre of the Criminal Justice System. This has meant introducing measures which will ensure that the criminal justice agencies act in a consistent way in response to incidences of domestic violence. New guidance and training have been produced for the police, Crown Prosecution Service and the Judiciary, which will be rolled out in the next year. This guidance and training give clear recommendations as how services are expected to respond and provide insight into the times and events when victims are most at risk.

This will offer greater protection to victims and instill more confidence that the CJS agencies will take their concerns seriously.

Objective four:

Increase the rate at which domestic violence is reported either directly to the police services or through third-party reporting arrangements, particularly in high incidence areas and/or communities.

Objective five:

Increase the rate at which domestic violence incidents result in sanction/detections, particularly in high incidence areas and/or communities as well as in areas with high attrition rates.

Objective six:

Increase the rate at which sanction detections are converted into offences/offenders brought to justice, particularly in high incidence areas and/or communities as well as in areas with high attrition rates.

The achievement of these three objectives (Objectives 4, 5 and 6) is linked to the improvement of the Criminal Justice System.

Despite being a volume crime and a significant proportion of violent crime, much of domestic violence is invisible due to under reporting.

This is particularly true in some socio-economic classes and ethnic communities. The Government is particularly keen to encourage local partnerships and agencies to develop better relationships with the police to encourage third party reporting of domestic violence incidents.

The Domestic Violence, Crime and Victims Act 2004 recognised that the continuum of the Criminal Justice System often failed victims whose cases were brought to court. This resulted in extraordinarily high attrition rates amongst domestic violence cases. The Domestic Violence Crime and Victims Act 2004, seeks to redress this by introducing a series of new measures which improve the effectiveness of protection offered to victims and Police Powers to arrest perpetrators. The measures will be rolled out over the coming year. The Police and the CPS are also taking a more proactive approach to prosecution, even where the victim does not want to press charge.

Through the development of specialist court services and the integrated support services, the Government is seeking to make the CJS more effective in dealing with domestic violence cases. Specialist courts in Cardiff, Croydon and other areas have demonstrated that by organising cases differently and providing focused support through Independent Domestic Violence Advisors (IDVAs) the courts are achieving greater throughput of cases and securing more convictions. The Government will be rolling out the specialist court programme by having 25 specialist domestic violence courts running by the end of 2006.

It is also essential that domestic violence perpetrator programmes run by the probation services continue to be developed and rolled out evenly across the country, so that the Judiciary has effective sentencing options in all areas.

Objective seven:

Develop the evidence base to close key knowledge gaps, particularly around understanding the nature and scope of domestic violence.

Although the body of evidence about the extent and nature of domestic violence in the UK is growing, there is a need to keep learning about how it manifests itself across communities and what interventions are most effective. The Government is keen to establish a learning culture around domestic violence to fill in the gaps in knowledge, learn about effective prevention techniques, how to target particular communities, and which areas would benefit most from particular interventions.

The Plan is owned by a number of Government Departments and their agencies and will be delivered through a matrix of regional and local structures and stakeholders. Each objective and task have their own work stream and will be performance managed and monitored at regular intervals, to ensure that delivery stays on track.

Annex B

MEASURING PROGRESS

Performance Indicators

- Annual **number of homicides** as a result of domestic violence: On average two women a week are killed by a partner or ex partner. Since 1997, trends in domestic violence homicides have been broadly level, and though an upward trend can be detected in recent years, the numbers are too small to be statistically significant. In the medium to long term, we would be looking for a downward trend as agencies begin to focus more on early intervention and protection.

- **Headline prevalence of domestic violence:** measured by the British Crime Survey Inter-Personal Violence module, which estimates the extent of domestic violence, sexual assault and stalking in England and Wales. Changes in methodology from 1996 to 2001 mean it is not possible to compare prevalence rates directly, but the general trend remains the same, with between 18 and 25% of violent crime being domestic violence related.

- **Numbers of a) young people and b) all people who think that violence is acceptable in some circumstances:** Research from 1998 showed that 1 in 5 young men and 1 in 10 young women thought that violence towards a partner was acceptable in some situations. While we have no information on trends, we will use these figures as our baseline to measure this indicator annually using the Office of National Statistics Survey. We hope levels of acceptance will reduce as levels of awareness increase.

- **Percentage of domestic violence incidents with a power of arrest where an arrest was made related to the incident and, of this, the percentage of partner-on-partner violence:** Since April 2004, this has been a Statutory Indicator in the Policing Performance Assessment Framework. This year will give us a reliable baseline on which to build, and we want the underlying trend to be upwards, with increased training and guidance for frontline police officers.

- **The number of domestic violence offenders brought to justice:** This will measure outcomes in the Criminal Justice System, and will be a Key Diagnostic Indicator to inform the Policing Performance Assessment Framework from April 2005. We want to see the number of offenders successfully prosecuted increase, and the number of offenders successfully prosecuted against the number of arrests made to increase too, as evidence gathering and support for victims improve.

- **The number of civil orders made:** In 2003 around 30,000 non-molestation and occupation orders were issued and about 4,500 undertakings were given. The Domestic Violence, Crime and Victims Act 2004 should increase the number of orders made. We will monitor the impact of the Act to gauge whether the number of orders increase.

- **Actions against domestic violence:** A revised wider Best Value Performance Indicator (BVPI) will be introduced on 1 April 2005. For 2004-05, local authority performance on domestic violence is measured by the original Indicator 176, looking at refuge provision. This has been used since 2001-02. The average number of refuge places per 10,000 population was 0.5 in both 2001-02 and 2002-03 and 0.96 in 2003-04. The purpose of the revised BVPI is to assess the overall effectiveness of local authority services designed to help victims of domestic violence. It consists of a 'basket' of indicators, seeking information across a range of key local authority services, which are essential in order to tackle domestic violence effectively. They cover a mix of strategic and operational services.

- An indicator relating **to victim satisfaction with the support they have received from key agencies:** This is a new exercise, with no information on past trends. Data will be gathered from a sample of those who said they were victims in the British Crime Survey Inter-Personal Violence module and a pool of victims from refuges. It will be produced on our behalf by Women's Aid, as responses will need to be sensitive to the needs of victims.

BIBLIOGRAPHY

Butler Committee (1975) *Report of the Committee on Mentally Abnormal Offenders* (Cmnd 6244)

Crawford, MJ et al (2007) *Psychosocial interventions following self-harm. Systematic Review of their efficacy in preventing suicide.* British Journal of Psychiatry 190, 11-17

Deutscher, I (1966) *Stalin: A Political Biography.* Penguin Books

Ellis, L and Hoffman, H (eds) (1990) *Crime in Biological, Social and Moral Contexts.* Praeger

Ellis, L and Coontz, PD (1990) *Androgens, Brain Functioning and Criminality: Neurohormonal Foundations of Antisociality.* In Ellis, L and Hoffman, H (eds) *op cit supra*

Farrington, DP (ed) (1994) *Psychological Explanations of Crime.* Aldershot: Dartmouth

Fest, J (1982) *Hitler.* Penguin Books

Gekoski, A (1998) *Murder by Numbers.* Andre Deutsch

Golding, JM (1999) 'Intimate partner violence is a risk factor for mental disorders: a meta-analysis'. *Journal of Family Violence.* 14, 99-132

Hunt IM et al (2006) 'Suicide within 12 months of mental health service contact in different age and diagnostic groups'. *British Journal of Psychiatry* 188, 135-142

Itzin, C et al (2008) 'The effects of domestic violence and sexual abuse on mental health'. *Psychiatric Bulletin.* 32, 448-450

King, NS (2003) 'Post-concussion syndrome: clarity among the controversy?' *British Journal of Psychiatry Editorial.* October 2003

Law Commission (2005) *A New Homicide Act for England and Wales?* Law Com No 177

Mahendra, B (2006) 'Adult Psychiatry in Family and Child Law'. *Family Law*, Jordan Publishing

Mahendra, B (2008a) 'Risk Assessment in Psychiatry: A Guide for Lawyers'. *Family Law*, Jordan Publishing

Mahendra, B (2008b) 'Substance Misuse in Psychiatry: A Guide for Lawyers'. *Family Law*, Jordan Publishing

Mahendra, B (2008c) 'Behaviour, not diagnosis, the key: some misconceptions in the psychiatry of family and child law'. *Family Law*. 38, 159-162

Power, DJ et al (1996) *Dangerous Patients and the Public. In Criminal Law and Forensic Psychiatry*. Barry Rose

Salib, E (2003) 'Suicide terrorism: a case of folie a' plusieurs?' *British Journal of Psychiatry* 182, 475-476

Swinson, N et al (2007) 'National Confidential Inquiry into Suicide and Homicide by People with Mental illness: new directions'. *Psychiatric Bulletin*. 31, 161-163

Van Rooyen, CL and Mahendra, B (2007) 'Psychology in Family and Child Law'. *Family Law*, Jordan Publishing

Webster, CD et al (2002) 'Violence risk assessment using structured clinical guidelines professionally'. *International Journal of Mental Health*. 1, 185-193

Whalley, MG and Brewin, CR (2007) 'Mental health following terrorist attacks'. *British Journal of Psychiatry*. 190, 94-96

INDEX

References are to paragraph numbers.